# LESSING'S *LAOCOON*

ANGLICA GERMANICA SERIES 2

*Editor* M. SWALES

## *Other books in the series*

# LESSING'S *LAOCOON*

## SEMIOTICS AND AESTHETICS IN
## THE AGE OF REASON

### DAVID E. WELLBERY

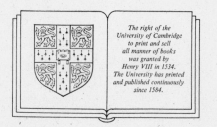

The right of the
University of Cambridge
to print and sell
all manner of books
was granted by
Henry VIII in 1534.
The University has printed
and published continuously
since 1584.

CAMBRIDGE UNIVERSITY PRESS

CAMBRIDGE
LONDON    NEW YORK    NEW ROCHELLE
MELBOURNE    SYDNEY

Published by the Press Syndicate of the University of Cambridge
The Pitt Building, Trumpington Street, Cambridge CB2 1RP
32 East 57th Street, New York, NY 10022, USA
296 Beaconsfield Parade, Middle Park, Melbourne 3206, Australia

First published 1984

Printed in Great Britain by New Western Printing Ltd, Bristol

Library of Congress catalogue card number: 83 – 15055

*British Library Cataloguing in Publication Data*
Wellbery, David
Lessing's Laocoon; semiotics and aesthetics in
the Age of Reason.—(Anglica germanica. Series 2)
1. Lessing, Gotthold Ephraim, 1729–1781.
Laokoon
I. Title  II. Series
701'. 1'7  N64
ISBN 0 521 25794 8

WP

*For Peter Demetz*

# CONTENTS

# CONTENTS

# PREFATORY NOTE

Since this book was written with a broad readership in mind and not just for specialists in the eighteenth century, I have translated quotations from German, French and Latin into English. In the case of Lessing certain passages are also given in the original. This practice seemed justified not only because Lessing's *Laocoon* is my central object of study, but also because Lessing's prose style is in itself an immense cultural achievement.

# INTRODUCTION

In a recent book, which in its elegance and forcefulness testifies to the renewed vigor of philosophical aesthetics in the United States, Arthur C. Danto argues 'that there is an internal connection between the status of an artwork and the language with which artworks are identified as such...'[1] The kind of language meant here is a theoretical one: works of art are the sorts of things that presuppose theories. But it is not only the identification of works of art as such that requires, in Danto's view, an antecedent theory; the theoretical language also determines which properties of the works will be found aesthetically relevant. Even living aesthetic experience breathes in an atmosphere of theory. My enterprise in this study involves putting Danto's argument to historical use by attempting to describe the set of theoretical parameters that, in a particular age, programmed what counts as a work of art, an aesthetic quality, or an aesthetic experience. The age in question is the German Enlightenment, the writers I shall be principally dealing with are such figures as Alexander Baumgarten, Moses Mendelssohn, and Gotthold Ephraim Lessing. Stated this abstractly, of course, the project rings familiar. For a long time cultural historians have endeavored to reconstruct the system of aesthetic norms (generic, thematic, stylistic, etc.) that hold for a given era and there would be little point in invoking Danto if this were what I intended to do. But the theoretical framework I am out to describe needs to be distinguished from the Enlightenment order of aesthetic preferences (to which, however, it is profoundly related). The tantalizing possibility that Danto's work suggests – to me at least – is that the fundamental determinations regarding the nature of art works and aesthetic experience within a particular period are formulated in terms of a theory of language.

In this sense, Danto's ontological analysis of what a work of art is lends support to two fundamental hypotheses of contemporary structural-semiotic research: (1) that the production, circulation and interpretation of signs within a culture are governed by a kind of deep-structural theory, a system of assumptions, let us say, about what constitutes a sign and what it is proper to do with one; and (2) that this general theory of language and signs lays down guidelines for the organization of the aesthetic field (as well as of other domains). The two scholars whose work has most powerfully demonstrated the fecundity of these hypotheses are Michel Foucault and Juri Lotman, both of whom, in the formulation of a recent 'dictionary,' attempt to describe a 'metasemiotic of culture, that is to say. . . the attitude which a socio-cultural community adopts in relation to its signs.'[2] The antecedent theory, which according to Danto is presupposed in every identification of an artifact as an art work, has its historical reality in the patterns of sign use which a given culture sanctions. The structure of aesthetic experience is always rooted in an historically specific codification of the relations between signs and their users. My purpose here is to show how, as regards a single example, this patterning occurs; how broadly held assumptions regarding signs influence theorizing about the arts.

As it happens, Enlightenment culture articulates 'the relations it entertains with the sign'[3] in terms of a semiotics, a theory of signs. This need not be the case. In the work of Johann Gottfried Herder (1744–1803), for instance, a predominantly hermeneutic approach to texts begins to replace the semiotic approach of the Enlightenment. The very fact that language is viewed as a repertoire of signs is a distinguishing feature of eighteenth-century culture before Herder (that is, prior to 1770). The Enlightenment possessed an explicitly formulated semiotic theory, and it is this theory in particular, as a conceptualization of linguistic and other sorts of representations, that the term 'semiotics' in my sub-title designates. Thus, I start from the assumption that, within the representational paradigm of knowledge characteristic of the Enlightenment, the notion of the sign plays an essential, organizing role –

2

something which Foucault's work has shown very forcefully. The classical model of language as a system of signs engenders those forms of knowledge, those aims, methods and even objects of inquiry, that dominate Enlightenment thought.

One such configuration of knowledge is aesthetic theory, the object of my investigation here. Clearly aesthetics is a child of the classical age. The term was coined in 1735 by Alexander Gottlieb Baumgarten (1714–62) and was adopted so readily that by 1804 the wry Jean Paul – himself one of the finest – could remark: 'Our age abounds with nothing so much as with aestheticians.'[4] With the gradual breakdown of the rhetorical tradition and with the increasing diffuseness and indefiniteness of the artist's social role, the need for philosophical definition of art and poetry became pressing. In England, David Hume, Adam Smith, James Harris and Edmund Burke offered substantial contributions to the developing discipline while in France the discussion was carried on by Jean Baptiste Dubos (one of the first and most influential writers on aesthetics, an aesthetician before the science was invented), Charles Batteux and Denis Diderot.[5] The present study is limited solely to the development of aesthetics in Germany, to the work of Baumgarten and his student and popularizer Georg Friedrich Meier (1718–77), to Moses Mendelssohn's (1729–86) writings on aesthetics, and in particular to the *Laocoon* of Gotthold Ephraim Lessing (1729–81). My aim is to show the relationship which obtained between the aesthetic theories of these writers and classical or Enlightenment sign theory.

At one point in his philosophical itinerary Danto devotes some fine pages to the dismantling of what he calls the 'transparency theory' of the arts, among whose advocates he rightly numbers Lessing.[6] But refutation – as Heine noted with regard to Lessing's own opponents – is itself a form of historical afterlife: in exact proportion to its incisiveness Danto's criticism confirms its target as a classic. This example of philosophical interanimation across two centuries highlights the obvious (though complex and thickly mediated) cultural fact that

Lessing remains to this day an active intellectual and artistic presence. His dramas still engage German theater-goers, his *œuvre* as a whole continues to elicit remarkably creative interpretive responses, and his *Laocoon* – my main exhibit here – still commands a place among the standard texts in aesthetic theory.[7] I have no intention in the present study of assailing Lessing's prestige; indeed, I will not regret at all if my admiration for him shows through. However, it is important to emphasize that, although half this book attends to the *Laocoon*, I am not arguing for its essential truth or contemporaneity. On the contrary, what I am principally after is the *otherness* of Lessing's great work in aesthetic criticism, its position outside our own order of words and things. From my perspective, Lessing's vital intellectual presence stems less from the perennial truths he disclosed than from the systematic consistency and precision with which he modelled the order of his culture. I fully accept Danto's refutation of the transparency theory. The question I want to pursue is why, in the Enlightenment, this theory seemed so absolutely self-evident.

The first phase of this pursuit leads to the recondite philosophical compendia of Christian Wolff (1679–1754). Although not immediately relevant to questions of aesthetic and poetic theory, Wolff's philosophy plays an essential role in the development I am studying here. Wolff's influence in Germany was both profound and abiding and extended beyond the confines of academic philosophy. It was from within the systematic framework of his philosophical doctrine that the discipline of aesthetics was first elaborated. Wolff's influence can also be registered in the discussion of semiotic theory in Germany. The article 'sign' in the encyclopedic *Universal-Lexikon* published in 1749 by Johann Heinrich Zedler, for example, consists in its systematic portion largely of unacknowledged quotations from Wolff.[8] The 'Semiotik' which makes up the third part of Johann Heinrich Lambert's *Neues Organon* (1764),[9] perhaps the most important work on sign theory and language theory in Germany before Herder, likewise owes a great deal to Wolff. I do not contend that Wolff was an especially original semiotic theoretician. His importance seems to me to lie in the authority of his texts throughout the first half of the eighteenth century and in the systematic shape he gave to doctrines borrowed from Leibniz, Locke and Descartes. Accordingly, my discussion in the first chapter has less to do with Wolff as an individual than with broad tendencies which, as it were, speak through his texts. What I attempt to sketch is the systematic coherence of eighteenth-century thought about signs and language, and it is for this reason that I freely supplement Wolff's statements with passages from Condillac and Lambert, Mendelssohn and Rousseau. The analysis not only explicates basic semiotic terms but also points out the fundamental ambiguity of the notion of the sign in Enlightenment culture. The sign proves to be at once that which allows man to elevate himself beyond immediate experience, to conceptualize and to perfect his knowledge, as well as that which points out his essential limitation, the finiteness of his soul, his propensity for delusion and error. In this sense, the Enlightenment exhibits a deep suspicion of its own conditions of possibility (signs and language). It resolves this conflict with itself by projecting an ideal future state free of the deceptive opacity of sign use.

The second chapter is narrower in scope and more intensely focussed. It deals with the classical rationalist view of art, the aesthetic theory first articulated by Baumgarten and his amanuensis Meier and subsequently elaborated by Mendelssohn. This body of theoretical work, written for the most part between 1735 and 1770, might be characterized as the dogmatic ancestor of the magnificent Kantian *Critique of Judgement* (1790). These are philosophers whom Kant read and admired and whose works, year after year, he taught.[10] But I have not set out here to narrate the development of eighteenth-century aesthetic theory and it is for this reason that I ignore the Kantian connection. For the same reason, I do not discuss the earlier and highly significant efforts to rationalize poetic theory, the *Critical Poetics* (1730) of Johann Christoph Gottsched (1700–66) and the work by the same title which Gottsched's Swiss counterpart Johann Jakob Breitinger (1701–76) published a decade later.[11] What the chapter describes is not the progressive unfolding of eighteenth-century notions of art and literature, but rather the systematic coherence of a particular type of theoretical discourse. The works of Gottsched and Breitinger (especially those of the former) fall outside the paradigm I am concerned with and I will therefore refer to them only for purposes of contrast. The same applies to Kant, whose aesthetics transforms in decisive ways the theoretical structure informing the writings of his rationalist predecessors.

In the traditional view, the emergence of aesthetic theory around mid-century (the first part of Baumgarten's *Aesthetica* appeared in 1750) expresses the growing interests of subjectivity.[12] My notion is that the rationalist theory of the aesthetic belongs to, and actively participates in, a reorganization of the culture, a transformation of its patterns of sign production and use. Enlightenment aesthetic theory is not the mere expression of an antecedent, animating force; it is itself, as a structured body of discourse, a cultural reality with definite functions and effects. My interest here is directed principally toward the cognitive function of this discourse, the fundamental model in terms of which it circumscribes and partitions the aesthetic field. I call this the representational model of the aesthetic. In my analysis, I devote special attention to two aspects of this model, the theory of aesthetic representations and the theory of aesthetic signs (aesthetic semiotics). My purpose is to show how the works of the rationalist aestheticians locate art works and the behavior associated with them within the array of values that characterizes the Enlightenment 'meta-semiotic' or attitude toward signs. In this way, it becomes clear that the discourse on aesthetics provides a theoretical codification of the being of art within Enlightenment culture. A tendency to idealize aesthetic representations and signs emerges into view: the Enlightenment attributes to art the capacity to

6

renew the life of the culture by reactivating its most archaic mechanisms as well as to anticipate the goal of cultural progress by virtue of its transparent form of signification. If, as the first chapter argues, the *telos* of Enlightenment culture is a system of natural signs, then art becomes the locus where this *telos* is proleptically achieved.

The final chapter presents a detailed analysis of Lessing's *Laocoon*, the published portions of which appeared in 1766. I show that Lessing's distinctions between poetry and painting (actually the plastic arts in general) constitute a global model of aesthetic signification, a remarkably penetrating and articulate development of the aesthetic semiotics which Baumgarten first imagined and which Meier and Mendelssohn began to work out. Lessing adopts the notions of sensate intuition and natural sign that played such a prominent role in the work of the rationalist aestheticians, but applies them with a systematic rigor and, at the same time, an attention to detail that surpass anything produced by his immediate precursors. Particularly important is Lessing's attempt to evaluate the arts in terms of the degree of imaginative freedom they afford both artist and audience. The superiority of poetry over the plastic arts in this regard is derived from the more refined form of semiosis (or process of signification) the poet employs. It is here that the anticipatory (or utopian) function of the aesthetic within Enlightenment culture becomes especially apparent. While he distinguishes poetry and painting as regards the material constitution of their signs, their syntax and their contents, Lessing nevertheless insists on the fundamental unity of the two art forms. He traces this unity to the structure of signification they share, sign motivation or natural signification. The doctrine of *ut pictura poesis* is not abandoned, but is relocated on a higher level of generality: in the principle that all the arts, poetry included, draw their efficacy from their status as natural signs.

There are texts which, with special force and lucidity, exhibit the tacit patterns of thought that dominate a culture; which map out, as it were, the major islands of value that a culture recognizes and the channels that link them. Lessing's *Laocoon* is, I believe, such a text. The elaborate model of aesthetic signification it establishes reveals – when viewed from the outside – the systematic closure of Enlightenment culture. The 'transparency theory' of the arts, which Danto so handily disproves, is an imperative of eighteenth-century thought. This thought, organized by and articulating itself within a particular 'metasemiotic,' is certainly no longer our own; but it is not for that reason a matter of antiquarian interest only. On the contrary, the very otherness of Enlightenment aesthetics allows us to glimpse what we otherwise cannot possibly see: our own ensconcement within a finite cultural horizon.

# 1 · THE FRAMEWORK OF ENLIGHTENMENT SEMIOTICS: CHRISTIAN WOLFF

## *The structure of representation*

In this chapter I shall not be concerned with Wolff's entire philosophy, but merely with his theory of language and signs; and even this restricted domain I shall only briefly sketch. It is a matter of setting forth the key semiotic terms that later enter into the discussion of aesthetics, of pointing out the important non-semiotic concepts to which these terms are related, and of grasping – if only in silhouette – the systematic context in which they acquire their value. I start from the notion of representation, which, following Heidegger, Foucault, and Hacking, I take to be a fundamental category of thought in the eighteenth century, a governing notion, or rather a matrix of notions, that pre-structures the fields in which thought and inquiry move.[1]

The first term that needs to be drawn into an analysis of eighteenth-century 'representation' is the 'soul'. For Wolff, representation is the essential activity of the soul. A soul, in fact, is a power of representing (*vis repraesentativa*) and all mental activities, such as sensation, imagination, memory, reflection, reason, desire, willing, have their source in – are modifications of – the soul's representational activity. What I attend to when I reach for this pen, catch a whiff of coffee, or feel a pang of hunger, is neither pen, nor aroma, nor impulse, but in each case a representation, an idea. The subject, the soul, has as its immediate objects not the things of the world but representations; the function of representing gives unity to the entire psychological sphere. What this means is that beneath all the appearances of 'doings' – writing, walking, building, etc. – there is another, occult sphere of activity in which a soul is attending to representations. Furthermore, this sphere is the

9

more real one and therefore it is at this level that investigations of the most various sorts situate themselves. It ought to come as no surprise then, when this soul, this individual representational power that is independent of institutional contexts and even of the materiality and externality of a representational medium, later assumes its position at the productive and receptive poles of the representational model established in eighteenth-century aesthetic theory.

As for representation itself, Wolff understands it as duplication, as the thing once again. Today we tend to emphasize the projective character of anything that purports to represent something else: representations select aspects that are pertinent to the interests of inquiry; they do not simply pick up the object untouched. Wolff was not troubled by such considerations. For him a representation duplicates the thing represented; it is fully characterized by reference to its object. Representations are surrogative, referential and neutral. They take the place of the object and point to it, but contain no intrinsic element which might prejudice their duplicative function. What is most instructive, from a contemporary point of view, is the lack of any necessity to explain the representative relation. Indeed, it is the tacit character of this notion that signals its power: it names something which, however contrived it might appear to us, to the Enlightenment seemed as self-evident as nature.

The soul stands vis-à-vis these mental duplicates of things as if they were portraits, projections on a screen: 'Both sensations and imaginings are like images, such as paintings and statues, in that they all are representations of composite entities: and for this reason representations of corporeal things are called images.'[2] Wolff here quite properly limits the analogy between pictures and mental representations to those ideas produced by the faculties of sensation and imagination, but the decisive point is that the model of vision applies even when the soul does not literally see. Even when its representations are not imagistic in nature, the soul relates to them as if they were objects of vision. *All mental activity, all representation, is essentially specular.* Thus, representations exhibit themselves to the 'light of the soul' (*lumen animae*) and even our abstractions are 'perceptions' of class notions (*perceptiones specierum ac generum*).[3] George Friedrich Meier, in the logic textbook which Kant would still use, could characterize representation as follows: 'Experience teaches us that we represent infinitely many things. A representation (*repraesentatio, perceptio*) behaves like an image which the painterly skill of the soul draws on its own inside.'[4] We must not suppose today that the classical age labored toward this notion of mental activity as quasi-vision, or debated its merits, or weighed its heuristic value. The visual metaphor is not so much the result of inquiry as its precondition: an entrenched model that opens up a field of investigation. Nor must we suppose that an 'experience' which we share with the eighteenth century – say, the experience of 'seeing' – was unwarrantedly generalized to interpret all types of thought. Perception itself was a sub-class of representations and this affected its definition. As Foucault has argued, perception too has a history.[5] In the age of rationalism and empiricism it is the preeminent example of representation in general; like all forms of representation, perceptions make their object present to the subject by placing the object, in an ideal form, before the light of the soul. Today – one need only consult the work of Nelson Goodman – neither perceptions, nor portraits, nor representations remain the same.[6]

The purest expression of the representational paradigm is the metaphysical system of Leibniz in which the activity of representing is attributed to all of being. Each monad – and monads are all that there is – represents the world from its own unique perspective, with its own degree of strength. But Leibniz was by no means the only one to concentrate on the theme; the British empiricists Locke, Berkeley, and Hume exemplify the 'heyday of ideas'[7] just as well. Indeed, the fact that Wolff's writings are such a hybrid of rationalist and empiricist strains points to the underlying unity of these two main philosophical schools of the Enlightenment. And Wolff's philosophy itself is entirely built upon a foundation provided by the representational paradigm. We can gain a firmer notion of how that paradigm functioned if we look at the internal articulation of the representational field as it is revealed in Wolff's classification of ideas.

The office of the soul is to reproduce within itself, through the activity of thought, the objects of the world (*Sachen*). This representation is an idea (*Begriff*). In his logic handbook, *Rational Thoughts on the Powers of Human Understanding and their Correct Use in the Cognition of the Truth* (1713), Wolff subdivides the realm of ideas into several types, as illustrated in Figure 1.[8] Perhaps no set of distinctions is as

Figure 1

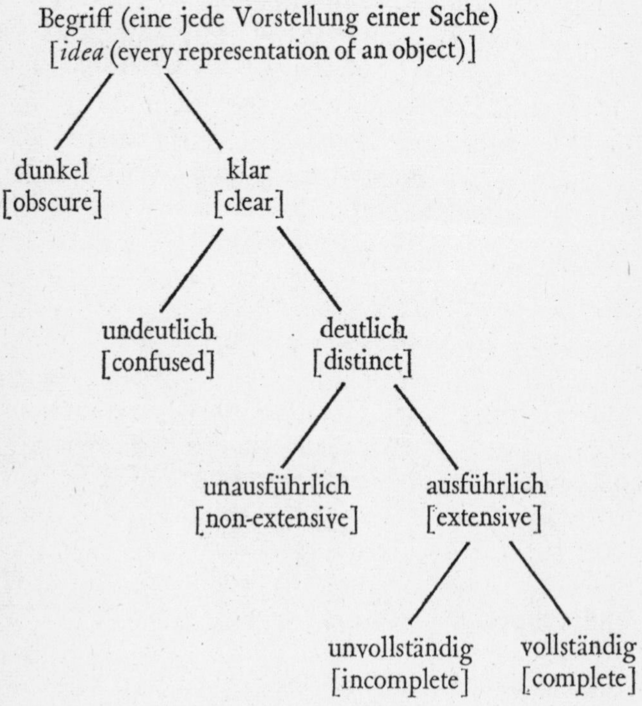

Begriff (eine jede Vorstellung einer Sache)
[*idea* (every representation of an object)]

dunkel
[obscure]

klar
[clear]

undeutlich
[confused]

deutlich
[distinct]

unausführlich
[non-extensive]

ausführlich
[extensive]

unvollständig
[incomplete]

vollständig
[complete]

important for eighteenth-century thought – this is true, in any case, for aesthetic theory – as that schematized by this inverted tree. Note first of all how the notion of representation governs and gives unity to what today would fall into entirely disparate realms: the obscure representations can be as subtle as the functioning of our bodily organs and completely distinct representations would have the look of a calculus, but nevertheless both qualify as representations. However, it is not merely scope which signals the importance of the schema, it is its poly-functionality as well. We have here first of all a set of formal distinctions, second a map of the progress of knowledge from crude sensations to refined conceptualizations, and third a schema for progress in history (as Lessing's *On the Education of Mankind*, for example, reveals). Whether talking about psychology, language, history, or art, the early eighteenth century was usually retracing the branching paths of this schematization. Finally, note that the metaphor which makes the classification possible is a visual one: the object represented is 'seen' in an ever brighter light.

Regarding the formal aspects of the classification, I will discuss only the two most decisive points, the distinctions between 'obscure' and 'clear' and between 'confused' and 'distinct.' These are the articulations that will prove decisive for aesthetic theory.

An obscure representation is one which remains unnoticed by, unthematized for, the subject. It does not bring its object to a point where it can be distinguished from others; it does not suffice to discriminate or isolate its object. Clarity is a function of recognizability. We have a clear idea of something, 'when the idea we have suffices to recognize the objects as they occur, as when we know it is just that thing that bears this or that name.'[9] When the representation is sufficient to identify the instances of an object, then it is a clear representation. Clear cognition recognizes without explicating; it merely takes note of the presence or absence of an object in a given situation.

If we remain at this stage of simple acknowledgement,

our idea of the object is confused. (The Latin term employed by Leibniz for such ideas is 'confusa.' In German the term 'verworren' [confused] is often substituted for Wolff's 'undeutlich' [indistinct].) Merely clear ideas are confused. We have distinct cognition of the object when we can account for or justify our initial recognition: 'in such a case we are capable of enumerating for someone else the properties by virtue of which we recognize the object, or at least of representing these features to ourselves individually and in sequence.'[10] Whatever item is the object of cognition, it announces itself by its properties or features, which are, as it were, bundled together. Distinct cognition entails the ability to unravel this bundle of features so that they can be distinguished one from another and in their interconnection. In clear cognition the object is *con-fused*; it is a compound of features considered globally. In distinct cognition the object is distinct, that is, it is analyzed in terms of its features, which are themselves represented clearly. The clarity of representation is distributed among the features: 'Accordingly, distinctness is based on the clarity of the features of the object.'[11]

Thus, the formal distinction between clarity and distinctness is entirely relative, a matter of wholes and parts which can themselves be considered as wholes with their respective parts. If the whole object is manifested as such, the cognition is clear. If the object is manifested in terms of its constituent features, the object is distinct, the features clear. Wolff's account in the logic handbook, of course, has principally to do with the clarity or distinctness of concepts. The same formal distinctions, however, can be made on the perceptual level as well. The isolation of a tree within the perceptual field is a clear perception. If the perceptive focus moves through the features of the tree – e.g. the leaves, the branches, the trunk – then the perception of the tree is distinct.[12] In formal terms, it is perfectly consistent to speak of a distinct perception in the context of Wolff's doctrine.

Having summarized this formal distinction between clear

and distinct ideas, we are in a position to isolate certain important aspects of the structure of representation. The opposition between 'clear' and 'distinct' does not reflect a state of affairs in the world; we cannot interpret the terms by saying, for instance, what a clear idea might *really* be. Rather, the opposition in question acquires its meaning from a set of related oppositions; and these oppositional pairs constitute part of the conceptual grid which, in the Enlightenment, governed and organized inquiry in various domains. Indeed, my central argument in this study is that the questions raised and the answers found in Lessing's *Laocoon* were made possible by the representational structure of knowledge in the eighteenth century. As far as the distinction between 'clear' and 'distinct' is concerned, three conceptual pairs seem to me decisive in lending each of the two terms its meaning. First, the distinction involves the notions of whole and part: in clear (and confused) cognition the whole object is attended to as such; in distinct cognition it is attended to in terms of its constituent features. The second important aspect has to do with time: clear cognition presents the object as a simultaneous representation whereas distinct cognition distributes the features of the object along a succession so that they can be attended to 'individually and in sequence.' Finally, – and this aspect will naturally receive a great deal of attention throughout this study – the distinction can be drawn in terms of language. Clear cognition involves the 'lower' border of language, in Wolff's example the names of things which predicate nothing of their object but merely convey the mind toward the object as a whole. Distinct cognition, on the other hand, involves the ability to 'enumerate for someone else' what the individual features of the object are. Clear and distinct cognition, then, are opposed: (a) as a whole is to its parts; (b) as simultaneity to successivity; and (c) as designation to discourse. These three oppositional pairs are among the most important elements in the conceptual repertoire of Enlightenment aesthetics.

Wolff's classification of ideas, as I have schematized it,

also exhibits the Enlightenment conception of the progress of knowledge. From our as yet unconscious (and therefore 'obscure') representations of the world this progress moves toward a state of knowledge in which not only the features of the object are known, but also the features of those features. 'Our idea is complete when we also have clear and distinct ideas of the properties by virtue of which the object is known.'[13] Knowledge moves forward as an ever more penetrating, ever more refined analysis, finally arriving at that point where the object is known as a collocation of irresolvable notions, logical simples themselves immediately clear and distinct. If we think of each level of our branching diagram as a stage in this progress, then the notions clear and distinct lose their relative character and come to designate fixed positions within a hierarchy of types of representations. 'Clear' applies to those representations which are characterized by their wholeness. Such are the representations generated by the lower faculties, sensations, perceptions, imaginings, imagistic memories and anticipations. 'Distinct,' on the other hand, applies to those representations in which the parts of the object, its properties and features, are set forth, as is the case, for example, in definitions. Such are the representations produced by the intellect. Thus, insofar as they are taken to mean definite stages in the development of knowledge, the terms 'clear' and 'distinct' denote the representations produced respectively by the inferior and superior cognitive faculties. They name the two great domains of our knowledge, knowledge by the senses and knowledge by the intellect.

Broadly speaking, the intellect is the power to represent possible objects distinctly. The senses and the imagination can only bring their representations to the level of clarity.[14] A pure intellect achieves its representations entirely without sense images. The intellect of man is mixed; man always has recourse to some degree of sense imagery in his representations of possible worlds.[15] Indeed, it can be claimed that for the Enlightenment man is the figure who straddles the border between 'clear' and 'distinct.' And therefore it is no accident that thought in the Enlightenment addressed itself in the most diverse ways to the liminal stage between these two realms, to the passage – always already made but always to be made anew – from nature to culture. As we shall see, it is the invention of language that carries man across the line.

## The themes of Wolff's semiotics

Looking through Wolff's various treatises on logic, metaphysics, and psychology, we find that there is frequent talk about signs. To be sure, there is no fully developed semiotic theory such as is elaborated in J. H. Lambert's *New Organon* (*Neues Organon*, 1764). But Wolff's remarks on signs are for that reason not just occasional: they reveal, on the contrary, the centrality of the sign to Enlightenment thought. In this section I will make a case for such centrality by discussing what I consider three major themes of Wolff's semiotics and by showing how these themes function within the representational paradigm. By theme, I mean a local area of inquiry, something felt to be an important problem or question. In the long run, of course, my argument will be that the themes of Enlightenment aesthetics are related in important ways to the themes of Enlightenment semiotics.

## The arbitrary signs of language

Wolff is typical of the eighteenth century in that he characterizes the linguistic sign as arbitrary (*willkürlich*). This notion of arbitrariness is quite different from the concept of the arbitrary sign that is current in post-Saussurian linguistics and semiotics. As Saussure insisted: 'The term [arbitrary] should not imply that the choice of the signifier is left entirely to the speaker... I mean that it is unmotivated, i.e. arbitrary in that it actually has no natural connection with the signified.'[16] But precisely this element of free choice, which Saussure eliminates from his definition, is central to the eighteenth-century sign concept. Furthermore – Jonathan Culler has emphasized this – the arbitrariness of the sign in Saussure is linked to the relational or differential constitution of both signifier and signified.[17] Indeed, for contemporary semiotics the sign is not a given, not a positive entity, but is produced by the intersection of two systems. It is 'the meeting ground for independent elements (coming from two different systems of two different planes and meeting on the basis of a coding correlation).'[18] This systematic (relational, differential) quality of the sign is entirely foreign to Enlightenment semiotics.

It would be senseless to evaluate this discrepancy as a matter of right and wrong; the contemporary definition of the sign does not refute that of the eighteenth century. Rather, the two definitions are drawn within diverging, perhaps incommensurable, theoretical frameworks. For Saussure and for contemporary semiotics, language is a social institution, a semiotic (or semiological) system that is sustained by and sustains the collective. But language in this social, systematic, institutional sense is not known – is not an object of study – in the eighteenth century. In the eighteenth-century view, language is one set of instruments (perhaps the most prevalent one, but not the most 'perfect' one imaginable) which rational beings use to mark, externalize, manipulate, and communicate their mental representations. The objects studied by contemporary and by Enlightenment semiotics are not at all the same. It is for this reason that we cannot say that one is correct, the other mistaken.

As I mentioned, the element of free choice is the essential component of the eighteenth-century sign concept. Consider Wolff's definition: 'We also have the practice of bringing two entities together in one place as we please – entities which otherwise would not come together – and making one the sign of the other. Such signs are called *arbitrary* [*willkürliche*] signs...Words belong among the arbitrary signs: for that a word and an idea are present together at the same time or that one of the two follows upon the other rests on our free choice [*Willkür*].'[19] In the Latin *Ontologia*, these arbitrary signs are called 'artificial' (*signa artificialia*) and their signification is said to 'depend on the free choice' of intelligent beings.[20] The sign is essentially a name, freely chosen to mark a representation itself directly knowable; language is a nomenclature for the realm of ideas. For this reason, the sign in eighteenth-century thought is inextricably bound up with a primordial act of naming. The question of the origin of speech in an 'act by which, at a given moment, names were assigned to things' – the very question which for Saussure is 'not even worth asking'[21] – becomes one of the Enlightenment's most intensely debated issues.

Wolff himself does not address the question of the origin of speech as such, but he does position sign-use within the ascending hierarchy of mental representations his *Psychologia Empirica* unfolds. The sign is introduced into the discussion at that point where the subject's dependence on the contingency of sensations and images yields to deliberate inquiry. For Wolff, the ability to achieve this distance and freedom from the thrall of sensation is manifested by the deliberately effected focus of attention (*Attentio, Aufmerksamkeit*) and its protracted form, reflection (*Reflexio, Überdenken*). Within the suspension of contingent sensation provided by reflection the world manifests itself in such a way that its various parts are distinguished. As Wolff phrases it, when we reflect on an object, we perceive it distinctly and, perceiving it distinctly, we discriminate several individual 'enunciables' within it.[22] These intuited enunciables are then marked by signs which function essentially as names.[23] Here we see why the definition of the conventional or arbitrary sign (Wolff speaks of 'signa artificialia') necessarily implies an element of free choice: the sign is instituted at that moment when the distance achieved in reflection allows us to attend to representations over which we have free control ('apperceptiones dependentia a nostro arbitrio') and to mark these with signs the meaning of which is therefore also a matter of our free selection ('vis significandi eorum prorsus ab arbitrio nostro pendet').[24]

Thus the sign is defined in terms of an intuition which itself is prior to any act of signification. Because man enjoys the freedom of reflection, he can choose to name – with a sign of his own making – the various features or objects he discriminates. Since the name is, in a sense, gratuitous, being merely a mark for an idea already entertained, then we can say that it derives its significative force from our arbitrary choice. In fact, the arbitrary nature of the verbal sign is necessary for Wolff's theory. If the sign were other than arbitrary in this sense, if its coming into being depended on factors other than the free choice of the soul; if, in short, it had any intrinsic history or were itself in any way productive, then the status of the presignificative moment of intuition would be threatened. The doctrine of the arbitrary sign in Wolff's philosophy serves to guarantee the epistemological primacy of intuitive apprehension by relegating the sign to the status of a gratuitous name. In effect, Wolff raises the question of the sign in order to dispense with it as bearing no intrinsic relationship to the acquisition of knowledge. The sign is arbitrary because it is engendered in the reflective freedom preceding its institution.[25]

Given this definition of the arbitrary sign, we can begin to describe the structural position of the sign concept in Enlightenment thought: the institution of the sign signals the dawning of reflection, the achievement of a degree of freedom from the contingent flux of sensation and imagination, the first, tentative efforts of deliberate inquiry and rationality. The sign, in other words, is introduced at the point of man's passage from nature to culture. This hypothesis as to the structural position of the sign concept can be confirmed by comparing Wolff's account with theories which explicitly take up the question of the origin of language. As we have seen, Wolff presupposes attention and reflection as those mental operations which liberate man from the contingency of sensation and imagination and create a free arena in which the sign can be instituted. If we turn to Condillac's *Essai sur l'origine des connaissances humaines*, we encounter a view that is symmetrically the reverse: rather than presupposing reflection, the sign is the prerequisite of reflection.[26] And Herder, in his prize essay on the origin of language, synthesizes the two views (thereby solving the dilemma of priority) by having the freedom of reflection (*Besonnenheit*, *Reflexion*) and sign-use emerge together as two aspects of human being-in-the-world.[27] As in the case of Wolff, we find that for both Herder and Condillac the institution of the sign is correlated with the freedom from sheer contingency that inaugurates human learning, inquiry, and culture.

It is possible to give this structural position of the sign a finer articulation. The passage from nature to culture through the invention of a language of arbitrary signs implies a radical transformation which to many appeared paradoxical. How could it be that nature produces culture out of itself? Condillac himself notes that sign use would seem to be made possible only by the very reflective operations of which it is the precondition.[28] To solve the problem, a number of gradualist accounts attempted – in lieu of appeal to a more or less fictional hypothesis of divine instruction – to interpolate transitional stages between the radically opposed poles of nature and culture, sensation and thought, dependence and freedom. Condillac's own 'language of action' is one such intermediate phase: a language, and yet pre-conventional.[29] Another solution is put forward by Moses Mendelssohn in a text publicly addressed to Lessing and presumably relating their joint views.[30] Mendelssohn imagines the following sequence: First, the mimesis of natural sounds (onomatopoeia) and the natural expression of emotions (interjection-like cries) provide an entirely pre-conventional repertoire of terms. Then the meanings of these first terms are expanded and displaced in a quasi-natural process that moves along associational paths and that corresponds to the rhetorical (tropic) transformation of meanings. Mendelssohn's account, therefore, develops (without much originality, actually) three terms which could be said to occupy the lower limit of language, its contact with nature. Beneath the level of arbitrary signs proper he locates the quasi-natural signifying procedures of mimesis, expression and trope. The interesting point to note is that all three of these terms designate poetic or aesthetic concepts. Mendelssohn's brief reflection on the origin of language indicates the structural position that the Enlightenment assigns to aesthetic representations. The aesthetic mediates between the flux of sensations and images, the sheer contingency of our natural being on the one hand, and the ordered unfolding of our knowledge in civilized discourse on the other. In terms of Enlightenment semiotics, this means that aesthetic representations are characterized by the fact that they reactualize an archaic stratum of pre-conventional signifying procedures.[31]

The definition of the arbitrary sign is related to a second conceptual opposition that governs Enlightenment semiotics. The sign, as we have seen, is an indifferent mark freely selected to name an idea or representation that can itself be directly intuited. It is possible, therefore, to distinguish between those cases when we directly attend to our ideas and those when we attend merely to the signs that have been substituted for them: 'It should be noted that words are the basis of a special type of cognition which we call figural cognition [*die Figürliche*]. For we represent things to ourselves either themselves or through words or other signs. The first type of cognition is called *intuitive* cognition [*anschauende Erkäntnis*]; the second is figural cognition [*figürliche Erkäntnis*].'[32] It is this notion of figural cognition – the Latin *cognitio symbolica* is later, with Meier, Mendelssohn and Lessing, translated as 'symbolic cognition' [*symbolische Erkenntnis*] – which in the Enlightenment subsumes (and effaces) the entire experience of the objectivity of discourse, its opacity, its otherness to lived experience. And, as I shall argue in the next chapter, it is the distinction between figural and intuitive cognition which provides the emerging discipline of aesthetics with one of its foundational conceptual pairs.

The primacy of intuition in classical thought from Descartes on is well known. Only intuition (or deductions proceeding from intuitions) guarantees truth and certainty. However, if we substitute for our intuitions the mediated representations of figural or symbolic cognition, we sacrifice that self-evidence which alone anchors thought in truth. The unmotivated quality of the sign ('in itself indifferent. . . to whatever it signifies')[33] brings with it the consequence that discourse is deprived of certainty. Wolff states the matter in a typically laborious sentence: 'Since the words which mean something do not represent any distinguishing feature of that thing (for, to take one example, the word *truth* represents no aspect of truth), and since, for that reason, the word is only intelligible insofar as we remember that it signifies a certain thing of which we have had an idea, that is, in memory of the intuitive cognition; then it can be concluded that the *figural cognition based on ordinary language has in itself no clarity and certainty.*'[34] Because it is interposed between the attentive soul and the idea or meaning, the sign is the source of error and false belief. Constant vigilance is required lest the mind be led astray by the merely functional surface of discourse and blindly accept signs without inquiring what ideas they represent: 'In order that each person might learn whether he knows what he is saying or whether his words are only an empty tone it is necessary that he ask himself, in the case of every word he speaks, what idea he associates with that word.'[35] The passage signals a dual attitude as regards signs and language that is characteristic not only of Wolff but of the entire era. Indeed, we shall encounter it again in Christian Garve's review of Lessing's *Laocoon* as well as in the *Laocoon* itself. On the one hand, sanguinity: if the sign is merely the sign-of-an-idea, then we need only trace the contours and contents of our ideas and knowledge can progress forthrightly, unimpaired by the needless haggling and misunderstanding of 'word-battles.'[36] A word which cannot be related to a definite idea is no sign at all; it is the empty shell of a sign, mere noise, and can be dismissed from consideration. On the other hand, a suspicion of the 'glozing deceits'[37] of signs: Where words are used without circumspect attention to the ideas they mark, minds are confounded, chimeras taken for truth, and inquiry is led astray into a labyrinth of senseless dispute. A sign which is no genuine sign but only 'an empty tone' can still seduce speaker and listener into believing that the discourse is really about something. Our confusions are the products not only of the careless use of signs but also of a certain inertia that is endemic to sign use.[38] Even nonsensical signs insist on being spoken and accepted. Thus, the fervency with which the age discusses the nature of signs is sparked by the hope of liberating man from their thrall.[39] The intuitionist doctrine of the sign is essentially critical and curative. The last avatars of Enlightenment semiotics are to be sought among the nonsense-slayers of the Vienna School.

## Classification of signs: natural signs

Perhaps the primary theme of Enlightenment semiotics, its central task, is the classification of signs. The actual details of these classifications are not extremely important. The typologies tend to be wide-meshed: language, for instance, is simply given a global classification (arbitrary) and the matter is left at that. Rare, it seems to me, is a thinker such as Lambert who, in his 'Semiotik,' actually tries to discern what various signifying procedures are at work within that deceptive unity we call language. Among works published in Germany, only Lessing's *Laocoon*, which appeared two years after Lambert's work in 1766, evinces comparable subtlety. What interests me about these classifications, then – and Wolff continues to provide my central case in point – is less their results than their overall strategy. My question is not: how is a particular signifying practice classified; rather: what are the presuppositions that allow the classification to be made?

But perhaps the term 'presupposition' is inadequate; perhaps what I'm getting at exerts its constraints at a deeper level than what we normally call 'presuppositions' do. For the central fact about Enlightenment semiotics, that which constitutes it from one end to the other, is *the functionalization of discourse and language*. It is not as if a group of researchers undertook to study a set of objects (signs) with a certain set of presuppositions in mind. Rather, it seems that prior to the formation of any such presuppositions, that is, as their precondition, language and discourse had to be *made functional*. Beneath the level of what people thought about language an event took place which remade language. This is how I understand Foucault when he speaks of the 'being' of language as that which characterizes a particular *episteme*: it is not that men have had different views about an invariant object called language, but rather that the relationships – both practical and theoretical – between language, knowledge and experience are organized in historically specific patterns. A change in these patterns is of the order of a real event, not of the order of opinions or presuppositions.[40]

The notion of the sign – regardless of what type of sign we are dealing with – is only the explicit formulation of this functionality: 'A *sign* is what we call an entity from which another entity, either present or future or past, is known.'[41] The sign is a means to an end, a vehicle that allows us to get somewhere else, a transparency almost, something to be passed through. The sign is defined entirely within the framework of an instrumental rationality. From his position within a different organization of knowledge, Wilhelm von Humboldt clearly recognized the limitations involved in this subsumption of language to the means–end logic of the sign and he criticized it as reductive and oversimplifying.[42] But Humboldt himself erred when he interpreted this reduction as a philosophical naiveté, an almost natural, pre-reflective way of talking about the language we speak. The functional definition of language as a set of instrumental signs is in no way natural; it is a

25

construct specific to the culture of the Enlightenment. Furthermore, it is hardly naive: it is one of the central concepts by means of which the progressive, critical moment of eighteenth-century thought establishes itself.

The most important internal division of this field of functional signs is that which separates natural signs from artificial or arbitrary signs. The first thing to note about this distinction is that it does not operate as one expects. It does not – at least not initially – distinguish mimetic signs from unmotivated signs. Rather, the classification is based on origin: arbitrary signs are instituted by intelligent beings while natural signs are given in nature. For this reason, Wolff argues, the very notion of what a natural sign is in itself contains the reason for its signification.[43] From the nature of the thing it is possible to infer what it signifies. What is meant by this somewhat obscure definition can be clarified by looking at concrete examples: natural signs precede, follow upon (or are co-present with the things they signify and the reason the two are linked together is typically that one is a cause or effect of the other. Smoke, then, is a natural sign of fire; symptoms are signs of a particular disease. As long as we are informed about the causes and effects of the things we encounter in experience we are in a position to read those things as natural signs. We can infer from what they are what they signify.

This notion of natural signs reveals the interaction of pragmatic and theological impulses that is so characteristic of Enlightenment thinking. In the first place, the notion seems to capture a general sense of the world's communicativeness. Because they are related to their signifieds by causal, or otherwise guaranteed, connections, natural signs are a source of worldly information to the beholder who interprets them. Aspects of behavior indicate a person's virtuous or vicious character; facial expressions signify the passions that move beneath their surface. Because of their informativeness and their reliability, natural signs help man orient himself and prepare for future contingencies. For this reason Wolff argues that the interpretation of natural signs is by far the most prevalent form of sign use in our experience.[44] Indeed, reading natural signs is something we do automatically merely by assessing the situation in which we find ourselves. 'Everyone infers effects from causes, and vice versa.'[45] In the British tradition the concept of the natural sign plays a similar role. Locke holds that the 'secondary qualities' such as color, odor or warmth are signs of the inaccessible events which produced them.[46] Berkeley conceives of the entire visible world as a sign system: visual signs are so constructed as to allow man to anticipate the nature of tactile contact with distant objects; sight is foresight.[47] In all these cases, natural signs constitute a worldly nexus of messages the comprehension of which allows us to evaluate our present situation, to make inferences about things we can't immediately see, and to align our expectations with probable eventualities. Thus, what the world communicates to man through these omnipresent natural signs is not a hidden, spiritual message, not a theological sub-text, but merely the world itself. Natural signs simply encode the kind of information that a practically – in some cases, scientifically – oriented community of experiencers and observers has managed to glean. This information is entirely immanent to the world which conveys it. Both the natural signs and what they signify are located within the sphere of natural causes and effects. They have their entire functionality within the sphere of knowledge.[48]

The concept of natural sign would therefore seem to have undergone a process of total secularization. No longer do the things of the world convey the spiritual meaning of Divine Love;[49] they merely signify themselves, their causes and effects, their hidden aspects. And yet a theological moment is unmistakably present in the notion of natural signs. We see this very clearly in Berkeley, for whom the visual sign system of nature is in fact a system of arbitrary signs instituted by God, a language so efficient and so transparent that all men can read it without difficulty. In Germany, Baumgarten and Meier represent a similar theological view. According to Baumgarten, the world can be thought of as a perfect 'nexus significativus.'[50] This notion follows from the metaphysics of the Leibniz-Wolffian school. Assuming the Creator's rational and benevolent selection of this world over all alternatives, we must conclude that this is the best of all possible worlds. One aspect of God's selection involves the patterns of signification inherent in the world to be created. What human beings call a natural sign – because it is part of created nature – is in reality an arbitrary sign selected by God. And given the wisdom and benevolence of God's choice, natural signs must be characterized by the highest degree of perfection possible. '*God* is the *author* of the significant nexus in this world, and therefore every natural sign is an effect of God's action, and from God's perspective it is an arbitrary sign, and therefore a consequence of the wisest choice and the most benevolent will.'[51] Thus, the notion of a natural sign does indeed preserve the theological view of a divinely instituted language of nature, but what this language of natural signs communicates is nothing but nature itself. Natural signs express the perfection and order of the natural world and they make this order transparent and knowable to man. Nature is a sign system which – free of all the deficiencies and limitations of culturally instituted sign systems – expresses only itself. And this brings us to what I consider the decisive point regarding the distinction between arbitrary and natural signs: they are not essentially different from one another. Indeed, natural signs are themselves arbitrary, that is, chosen, instituted by an intelligent being. The distinction between the two types of sign lies solely in the breadth, thoroughness and transparency of each, in short in their respective degrees of perfection. For this reason, *the system of natural signs is the telos of all our culturally instituted systems of arbitrary signs*. The point where the two types of sign coincide, where natural and arbitrary signs become indistinguishable, is the mind of God. To perfect human language would be to render it equivalent to (a complete translation of) that divinely instituted nexus of signification through which nature exhibits itself.

The point of convergence where the arbitrary signs of human institution attain to the status of natural signs remains, needless to say, an ideal. Yet, as an ideal, it is culturally efficacious, serving as a constant stimulation to research and speculation. In my view, this ideal of a fully perfected, quasi-divine language is one of the most profound imperatives of Enlightenment culture. Certainly it exerts its constraints on the emerging theory of art and aesthetic representation, as I shall subsequently show. At this point, however, I merely want to comment on one final aspect of the Enlightenment notion of natural signs. This aspect has to do with those natural signs which man himself commonly produces. These are essentially two: mimetic signs and expressive signs.

I have already mentioned that natural signs are not to be equated with mimetic or what today we would call iconic signs. Indeed, many of the instances which the Enlightenment classified as natural signs would today be considered indices, signs that have some existential connection with their signifieds. The eighteenth-century concept which most closely approximates the contemporary notion of iconic sign is introduced by Baumgarten and Meier: 'Essential signs [*signa essentialia, wesentliche Zeichen*] are those signs the parts and mode of composition of which are similar to the signified objects to a great degree. One thing among two similar things can easily be cognized from the other, and indeed all the more easily the more similar they are to one another.'[52] Here we find a concept that is quite distinct from that of a natural sign and which isolates those signs which imitate the things they refer to. In practice, however, the two concepts merge. First of all, natural signs are inevitably essential signs, as Meier notes, since there is throughout nature a proportionality or similarity between cause and effect.[53] Secondly, those essential signs which man fashions – pictures and diagrams, for instance – are natural signs because the nature of the sign vehicle itself contains the reason for its signification. Wolff therefore refers to signs which 'naturally imitate' their signifieds as natural signs even though they are produced by man.[54] And for Dubos, Mendelssohn and Lessing – to name only three – paintings qualify as natural signs. Thus, not only are the signs produced by nature imitative, but also all the imitative signs produced by man – from mimetic sounds to paintings – are natural.

The second type of natural sign that man produces consists of those signs which nature emits through man: cries and other vocal gestures, facial movements that express the emotions. References to this type of natural sign can be found throughout the century, for instance in the work of Meier, Mendelssohn, Lessing and Herder in Germany, Condillac and Rousseau in France. The interesting thing to note is that these expressive signs are classified side by side with imitative signs beneath the concept natural. Again, this has to do with the proportionality inherent in nature: expression is a form of mimesis that mobilizes non-visual similarities. 'Nature signifies the passions through changes in the body, which are essential signs, and for that reason it is easy to see whether a person is happy or sad.'[55] These expressive gestures are 'as it were paintings or hieroglyphic signs'[56] of the movements of the soul they represent. Thus, there is no essential difference between imitative and expressive natural signs. Both are linked to their signifieds by the isomorphism that reigns throughout nature and that characterizes the divinely instituted nexus of signification.

### Sign-use and distinct cognition

The language of arbitrary signs – that object of study proper to the Enlightenment – is not a system that underlies and makes possible individual speech performances in the sense of Saussure's *langue*; nor is it the characteristic expression of a cultural identity or spirit as it would be for Herder. It is, rather, a more or less efficient means for the marking, manipulating and communicating of mental representations. Language externalizes and represents mental discourse, that unfolding of ideas with which we represent the world. And the more distinct our ideas become (the more finely we discern the features of things), the more we depend upon language as the medium of our thinking. The progress of knowledge as an ever more penetrating analysis of representations is indissociably linked to the codification of knowledge in linguistic (and other) sign systems and to the predominance of symbolic cognition as the mode in which that knowledge is subjectively appropriated. This correlation of sign use and distinct cognition is the third and final theme of Enlightenment semiotics I shall discuss here.

According to a Wolffian classification of signs in terms of their function, signs can be used (a) to abbreviate (b) to keep secret (c) to represent things distinctly, and (d) to discover new truths.[57] The first two types are of little interest (examples mentioned are, for (a) astronomical and chemical symbols, and for (b) secret codes and alchemical emblems) but the third takes us to the center of the Enlightenment view of language. Wolff offers as an example of function (c) (distinct representation) the system of dance notation introduced in 1700 by Raoul Anger Feuillet. In dance notation the features of each step – which in their simultaneity and evanescence are hard to distinguish – are isolated and marked. The notation can then be used to expose, in an easily perceptible manner, the nature of each step as a composite of certain fundamental features. Language, for Wolff, functions in precisely this way. Its articulation parallels the articulation of the object when the object is cognized distinctly; the 'enunciation' of the signs corresponds to the arrangement of the 'enunciables' in the object itself. It is for this reason that distinct cognition can be defined as the ability to 'enumerate for someone else the properties by virtue of which we recognize the object.'[58] A distinct concept is intrinsically communicable. There are, of course, ideas that are inherently global, irreducibly con-fused ideas such as we have of colors, and these cannot be communicated discursively, cannot be defined intensionally. The only means of instructing someone what 'red' means is to show him something red. For Locke, such 'simple ideas' as the sense datum 'red' are the semantic primitives upon which all language is built. Wolff, however, regards them as symptoms of our intellect's limitations. There simply are representations which we, by virtue of the restricted scope and acumen of our understanding, cannot analyze: 'Such confused concepts are for example the roar of the wind, the rushing of the water, the pounding of the waves. Indeed, distinctions of taste and smell can only be noted clearly, but not distinctly.'[59] Such intrinsically clear ideas exist beneath the threshold of language; they can only be pointed to and named.

In the initial stages of knowing, of course, signs merely mark those enunciables which we intuitively attend to. Wolff speaks of a 'dependency of symbolic on intuitive cognition in the first operation of the mind.'[60] But gradually sign use becomes productive. Rather than merely cataloguing ideas we have already entertained, it serves as the vehicle through which our knowledge acquires increasing distinctness:

Figural cognition however has many advantages over intuitive cognition when the latter is not complete, that is, when it does not distinctly set forth as if before our eyes what a thing contains, how it is associated with others, and how it relates to them. For, since our sensations are for the most part confused or obscure, so it is that words and signs serve the end of distinctness insofar as we distinguish by virtue of them what the different aspects in and among things are. But since in this manner the similarity that is to be met with between individual things shines forth, so it is that one arrives in this manner at general concepts. And therefore it is through words that knowledge of the universal becomes distinct.[61]

The features which cohere within the perceived object are distributed along the horizontal axis of language where they are easily distinguishable one from another. In this way, figural (or symbolic) cognition actually brings about distinctness; its form is analytical. Furthermore, since the signs expose the features in a manner that can be easily surveyed, those properties several things hold in common 'shine forth' –

offering themselves for abstraction. Thus, language carries thought into the dimension of the universal, of conceptualization proper.

In this dimension sign use is indispensable. Johann Christoph Schwab, a late representative of rationalist thinking, merely echoes Wolff's views when he writes:

Since these [general concepts] are not only difficult to form but also difficult to reproduce and to fix, we must attach them to easily reproducible and fixed audible and visual ideas in order to make use of them. That is, we must attach them to articulate *sounds*, or *words*, and to *characters*. Insofar as we deal in our thinking with words and characters, we are dealing simultaneously with the concepts that are attached to them. And in this way thinking is made a great deal easier; or rather it is made possible, for to think without these signs would be extremely difficult for us, if not altogether impossible.[62]

Signs guarantee the easy reproducibility of abstract notions, which, without such fixed vehicles, would slip into oblivion. Sign-use is also essential in the formation of judgements since the third component of any judgement in addition to subject and predicate, that is, the act of affirmation or negation, emerges only in symbolic cognition. For this reason Wolff emphasizes the 'prerogative of symbolic cognition in the second operation of mind.'[63] Finally, discursive reason, which operates with distinct and abstract concepts and which compares judgements and links them in syllogistic argumentation, is thoroughly dependent on sign-use: 'The use of language facilitates and enhances the use of reason: apart from the use of language the use of reason could hardly be conceded.'[64]

For Enlightenment semiotics, then, the progress of knowledge toward ever greater distinctness of thought, toward an ever more refined analysis of our representations, is likewise a progress into language, a transition from perception and imagination to the manipulation of arbitrary signs in symbolic cognition. But this progress can also be thought of as a progress of language itself. In its earliest stages of development, language was a collection of names for clear, sensate ideas. It was full of tropic designations in which random associations determined what was being said. Indeed, it still preserved many of those mimetic (onomatopoetic) and expressive-gestural signs that constituted its first, quasi-natural beginnings. Through time, however, it was made both more 'philosophical' – terms are given secure definitions, abstract terms are increasingly introduced – and more 'grammatical,' more subject to law. The advance of knowledge and enlightenment is at the same time a refinement of language. Rousseau, of course, gives this 'progress' its most complete mythological interpretation, showing that it can as easily be understood as a 'decline.'[65] For the followers of Wolff, however, the indissociable link between the improvement of knowledge and the syntactic and semantic normalization of language becomes the justification for a powerful pedagogical program.[66] In this way, Enlightenment semiotics not only describes sign-use, but regulates and controls it. Some of the cultural efficacy of this enterprise can be measured in the sociolinguistic analysis of the 'Latinization' of the German language which Herder presents in his third collection of *Fragments on Modern Literature*.[67]

If knowledge progresses into language it can likewise move beyond it. The so-called natural languages, after all, are defective in many ways: all the terms are not securely defined; accidental factors (factors other than rational considerations) presided over the formation of many syntactic and semantic details. Perhaps an even more serious disadvantage is the fact that linguistic representations do not present their corresponding mental representations to intuition, thereby making error possible and necessitating constant vigilance on the part of speakers and listeners. But other sign systems are imaginable which do not suffer from these deficiencies. Let us assume that analysis has arrived at the inventory of irresolvable notions or logical simples which are at the basis of all complex representations. Let us assume further that the rules according to which these notions can be combined are known. Now, if we designate these notions with a set of primitive (atomic) signs and we codify the combinatorial rules as a syntax, then we have a sign system which can generate all possible (non-contradictory) concepts and judgements and which, through an algebraic form of calculation, can decide the truth of any proposed statement. Furthermore, this sign system would be absolutely transparent, for the derived signs formed through the combination of its primitive signs would be isomorphic to the notions they designate and the states of affairs these in turn represent. This is the ideal of the *ars characteristica combinatoria* which Wolff, following Leibniz and others, introduces in his *Psychologica Empirica*.[68] In such a perfect philosophical language, sign use would be more than an instrument for thinking; it would coincide with reason itself.

### *The place of the sign in Enlightenment culture*

The notion of the sign occupies an ambiguous position in the thought of the eighteenth century. The sign is at once essential and accidental, the medium of knowledge and the source of error. Thus, Michel Foucault can argue convincingly that 'Classical philosophy, from Malebranche to Ideology, was through and through a philosophy of the sign.'[69] And Juri M. Lotman can write with equal justification: 'The striving for de-semiotization, the battle against the sign, is the basis of the culture of the Enlightenment.'[70] The contradiction between these two statements is, of course, only apparent and it is my belief that, despite major methodological differences, Foucault's analysis of *epistemes* and Lotman's typology of cultures can be shown to be mutually supportive. Be that as it may, the quoted statements do dramatize the dynamic tension that any analysis of Enlightenment thought about signs and language must endeavor to capture.

Where does this tension come from? As I have emphasized, we are not dealing here with a particular cultural perspective on an invariant object (language or signs), but rather with the codification of the being of language within Enlightenment culture, that is, of the set of practical and theoretical relations that obtain between language, knowledge and experience. Two broad trends seem to me to be characteristic of the modifications that these relations undergo in the eighteenth century, trends which are probably inseparable from the notion of Enlightenment itself: on the one hand, the desacralization of language; on the other, the methodologization of knowledge.

By desacralization I mean that textual instantiation is not in itself a value, but rather merely an extrinsic and accidental vehicle for what is of genuine importance: the signified ideas, the content. There are two cultural sites where language and signs (for it is a matter of more than just linguistic signs) are sacred, where texts are auratic,[71] and these are, of course, the church and the court. The desacralization of language is the extrication of language from its place within the ceremonies of religious and absolutist authority and its transformation into a medium of communication and debate among equal subjects. Enlightenment semiotics, with its emphasis on the merely conventional character of institutional signs and the merely functional character of the signifier, provides both a theory of language as desacralized and an instrument of critique that can be used to bring about such desacralization. Eighteenth-century sign theory reinterprets language and in so doing helps remake it and bring it within the regime of an historically specific will to power. This aspect of the genealogy of Enlightenment culture is captured by Lotman's characterization of that culture as a 'battle against the sign.'

To denude texts (written or spoken texts, but also symbols of religious and political authority) of their aura is to expose them as instantiations of conventional signs which themselves are entirely external to the ideas they represent. It is only the ideas that count and they must exhibit rational coherence if they are to be acceptable. Enlightenment semiotics rejects the false coin of signs and accepts only ideational gold that can pass the judgement of reason. At the same time, however, rational inquiry finds itself in need of – and, as it progresses, increasingly dependent upon – sign systems as the medium and instrument of knowledge. The methodologization of knowledge – the replacement of erudition and the truth of authority with science in the broadest sense – can be accomplished only through the development of semiotic instruments that enable reason itself to progress. Thus, Descartes' fourth rule of method requiring a complete enumeration of the steps followed by the inquiring mind (interestingly, the rule is introduced as a prophylactic against forgetfulness, that is, against the finitude of human reason) is not at all the afterthought it appears to be: codification in a semiotic system is indispensible to the project of reason.[72] By the same token, language, as that semiotic system we most depend upon at present, must itself be remade so as to fit the needs of methodical thinking: 'In philosophical method only terms which have been fixed in exact definitions may be introduced, and nothing will be accepted as true which hasn't been sufficiently proved;...'[73] Rational inquiry is indissociable – this the Enlightenment recognized – from certain forms of semiosis. It is in this sense that the thought of the eighteenth century is, as Foucault says, 'through and through a philosophy of the sign.'

These two major trends that characterize the refashioning of discourse in the Enlightenment need to be studied in all their specificity. My own task here, however, is much more limited: I merely want to sketch the most general outlines of the theoretical codification that these developments assume in Enlightenment semiotics. It is a matter of formulating the myth of the sign as it emerges from the superimposition of various eighteenth-century texts dealing with sign theory.

The sign is always a means or medium (Baumgarten and Meier define it as a 'medium' or 'Mittel' [means]),[74] something to be passed through. It is characterized by its thoroughgoing functionality. Thus, as conventional sounds or characters employed for the purpose of representing ideas, linguistic signs (signifiers) in themselves are of little interest and not worthy of much attention or cultivation. (This implies, as I shall argue in the following chapter, that an art of the signifier is no longer

37

acceptable.) All dignity and importance accrue to the signified ideas, our more or less ordered, more or less distinct representations of the world.

This medial function and position defines the sign at every level of analysis. Viewed in simple pragmatic terms, the sign is a means for conveying our thoughts to an interlocutor:

We have the practice of making our thoughts known to others through words. And therefore words are nothing else but signs of our thoughts, out of which, that is, someone else can know them. For example, when someone asks me what I am thinking of and I reply: the sun, then I am giving to be understood through this word what thing I am at that moment representing in my thoughts.[75]

According to this scheme, the sender has certain ideas in mind which he can at will communicate to another through the use of signs. The receiver recognizes the signs as conventional stand-ins for ideas, decodes the signs accordingly and thereby attains to the ideas which the sender was entertaining. The movement is from a mental stage of intuition through material signs to a second mental stage of intuition equivalent to the first. It is easy to see why Meier referred to signs as 'canals through which thoughts pass from one mind to the other.'[76] The sign is the area of transit between two intuitions.

This priority of intuition – it is always both the origin and end of sign-use – can be observed throughout Enlightenment semiotics. Indeed, we can speak here of an intuitionist doctrine of the sign: the very notion of the arbitrary sign is formulated in terms of the notion of intuition; the sign is, at its origin, the freely chosen mark of a directly intuited idea. The ideal of intuition likewise guides the critique of confused or mystified sign use. Our errors and disputes follow from our inattention to the ideas signified by our words: 'it often happens that men, even when they would apply themselves to an attentive consideration, do set their thoughts more on words than things . . . But so far as words are of use and signification, so far is there a constant connection between the sound and the idea, and a designation that the one stands for the other; without such application of them, they are nothing but so much insignificant noise.'[77]

But of course intuition is not always possible. The limitations of the soul are such that it must rely on instruments which, though extrinsic to thinking itself, nevertheless allow thought to progress well beyond the point attainable without such aids. Sign-use – however secondary it might be in comparison to intuition – introduces into thinking an economy that enables inquiry to progress. The signs we employ are constituted materially in such a way as to facilitate their memory and use: the 'material ideas' that function as signifiers (e.g. articulate tones and characters) can be easily summoned up by the imagination (the faculty of recall) and easily manipulated and combined. Thus, if we denote a confused perception with a word, then the imaginative operability inherent in the word (as signifier) is substituted for the imaginative intractability of the perception. Such substitution, Wolff remarks (laying the foundation of a rationalist poetics which Lessing will later build on), allows for the rapid and economical combination of several confused ideas into a fictive entity.[78] The same economic virtues of the sign (dispensation from mental labor through sign-use) enable us to manipulate abstractions, indeed to form abstractions and thereby to find access to the universal in the first place. *The form of the signifier itself enables thought to proceed*. By virtue of its articulate or analytic structure, the organization of the signifier anticipates the progress of thought. It is the linguistic sign – this sense image that is attended to not in itself but for the sake of what it signifies – that allows the mind to free itself from sense images.

'Speech distinguishes man among the animals. . .'[79] 'The usage of signs is the true cause of the progress of the imagination, of contemplation and of memory.'[80] 'Apart from the use of language the use of reason could hardly be conceded.'[81] The sign elevates man out of nature, frees him from dependence on the present moment of sensation or perception, allows him to expand the scope and to increase the penetration of his knowledge. The progress of knowledge can only occur where man substitutes for his original, naturally endowed intuitions a symbolic cognition that relies on conventionally instituted, arbitrary signs. Here too sign-use is a means, a middle term between origin and end. It is the detour which the soul takes rather than proceeding directly, that is, rather than employing intuition alone. This does not mean, however, that knowledge and reason are left dependent on a form of representation which, as Wolff said of symbolic cognition, 'has in itself no clarity and certainty.'[82] On the contrary: just as arbitrary signs are defined in terms of a moment of intuition in which they originated, so too is the symbolic cognition that carries our knowledge oriented toward an ideal of cognition which is purely intuitive: the *telos* of rational inquiry is divine knowledge in which the symbolic cognition of human knowing is reconverted into an intuitive form. God's knowledge is at once intuitive and completely analytical. He does not require signs or the successive process of analysis which characterizes man's knowledge.[83] In divine knowledge, the extended sequences of signs in which the results of human inquiry are codified are transformed into the simultaneity and immediacy of intuitive apprehension. The fact that the intuition characteristic of God's knowledge is the immanent *telos* of human sign-use is made clear by the linguistic ideal of an *ars characteristica combinatoria*. As Herder critically noted, a thoroughly philosophical language in the sense of such a 'characteristic' would have to be formed from a standpoint equivalent to that of God.[84] And indeed, in the 'characteristic' Wolff imagined, knowledge would shed its semiotic character and return to the immediacy of intuition: 'By virtue of the *ars characteristica combinatoria symbolic cognition is converted as it were into an intuitive cognition*, even in those cases where a distinct intuitive cognition cannot ordinarily be attained.'[85]

The Enlightenment myth of the sign, then, positions sign-use between two forms of intuition, perception and divine cognition. Considered in a purely synchronic fashion, sign-use can

therefore be said to mark the position of man within a hierarchy of souls. Man is distinguished from the animals because
he has the requisite strength of attentiveness to form signs and
to inquire rationally. Yet he is distinguished from God because
he lacks the representational capacity sufficient for an intuitive
and thoroughly distinct grasp of all things. The sign is the
mark of man's finitude: 'But precisely this necessity of abstraction and signification (that is, of symbolic cognition) proves
that we are dust. Presumably, higher beings require these aids
less than we do, and the highest of all sees through all possible
worlds with a single look.'[86] The same structure, however, can
also be projected onto a diachronic axis. Such a projection would
yield a philosophical interpretation of history (a *Geschichts-
philosophie*) as *progressive semiosis*. In this scheme, it is the use
of arbitrary signs which allows man to extricate himself from
nature and to embark upon the history of his own self-
perfection. (The transition to sign-use is facilitated by the
natural signifying procedures of imitation and expression.)
But this history has as its immanent *telos* the reconversion of
conventional signifying operations (symbolic cognition) into a

## Figure 2

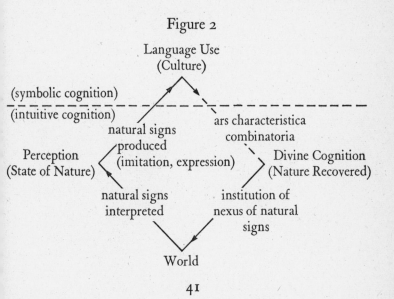

41

language that 'exhibits notions as if before the eyes.'[87] This fully perfected sign system or *ars characteristica combinatoria* would be equivalent to the divinely instituted nexus of signs that nature itself is. *Through progressive semiosis nature is recovered in the form of a completely transparent language that is equivalent to divine cognition.* Thus, the conventional signs of human institution occupy that middle ground of discourse that emerges out of man's pre-semiotic knowledge in intuition and that eventually returns to intuition in the form of a post-semiotic experience of the world as a logical structure. (Figure 2 summarizes these relations.) Such is the myth of the sign in Enlightenment culture.

# 2 · SEMIOTICS AND AESTHETICS IN THE WORK OF BAUMGARTEN, MEIER AND MENDELSSOHN

## Introduction

Historians of ideas have typically treated the works of Baumgarten, Meier and Mendelssohn as successive stages in the development of psychological, as opposed to logical and metaphysical, explanations of the beautiful.[1] The line of historical movement is thus pictured as running from an 'objective' notion of the aesthetic to an increasingly 'subjective' one. In this chapter I shall take another approach to the matter and discuss the work of all three philosophers as participating in the elaboration of an integral theoretical field. From their collective statements on aesthetics, in other words, I shall reconstruct a single type of theory, an invariant structure of which their works are variant manifestations. My approach does not efface the differences between these writers – differences which are certainly significant in several respects. Mendelssohn wrote, for instance, within a different institutional setting and with different pragmatic intentions than did Baumgarten, a fact which distinguishes the texts of each as regards both content and style. These are indeed important issues, but my analysis here is situated at a level where such differences are not pertinent: the level of what I call a theory-type. My intention, then, is to discuss the work of Baumgarten, Mendelssohn and Meier in terms of a shared theory-type.

We can informally define a theory-type as an organized set of factors that regulates a cohesive body of theoretical work.[2] Among the parameters constituting a theory-type are, for example: the objects described by the theory, the immanent conceptual system employed, the supporting disciplines the theory relies upon, the relationship to practice that the theory entertains, the structures of subjectivity for which the theory is

43

relevant. Such variables as these engender the multiple determinations that, in their specific organization, give a theory-type its identity. The key factor providing such organization, it seems to me, is the predominant model according to which the phenomenal field in question (in this case, the aesthetic field) is conceived. The model reduces the potentially infinite complexity of the phenomenal field to a limited set of components that entertain regular relationships to one another. It is the predominant model which gives a particular theory-type its unique physiognomy.

Aesthetics, in its emergence as an independent philosophical discipline in the eighteenth century, is a *representational* theory; that is, the organizing model that lends this theory-type its character depicts the aesthetic field in terms of the category of representation. The task of this chapter is to describe the most important aspects of this model, with special emphasis on the role of semiotic notions. Before I set out to do this, however, I want to give an external account of representational aesthetic theory by contrasting it with two other theory-types: with a *performance* theory (which models the aesthetic along the lines of a public performance) and an *expressive* theory (which models the aesthetic as an expressive event). The performance theory is the theory-type that develops out of the courtly-aristocratic culture of European absolutism while the expressive theory-type appears in the last quarter of the eighteenth-century, most notably in the work of Johann Gottfried Herder (1744–1803), to compete with representational aesthetics for predominance within bourgeois culture. The performance theory is, of course, almost totally moribund today, having passed from the scene along with the courtly-aristocratic milieu which supported it. Both the representational and the expressive theory-types, however, can claim vital, culturally significant heirs: the former is the ancestor of much work in philosophical aesthetics and, more generally, of all varieties of aesthetic formalism; and from the latter descends the massive and ongoing accumulation of work in the fields of literary, music and art history. My comparison of these three theory-types will be extremely cursory and general. Its function is merely to profile representational aesthetic theory against the background of two alternative theory-types and thereby to outline a context for what will be the primary task of this chapter, the internal analysis of the representational model.

We can begin the contrast by considering the sort of subjective behavior *vis-à-vis* art works that each theory-type starts out from and seeks to account for. In the case of the performance theory, such behavior might be called appreciation: the subject is essentially a connoisseur (often an amateur producer) who awards praise according to a finely tuned sense of what constitutes a performance of quality. This appreciative sense is itself a social accoutrement, a mark of distinction; it has its being not so much as an internal faculty but rather as something exhibited and esteemed. Likewise, the primary functions of art works for the appreciative receiver are eminently public: art entertains him within the context of a group *divertissement* and it rehearses (often glorifies) for him the values of his social class.[3] Aesthetic consumption thereby serves to enhance solidarity with a locally defined social group, but also to profile individual accomplishment: taste, status, wealth. The representational theory accounts for a receptive behavior of an entirely different order. Here the receptive attitude of the subject is oriented toward the reactualization of the artistic representation, the experience of the illusionary presence of the represented object, and the activation of an intense emotional response to that object. Art does not function as an entertainment for this subject, it 'moves' him. And the aesthetic pleasure he feels does not derive from the appreciation of a well executed performance but instead from the intrinsic qualities of the represented object and from the stimulation and energizing of the subject's representational and emotional capacities. Furthermore, rather than integrating the subject within a particular group and allowing him to distinguish himself in that group context by virtue of his appreciative virtuosity, the reception of art socializes the subject on the level of his general humanity (that is, in terms of an idealized group) by developing and exercising those faculties which are at the basis of human community (e.g., sympathy) or which characterize man in his universal identity (e.g., the harmonious play of the representational faculties). Finally, the expressive theory-type introduces a form of receptive behavior I would characterize as divination. I borrow the term from Herder: 'When the effort is worth it, this vital reading, this divination into the soul of the author, is the only true reading and the most profound instrument of self-formation.'[4] The experiencing subject here seeks to understand another subjectivity, that individual creative spirit from which the work issued. By thus divining the identity of the other, the interpreter discovers and develops his own identity as a specific historical and cultural configuration of subjectivity. Art is, on the productive side, a medium of individual self-expression (especially for the author-genius) and, on the receptive side, a medium of self-understanding resulting from the confrontation with other possibilities of subjective experience.

In the case of each theory-type the theorizing itself has a different purpose and obeys different norms. The performance theory seeks to formulate rules for successful production, for achieving an appreciative audience response. Such directives are often most akin to rules of social propriety or decorum. They escape explicit definition and must be characterized by referring to some intangible sense of tact such as *bienséance* or *bon sense*.[5] The theorizing itself relies heavily on authorative examples and exhibits a didactic, exhortative tone. The theory can even assume an artistic form as in Boileau's *L'Art poétique*. The representational theory, by contrast, derives its rules from man's representational faculties. The rules are arrived at deductively by proceeding from indubitable and necessary first principles and their purpose is to establish the conditions of possibility of effective aesthetic representations. The standard of effectiveness is no longer to be found in the sense of propriety of 'la cour et la ville' but rather in the nature of the human soul. The form of presentation is syllogistic argumentation as bare as possible of rhetorical and/or aesthetic appeal. Theory is no longer a set of directives congenial to and participating in actual aesthetic practice; it is a philosophical account of the beautiful and it relates to practice only through its applied form, criticism. The expressive theory-type (to the degree it is concerned with rules at all) attempts to discover the inner logic of cultural and historical production. Works of art, music and literature are not viewed as exemplifying universal rules of aesthetic representation (as Homer, for instance, did for Lessing). Instead, they are studied as so many pieces of evidence, clues pointing to the hidden nature of the human spirit (Herder's *Geist*). The theorizing tends to favor narrative-historical modes of writing. The task is neither prescription nor deduction, but reconstruction and interpretation. In this way, theoretical activity becomes altogether secondary to aesthetic practice, which is the exclusive prerogative of the genius or creative spirit. But at the same time a secondary form of aesthetic practice emerges with the interpretive essay which presents itself as a simulacrum of the spirit expressed in the original work.

Each theory-type can be said to draw on particular disciplines or bodies of thought. The performance theory is intimately associated with the art and discipline of rhetoric. Rhetoric not only emphasizes the persuasive element that is so essential to performance theory, but it also provides directives that cover every aspect of the productive process from invention to public presentation. The representational theory replaces rhetoric with semiotics. Semiotics makes possible the comparative study of different types of aesthetic representation, the description of their intrinsic limits and possibilities, the measurement of their relative efficacy. Finally, expressive theory is supported by the discipline of hermeneutics, which investigates the nature and limits of the interpretive reappropriation of creative meaning intentions.[6]

## Table 1

| PREDOMINANT MODEL | PERFORMANCE MODEL | REPRESENTATION MODEL | EXPRESSIVE MODEL |
|---|---|---|---|
| RECEPTIVE ATTITUDE | appreciation | reactualization of representations | divination |
| EFFECT IN RECEIVER | entertainment | movement | understanding of other and of self |
| SOCIALIZING FUNCTION | reinforcement of class values; self-distinction | integration within universal, human community | expansion of awareness beyond own cultural/historical limits; increased awareness of own national/cultural identity |
| TYPE OF RULES | rules for effective performance; rules of propriety | necessary rules derived from nature of representational faculties | immanent laws of imaginative production, of historical development |
| MODE OF ARGUMENTATION | instruction by example and exhortation | syllogistic | narrative-historical |
| RELATION TO PRACTICE | fraternal: instructs, praises, blames, co-produces | separate but equal; explains or criticizes (judges) | separate and secondary; interprets and imitates |
| MODE OF TEXTUALIZATION | rhetorical/ aesthetic | philosophical | philological/ historical study or interpretive essay |
| ADJACENT DISCIPLINE | rhetoric | semiotics | hermeneutics |

These remarks should suffice to characterize representational aesthetics as one among several alternative theory-types. (Table 1 summarizes the points I have made.) The comparison makes no claim to completeness. As it were, before entering the edifice of Enlightenment aesthetic theory, we have cast a glance at its facade and contrasted it with the facades of the neighboring buildings. From this point on, however, I shall attend exclusively to representational aesthetic theory, discussing first the notion of aesthetic representation, and second the notion of an aesthetic semiotics.

## The theory of aesthetic representation

With Baumgarten, the aesthetic is defined as perfect sensate representation: 'The aim of aesthetics is the perfection of sensate cognition as such.'[7] Such perfection constitutes beauty.[8] In this section I shall circumscribe the theoretical domain that this definition opens up and locate the most important subdivisions within that domain. In other words, I shall reconstruct the representational model of the aesthetic that the works of Baumgarten, Meier and Mendelssohn, regardless of the nuances that distinguish them, elaborate. My thesis is that this model organizes the theoretical activity emerging in the second half of the eighteenth century as the philosophical discipline of aesthetics. This thesis is not without polemical edge. As I mentioned above, historians of ideas have typically situated the works of Baumgarten, Meier and Mendelssohn (as well as other eighteenth-century writers) along an axis running from 'objective' to 'subjective.' This may well be due to the influence of Max Dessoir who at the beginning of this century claimed that all aesthetic theories must of necessity be either subject-oriented or object-oriented.[9] To argue that aesthetics, in its beginnings, was a theory of representations implies not only that Dessoir's classification is not exhaustive but also that the historical studies have been based on an inadequate conceptual grid.

My insistence on the notion of representation merely takes the writers at their word. Mendelssohn, reviewing Meier, calls for a definition of beauty that would resemble 'a universal algebraic formula'[10] to which specific qualifications need only be added in order to derive the rules characterizing individual art forms. His own attempt at such a general definition echoes Baumgarten: 'The essence of the fine arts and letters consists in an *artistically produced sensate-perfect representation*, or in a *sensate perfection represented through artistic means*.'[11] And Meier's 'first principle of all the fine arts and letters' – except for the logical wobble that is so typical of Meier – is little different: 'Sensate cognition ought to be as beautiful as possible.'[12] It is thus the notion of sensate representation that defines the contours of the aesthetic field.

The term sensate is borrowed from Wolff, for whom it qualified that sort of appetitive-conative impulse that is stimulated by a confused representation of the good.[13] Baumgarten expands the application of the term to embrace all those representations generated by the lower faculties. Sensate representations are not merely the representations of sense; they are the combined work of all the 'inferior' faculties such as the ability to perceive similarities and differences, sensate memory, the faculty of anticipation, the imagination, the poeticizing or fiction-making faculty, the lower faculty of judgement or taste. Taken together these faculties operate according to an immanent logic; they constitute an 'analogue of reason,' which is the organ of aesthetic cognition.[14] The sensate representations produced by the lower faculties are what we attend to when we experience beauty, and aesthetics is the discipline which determines how these representations attain perfection. What characterizes these sensate representations – and what therefore allows the aesthetician to isolate his particular object of study – is that they fall beneath the threshold of distinctness. 'A nondistinct representation is called *sensate*,' Baumgarten writes, introducing his use of the term.[15] That is to say, sensate representations are *confused* (or clear and confused) in the technical sense. The distinction between confused and distinct representations is at the foundation of aesthetic theory.

As I argued in the previous chapter, this distinction, considered merely formally, involves three conceptual oppositions: whole and part, simultaneity and successivity, and designation and discourse. These conceptual pairs provide the instruments for a progressive-genetic account of knowledge as an ever more penetrating analysis: the dissolution of whole representations into their constituent features, the distribution of these features along a successivity which is unfolded as a discursive definition or description. Such is the process involved in making the transition from sensate representations to the distinct representations produced by the intellect, in refining our knowledge of the world by translating the jumbled images of perception into the ordered intelligibility of rational discourse. It is apparent that, since the aesthetic field is the field of sensate representations, it too will be distinguished by those conceptual terms – wholeness, simultaneity, designation – which define the notion of clear representation. Indeed, a good many of the issues discussed and the positions maintained during this first phase in the history of aesthetics derive from these terms and their opposites. However, it is important to note that, as we move from the disciplines of logic and metaphysics (Wolff) to aesthetics proper, the juxtaposition of clear and distinct representations is both *expanded to other factors* than the formal properties of the two types and *given an axiological dimension*. Aesthetics introduces an analysis of representations which is, in comparison to Wolff's logical analysis, at once more encompassing and more evaluative.

We can gain an overview of this broader and more combative analysis of representations – and at the same time of some of the central claims of aesthetic theory – by considering the oppositional pairs which, in the writings of Baumgarten, Meier and Mendelssohn, differentiate between sensate and distinct representations. Four pairs are of primary importance:

(1) *Contentually replete vs. contentually attenuated.* An enormous advantage of aesthetic cognition is that it does not abstract from the metaphysical richness of the world as distinct thought – due to the finite character of the soul (our metaphysical lack) – must inevitably do.[16] Aesthetic representations are replete with content because they represent individual

entities in the fullness of their multiple determinations. In comparison to the weak representations that result from the abstraction endemic to distinct thought, sensate representations are strong: containing many features of the object, they stimulate a good deal of representational activity in the soul that attends to them.[17]

(2) *Global vs. disjoint.* This opposition has to do with the mode of presentation that characterizes each type of cognition; it therefore can be said to recapitulate the whole/part and simultaneity/successivity oppositions discussed earlier. Sensate cognition remains *con-fused*, which is to say that it is a coalescence of features within a single representation. Distinct cognition, on the other hand, separates these features: the 'notae' or properties which inhere within the totality of the phenomenal appearance are individually rendered. The distribution of clarity among the features – which distribution constitutes distinctness formally – results in an articulate representation. Sensate representation is characterized by its globality, which allows the *Gestalt* of the object to emerge. Distinct cognition, on the other hand, is necessarily disjoint: 'Therefore distinct cognition represents the object of an affect to us in such an internally differentiated fashion that that aspect of the object through which our spirit is moved *comes apart and disappears*.'[18]

(3) *Engagement of the whole person vs. engagement of the intellect.* Baumgarten himself, polemicizing on behalf of his new discipline, draws the relevant distinction: 'As long as only my intellect is trained, only man in general is attended to; but in aesthetics man is represented in the complete set of his determinations.'[19] The idea is that logic, which schools the use of the intellect in distinct cognition, accounts for our experience and perfects us only as men-in-general, only as anonymous rational beings. Aesthetics, on the other hand, draws within its province a manifold of human activities, especially the senate and affective-conative dimensions of our experience. The sensate representations of aesthetic cognition engage the whole

person, bring all the representational faculties into play and allow man to recover his full and natural identity as a human – not merely a rational – being.[20]

(4) *Intuitive cognition vs. symbolic cognition.* This opposition does not have to do with the qualities of sensate or distinct representations in themselves, but rather with the representations of such representations in semiotic media. For a communication to constitute a genuinely aesthetic experience for the receiver it must lead to an intuitive apprehension of the represented states of affairs. Intuitive cognition is a necessary component of the aesthetic: our faculty for producing signs, Baumgarten writes, must not be so highly developed 'that it suppresses the necessarily intuitive quality of beauty.'[21] It is the intuitive quality of the cognition that makes possible the vitality (*vita, Leben*) of aesthetic thoughts, their highest perfection, that effective and affective dimension of aesthetic representation which actually moves us.[22] 'Symbolic cognition, as such, is notably inert, only intuitive cognition is moving.'[23] Distinct thought, on the other hand, is dependent on symbolic cognition; and increasingly so as it progresses. Thus, although aesthetic texts employ signs, they must do so in such a way that the representations these signs stand for can be actualized intuitively. To show how this is done is one of the central tasks of aesthetic semiotics.

In the writings of Baumgarten and Meier, these values are articulated in rather tedious, scholastic form according to the six categories of perfection that apply to all forms of cognition: richness, grandeur, truth, clarity, certainty, and vitality.[24] Mendelssohn, who writes analytic essays for a reading public rather than academic compendia to accompany lectures, develops the representational model much more explicitly than Baumgarten and Meier. In addition, Mendelssohn's formulations of the issues more closely correspond to Lessing's thinking in the *Laocoon*. For both these reasons, I shall refer primarily to texts by Mendelssohn throughout the remainder of this section, the task of which is to provide a more detailed account of the theory of aesthetic representation.

The basic representational model consists of three components: the soul, which produces the representation, the representation itself, and the object represented. The representation mediates between subject and object insofar as it is generated by the former and duplicates the latter. Mendelssohn makes the point succinctly: 'Every representation stands in a double relationship; on the one hand to the matter-at-hand, its object, of which it is an image or imprint; on the other hand to the soul, or cognizing subject, of which it is a determination.'[25] At the same time, the object elicits an affective-conative response in the soul, a response determined by the 'degree of pleasure or displeasure, which alternately accompany all our representations.'[26] The representation, then, also mediates the effect of the object on the soul, its stimulation in the soul of an affirmative or negative response.

This model, of course, applies to all representations. Since the aesthetic is a sub-class of representation-in-general, an adequate account of what defines the aesthetic will require that the model be specified in various ways. Mendelssohn's writings provide us with two detailed arguments that illustrate very clearly along what lines such specification occurs. These arguments can serve us as case studies in the theory of aesthetic representation.

### A formula for beauty

The first argument is developed in the brief treatise 'On Mastery over the Inclinations' (1756–7), which Mendelssohn wrote in the context of a debate on the nature of tragedy that he, Lessing and Friedrich Nicolai conducted by letter.[27] Mendelssohn later repeated the position he had taken in the treatise in his 'Rhapsody'[28] of 1761 and allowed it to stand unaltered in the 1771 edition of that work. We are dealing, then, with a line of thought that remained important and convincing to him throughout his career. The basic issue is an ethical-didactic one involving the relative moral efficacy of different types of representation. How should we represent the good to ourselves and to others so that we maximize our 'mastery over the inclinations?' What modes of representation are most efficacious in convincing us to act virtuously? Mendelssohn begins with definitions. Whatever moves us to act is a representation and a representation viewed in terms of its capacity to incite or encourage action is a motive (*Bewegungsgrund*). The motive representation, in order to move us, must be the representation of a positive value, a perfection or a beauty. This proposition defines the object relation, the referential function of the motive. As regards the subjective reactions which the representation mediates, Mendelssohn distinguishes between two broad classes of movements within the soul: desire and feeling. A motive which represents its object as absent affects our desire (*Begehrlichkeit*), which is a class term embracing several graded species from indifference to yearning. A representation of an absent virtue, a virtue I know I lack, might inspire in me a desire to achieve that virtue. In such a case I would be motivated by the representation to become virtuous myself. Should the object be represented as present, however, there would be no gap for desire to bridge. Representations rendering their objects as present engender gradations of feeling (*Empfindung*) from indifference to ecstatic delight. The increased strength of the affects, or movements of the soul, signals in both cases the greater efficacy of the motive. Since we are dealing here with good or beautiful objects alone, the corresponding negative effects, which negative value qualities in the object awaken, are ignored.[29]

These definitions and distinctions only serve to clarify the original problem. The question which the treatise sets out to answer can now be stated forthrightly: what conditions make a motive efficacious enough to arouse, say, yearning or ecstatic delight rather than indifference? Mendelssohn's solution:[30]

The more good is contained in the representation of an object, and the more distinctly we cognize that good, and the less time that is required to comprehend it completely, the more intense is the desire, the more pleasant the enjoyment.

   (a) The quality of the motive therefore is proportionate to the amount of the good and to its distinctness, and inversely proportionate to the time required to reflect on it.

   (b) Let us posit the amount of good $= m$.

$$\text{the distinctness} = p.$$
$$\text{the time} = t.$$

   Then the quantity of the motive $= \dfrac{mp}{t}$

This formula can be most easily explicated in terms of the overall model of representation which I outlined above. The magnitude $m$ refers to the object side of the model: the 'amount of good' is simply the sum of the objective value qualities, the so-called perfections, contained in the object of the representation. The magnitude $p$ designates an aspect of the representation itself, its distinctness. And the amount of time required to comprehend a representation with $p$ distinctness of $m$ value qualities is marked by the denominator of the ratio. Finally, the ratio itself is equivalent to the overall effect which the given quantity of value qualities represented with the given degree of distinctness will exert on the soul sponsoring the representation.

Mendelssohn's formula is not just an historical curiosity, a symptom of the quantifying bent of Enlightenment thought. Rather, it should be interpreted as a significant contribution to the project of a mathematical aesthetics, a project which today once again is attracting research interest. The one aspect of the formula which seems to militate against such an interpretation is the magnitude $p$, distinctness. Distinctness is clarity of the features, individual representation of the properties of an object. Because he sets distinctness in direct proportion to the efficacy of a representation, Mendelssohn appears to contradict Baumgarten's definition of beauty as sensate – that is to say, clear – representation. Here it must be kept in mind that the terms 'clear' and 'distinct' are relative and flexible. It is entirely possible, for instance, to have a representation of a tree which captures many individual features and is in this sense 'distinct,' but which remains, as a simultaneous perception, within the limits of 'clear' representation. Clear representations, in other words, can be more or less differentiated internally, more or less various in their texture. Baumgarten understood this and adapted the inherited Wolffian terminology accordingly. The perfect sensate representations of aesthetic cognition, he claims, are characterized by 'extensive clarity,' which is fundamentally different from 'intensive clarity.'[31] The latter signifies the dissolution of the *Gestalt*-quality of the perceived object into a series of individually represented features. The former, however, designates a manifold, internally rich representation of the features of an object that nonetheless maintains the wholeness of the *Gestalt*: a clear, sensate representation, then, but one which is not schematic. Exactly this sort of representation optimally fulfills the stipulations of Mendelssohn's formula. Note in this regard the third magnitude, t. It signifies the time required to comprehend the whole representation and grasp its unity. If the representation is to have a considerable effect on the soul, then this magnitude must be reduced as much as possible, which, of course, is precisely what occurs in extensively clear representations: here the content m remains large because there is no abstraction from the richness of the individual object; here the time t is as brief as possible since the entire representation is grasped as a simultaneity; and here maximum distinctness is achieved, but without crossing the threshold into the region of intensive clarity.[32]

In 1776, twenty years after the debate with Lessing and Nicolai, Mendelssohn took up his formula for representational efficacy once again. His notes on Hemsterhuis' *Lettre sur la sculpture* (1769) contain the following formulation:

Beauty, he [Hemsterhuis] says quite correctly, consists of a maximum number of ideas in a minimum amount of time; but this maximum number of ideas must be explained accurately. For it must be understood not only *extensively* (the amount of representations), but also *intensively* (the clarity, forcefulness, etc.). The maximum number of ideas corresponds to the manifold and the minimum amount of time to the unity. Also, this minimum does not apply just to the time, but to the force of exertion as well.[33]

What was only implied in the earlier version is here rendered explicit: the ratio measures beauty; it makes theoretically possible the calculation of aesthetic effect. The terms 'extensive' and 'intensive' correspond to the variables m and p respectively and can be thought of as analogous to the concepts of 'extension' and 'intension' employed in contemporary semantics. The first simply characterizes the richness of the object represented (the referent), the number of features it has, while the second refers to the way in which these features are represented. Mendelssohn understands his own emphasis on the intensional aspect of the representation as an improvement over Hemsterhuis' more simple analysis. A second clarification – one of some significance – can be noted here as well. Mendelssohn indicates that the reason time functions as the negative factor is in part that it reflects the subjective effort involved in processing the representation. A representation which is too complex, which pursues distinctness too far, cannot be subjectively appropriated and synthesized as a whole but rather must be taken apart and attended to bit by bit along a sequence.

In essence, Mendelssohn's ratio merely formalizes the set of conceptual values I listed at the beginning of this section. What it measures is aesthetic efficacy, the intensity with which the soul's representational and affective capacities are actualized, or what I earlier described as an effect on the whole person. What it stipulates is that this effect will be greater if the representation is both contentually replete (m) and global (p/t). The only predicate which is missing from the formula is the fourth in the series, the intuitive quality of the aesthetic representation. Mendelssohn does not include it in his formalization even though it is of central importance to the definition of aesthetic representation. Only in intuitive cognition can the replete and global cognitions of perfect sensate thought be actualized and achieve their effect on the sponsoring subject. Symbolic cognition, on the other hand, is unfolded along a temporal axis and therefore does not provide a simultaneous apprehension of the various aspects of the represented object. Indeed, in the subsequent sections of 'On Mastery over the Inclinations,' Mendelssohn attends to precisely this point: 'Intuitive representations follow more rapidly upon one another than symbolic representations and for that reason the quantity of their effect is greater.'[34] Intuition is the condition of possibility of aesthetic effect – a statement which the second argument I shall consider here demonstrates very clearly.

### The aesthetic as sensate intuition

In the case of the first argument applying the basic model of representation to aesthetics, our starting point was an ethical-didactic problem, the question of motivational efficacy. The second argument I shall consider in detail begins immediately with aesthetic issues. Mendelssohn's first systematic essay on aesthetics, 'Reflections on the Sources and Combinations of the Fine Arts and Letters' (1757),[35] takes the effects of art works as its point of departure. These derive, in Mendelssohn's view, from the two primitive appraisive reactions of the soul, 'pleasure and displeasure,' and are nothing but modifications and combinations of these. The efficacy of art is therefore rooted in the 'capacity to desire and to reject,' a 'fundamental capacity of our soul.'[36] Mendelssohn introduces these notions as accepted presuppositions, not as explanations. Then, in view of the acknowledged efficacy of art *vis-à-vis* the soul, the task of the inquiry is first articulated:

... if it cannot be denied that the fine arts and letters have the power to excite our affects, then they must all be capable of exerting in various ways an effect upon this fundamental capacity of our soul and of setting the most secret drive springs of the same into motion. But what do the various objects of the art of poetry, of painting, of rhetoric and dance, of music, of sculpture and architecture, what do all these works of human invention have in common by virtue of which they can coincide in this one, single purpose?[37]

The question is formulated with admirable clarity. It is a matter of the capability of art works to move us by setting into motion the primitive reactions of pleasure and displeasure. Mendelssohn takes the efficacy of art as a given and proceeds to ask: how is this efficacy possible? He realizes that, by insisting on the effect of the arts as their common purpose, he has eliminated the possibility of defining the aesthetic in terms of content alone. From his point of view, a referential notion such as Batteux's 'imitation' has no explanatory force, for to say that art is imitation merely displaces the question of art's efficacy. Even if we accept the thesis that art is imitation, we must still ask why the imitated originals have the power to please us, and this brings us back to our original question.[38]

The dignity of the imitated original, then, is insufficient as an explanation of art's efficacy. The problem remains: what do the arts have in common that allows them to achieve their shared end? This problem is best solved by asking the further question, what is it that in any soul awakens pleasure and displeasure?

Every representation of perfection, of harmony, of that which is free of flaws, is preferred by our soul to the flawed, the imperfect and the dissonant. This is the first degree of pleasure and displeasure which alternately accompany all our representations. The truth of this principle has been proven from the mere definition of what a mind is, and experience conforms to it completely.[39]

Pleasure and displeasure are activities of the soul which accompany, and even sustain and energize, the soul's representational activity. In the above passage, they are further defined as preferences that the soul manifests *vis-à-vis* its representations. The objects of these preferences are of a formal nature: 'perfections' are preferred by the soul over the 'imperfect.' Pleasure is therefore the conative response of the soul to a represented perfection. At this point in the argument, then, basic tenets regarding the nature of the soul and its preferences are called upon to clarify the necessary precondition of an affect. This places us in a good position to answer our original question: since we know what the requisite conditions of an affect are, and since we know that art affects the soul, we also know at least the minimal conditions for the presence of beauty.

In order to follow the next step in Mendelssohn's argument, we must review a basic tenet of rationalist psychology. That is: a representation can effect a conative response in the soul only if the perfections and/or imperfections are present to the soul in intuition. Intuition alone allows the represented value qualities to set the drive springs of the soul into motion. In the language of Baumgarten and Meier, intuition alone provides a vital cognition: 'All symbolic cognition is dead as regards the represented object...As a result, only intuitive cognition is vital.'[40] With this basic assumption in mind, we can understand Mendelssohn's definition of beauty:

If the cognition of the perfection is intuitive, then it is called *beauty*. A cognition is called intuitive either when its object is immediately present to our senses or when it is represented through such signs as allow us to attend more distinctly to the ideas of the signified object than to those of the sign itself.[41]

Beauty is defined as a cognition or representation distinguished in two respects. The object of the representation must be a perfection and the representation itself must be intuitive. Both conditions must be fulfilled; perfection on the side of the object alone is an insufficient criterion of beauty. 'Every perfection therefore, which is capable of being represented intuitively, or sensately, can provide an object of beauty.'[42] The admissibility of the object to the aesthetic field is determined by its representability in sensate intuition.

Mendelssohn defines beauty in terms of a relation between the represented object, the representation itself, and the resultant effect in the soul, in other words, in terms of the basic model of representation outlined above. We can therefore think of Mendelssohn's characterization of aesthetic experience as a series of phases. The first phase is the establishment of the representation as a specific determination of the soul. This representation must be intuitive, that is, it must present the object directly to the soul without the mediation of signs. Since the object, with its perfections, is presented to the soul in intuition, it can achieve a strong and vital response. It can please the soul and can thereby arouse the affects and emotions that characterize aesthetic experience (second phase). At this point in his discussion Mendelssohn does not mention what, on the basis of Meier's theory of the affects, we can consider to be the third phase in this process. The affects are themselves representation-generating. In Meier's terms: 'The effects brought about by the emotions themselves become causes of the same, and thus it is clear that a confused representation can be simultaneously the effect and the cause of the affect.'[43] What ensues is the ongoing, intense, conative-representational activity characteristic of 'vital' cognition, an energetic, self-sustaining attentiveness in which emotional response and sensate representation are enriched and ramified.

At this stage in his career (1757) we find Mendelssohn defining art as the sensate intuition of an object. The source of the pleasure which characterizes art's efficacy is the perfection of the object. Nevertheless, it is not the object alone which constitutes beauty, but rather *a particular form of the representational relation*. Objects are admissible as objects of art only insofar as they can enter into this relation, that is, only insofar as they can be intuited sensately. The definition of beauty is neither psychologistic nor objectivistic; rather, it is formulated as a specific modification of the basic model of representation.

The definition of beauty based on the representational model remains central to Mendelssohn's later writings on aesthetics. I feel certain, in fact, that the development of Mendelssohn's aesthetic theory subsequent to the 'Reflections' is only intelligible in terms of the model of representation that underlies both that essay and 'On Mastery over the Inclinations.' This can be shown by comparing the 1757 version of the 'Reflections' with the revised edition of 1771, which carries the title 'On the Chief Principles of the Fine Arts and Letters.'[44] The earlier essay draws the following conclusion as to the nature of the aesthetic: 'We have now found the general means through which our soul can be pleased, namely the *sensate representation of perfection*;...'[45] The related passage in the 'Chief Principles' reads:

We have now found the general means through which our soul can be pleased, namely *sensately perfect representation*. And since the purpose of the fine arts is to please, then we can presuppose the following principle as certain: The essence of the fine arts and letters consists in an *artistic sensate-perfect representation*, or in a *sensate perfection represented through art*.[46]

In the later formulation the perfection is located in the representation, and no longer in the object. The object is of interest to aesthetics only insofar as it can be the object of a perfect sensate representation. Even in the 'Reflections' the object's admissibility to the aesthetic field was determined by its capacity to be represented in a sensate intuition. Here, though, Mendelssohn's position is even less referential: the perfection, which is the source of aesthetic pleasure, resides in the representation itself. 'Perfect' is a predicate in aesthetic discourse which now applies to representations and not to objects. This alteration allows aesthetic theory to account for a wider range of phenomena: 'This representation through art can be sensately perfect even if the object in nature be neither good nor beautiful.'[47] Objects in themselves ugly or evil, that is, objects with predominantly negative value qualities, can nevertheless be objects of aesthetic cognition so long as the representation itself is a perfect sensate representation.[48]

It is this possibility which brings Mendelssohn to the most complete elaboration of his model of aesthetic representation. The opening pages of his 'Rhapsody' attend to the so-called 'mixed emotions' which arise when the object represented is characterized by negative value qualities. Mendelssohn's analysis of such cases runs as follows:

It is the same with all other good and evil properties, advantages and lacks, virtues and flaws of things. They must be considered in two regards: as regards the object or the subject matter outside of us to which they apply, and as regards the intention or the thinking being that perceives them. The good is pleasant in both regards, that is, it is not only an element of perfection in the object, but it also increases, regarded now as a representation, the affirmative properties of the thinking being, and it must in both respects excite pleasure. The evil, however, is unpleasant on the side of the object, regarded as the original of a representation outside of us, insofar as it, in this regard, consists of a lack, a negation of something in reality; but, regarded as a representation or image within us which engages the representational-conative forces of the soul, even the representation of evil becomes an element of perfection and brings with it something pleasurable which we by no means would rather not feel than feel.[49]

As I view it, the nerve of this rather difficult passage is the more careful and more severe distinction between the three terms of the representational model that was already the organizing paradigm in Mendelssohn's earliest essays. The empirical fact which demands the shift in the location of perfection (within this model) is the undeniable use of unpleasant objects as referents in works that Mendelssohn would like to label aesthetically valuable. The appearance of such objects in pleasing works necessitates the consideration not only of the soul's relationship to the object as mediated by the representation, but also of the soul's relationship to the representation itself, and therewith to its own representational-conative activity. The pleasure present in the mixed emotions derives from a second order of representation: it derives, in other words, from the soul's reflexive apprehension of its own perfection as that perfection is manifested in the first-order representation, the representational-conative activity involved in the apprehension and appraisal of the unpleasant object. The soul intuits the imperfections of the object and is affected by them, but at the same time intuits its own activity and is positively affected by the perfection (its own strength and harmony) it reflects upon.

In the characterization of aesthetic experience Mendelssohn provides here, the content or object of the first-order representation becomes a mere pretext which allows the real matter of interest in art to emerge – the soul as a spontaneous power of willing and representing. In aesthetic experience the final level of representation is the self-representation that comes to awareness by virtue of the reflexive relation obtaining between the soul and its own activities and products. This additional source of pleasure, the enhancement of the soul's reality ('Realität')[50] through actualization of its representational-conative potential, is, according to Mendelssohn, more universal ('weit allgemeiner')[51] than the perfection inhering in the object. Aesthetic experience, then, is not limited to the thematic perfections of particular representations, but affords access to the universal ground of all representations, the activity of willing and representing itself. If we take seriously Mendelssohn's claim that a soul is unthinkable apart from such activity, then we can say that for him aesthetic experience conducts us to an awareness of the transcendental ground of our experience.[52] In aesthetic experience we act as particular individuals here and now, but at the same time discover a transpersonal, universal dimension of ourselves which we can otherwise know only indirectly in theoretical speculation. This is the socially integrative function of art I alluded to in my introduction to this chapter: the subject discovers in himself the source of the idealized community of mankind.

I want to consider this account of aesthetic experience in one final connection. Just as in phenomenology access to the transcendental sphere is achieved by virtue of an *epoché*, an abstention from all mundane interests that dominate our 'natural attitude,' so too in Mendelssohn's aesthetic theory the reflective intuition of the soul's activity and products is only possible by virtue of a detachment from the demands that objects ordinarily make upon us.[53] The immediacy of intuition must be maintained, but not in such a way that the physical, natural, existential aspect of the object overwhelms us so much that a reflexive apprehension of our internality is precluded. The requisite bracketing of the existence of the object is guaranteed by the fact that the receiver encounters an object of art (*Kunst*) as opposed to a natural object, an imitation (*Nachahmung*) as opposed to an actual presentation. As an object of art (and not as an existent met in nature), the object is encountered in a field of security. The subject is in no way threatened or overwhelmed by the object because the object is distanced from him by art. An abiding awareness of the unreal quality of the object provides the necessary atmosphere for the object to present itself without the impinging immediacy characteristic of our entanglement in the empirical world. At the same time, the object is not distanced to such a degree that it is totally absent, in which case we would only experience the indifferent neutrality of theoretical reflection. Art presents its object as present, but as *present at a distance*.

This double achievement of art can be illustrated quite well in terms of Mendelssohn's use of the concept of imitation or mimesis. Mendelssohn did not think that all of aesthetics could be based on the concept of mimesis nor did he hold, especially later in his career, that all the arts are mimetic. Nevertheless the notion remained important to him throughout his writings and his understanding of it deserves some attention. There are two aspects to mimesis which, though related, must be distinguished: a referential aspect and an effective aspect. Considered referentially, an imitation partially *duplicates its object*. It not only denotes the object but shares pertinent qualities with it. However, even if we speak of an art work as an imitation of an original, the dignity of the art work cannot be derived solely from the status of the original. In addition to its function as a duplication, every imitation also has an effective aspect. Viewed in terms of its efficacy, the imitation functions so as to *make present to the subject* the particular object it imitates. The word for this evoked presence is 'illusion' (*Illusion*). An imitation presents the object to the intuitive apprehension of the receiver by creating an illusion. In this way, mimesis fulfills the dual function of art described in the previous paragraph: it *renders an absent object as present*. The absence of the object must be qualified as existential absence; it is not a real snake I see before me in the painting. The presence of the object is internal presence-to-mind; the full idea of the snake is present to me as the content of my intuition.[54] The illusion evoked by the imitation thus allows me to experience the representational-conative activity engendered in direct intuition while maintaining the existential security provided by detachment from worldly interests and demands. Paradoxically, I can experience the object as a presence and thereby experience myself as present to myself, only when the object is absent, only when I am not thrown outward among the things of the world. Mimesis, by neutralizing the pure present actuality of the object, provides the aesthetic distance necessary for the object to manifest itself and for the subject to become present to itself as the representational-conative power it in fact is.

The requirement of existential absence as the possibility of experiencing presence leads to a second apparent paradox. If the function of mimesis is to render an existentially absent object (or non-existent object) as present-to-intuition, then the best artistic medium in which to accomplish this is the one which corresponds least to the original it imitates. The effectively most mimetic medium will be the referentially least mimetic. This brings me to themes I will treat in the next chapter on Lessing, but I want to adumbrate them here in order to show the proximity of Lessing's and Mendelssohn's views. Painting is referentially highly mimetic because it shares physical properties (color, contour) with its original. Precisely for this reason, though, its mimetic efficacy is reduced, for painting brings something of the physical nature of the original with it. The materiality of the painting constitutes an existential aspect that is difficult to pass over. Because of this existential dimension the painting makes some of the same restrictive claims on the subject that a real object would. The ideal medium for an effective mimesis would be one which is immaterial, which is free of the existential determinations characteristic of painting and sculpture. The ideal medium for presenting ideas to intuition would be the medium of ideas themselves, for only in such a medium could intuitions be evoked without their being tied to particular existents. This medium is nothing other than the imagination with its ability to recall and recompose the ideas of absent objects. The imagination, however, cannot be called an artistic medium in the strict sense. Our ideal medium, then, must be one, the material qualities of which are extrinsic, irrelevant, non-constitutive; one which cleaves to the movement of the imagination while leaving its materiality behind. Our ideal medium must be language. Not just any language, though, but a transparent one that sheds its semiotic character and yields without resistance to an intuitive-ideational process in the soul. It must be a language in which the signified idea is rendered present and is not held in absence by the arbitrariness of its signs. It is precisely such a language that the aesthetic semiotics of the Enlightenment projects as its ideal.

## Aesthetic semiotics

Baumgarten divides the discipline of aesthetics into three branches: heuristics (*heuristica*), methodology (*methodologia*), and semiotics (*semiotica*).[55] The first treats the qualities of aesthetic thoughts or representations, the second discusses the arrangement of the representations, and the third the means through which they are signified. This subdivision is easily recognizable as an adaptation of traditional rhetoric with its central triadic organization into *inventio*, *dispositio*, and *elocutio*. It appears then that the writings of Baumgarten and

Meier do not at all offer us a new discipline of aesthetic semiotics, but merely a reedition of *elocutio* under a new name.[56] This appearance, I want to argue, is deceptive. One must keep in mind that a paradigm shift does not necessarily occur *between* theoretical texts, but can take place *within* texts as well; the line of theoretical fracture splits the texts in two. In my view, this is the case with the work of Baumgarten and Meier. The rhetorical triad that manifestly organizes their major writings on aesthetics is the remains of a theory-type which, as regards the basic thrust of those writings, has been thoroughly overcome. The use of the triadic organizational schema does not mean that the authority of the old theory-type remains unchallenged, but rather that the inherited theoretical paradigm is being dismantled from within. In the writings of Mendelssohn and Lessing, finally, it will be thoroughly abandoned.

The literature on Baumgarten has – unwittingly – confirmed this interpretation. A recently anthologized essay on 'A. G. Baumgarten's *Aesthetica* and Ancient Rhetoric'[57] concludes that two essential theoretical displacements separate Baumgarten's aesthetics from the traditional teachings of rhetoric: on the one hand, several points which the rhetoricians subsumed under the rubric *elocutio* are assimilated into the theory of aesthetic representations; on the other, the didactic aspect of rhetorical persuasion is underplayed and the affective-emotional dimension of aesthetic effect emerges into the foreground. Both of these changes – the greater accentuation of the representations and the increased emphasis on affective movement – indicate the presence of a paradigm-shift in aesthetic theory. As a representational theory, aesthetics has as its proper theoretical object aesthetic thoughts or representations, not the tactics for achieving successful performances. Aesthetics investigates how to present representations to the receiver in such a way that they elicit an optimal representational-conative effect; it does not teach how to transmit persuasively a pre-given set of values. In short, the scaffolding of traditional rhetoric is preserved in the writings of Baumgarten and Meier, but its major function is to make possible the construction of a new theoretical edifice – a theory of aesthetic representations rather than a collection of directives for rhetorically masterful performances. This is why it is possible for Mendelssohn and Lessing to adopt Baumgarten's major tenets, combining them with intellectual impulses from England and France, without according the rhetorical triad any importance at all.

The thesis that aesthetic semiotics constitutes a theoretical innovation *vis-à-vis* traditional rhetoric can be confirmed by examining the work of Meier, and especially of Mendelssohn. The rhetorical term *elocutio* designates a stage in the production of a communication; it embraces a corpus of stylistic rules and tropic and figurative devices that essentially amounts to a handbook of linguistic virtuosity. The question which the rules of *elocutio* answer is: what expressive strategies are to be employed in what communicative situations with what perlocutionary results?[58] Semiotics, however, is a general theory of signs. Within the context of aesthetics, it attempts to answer the question: what are the general laws of aesthetic semiosis and what are the specific laws that apply to the individual arts? *Elocutio* and semiotics belong to different classes of discourse, *ars* and *scientia* respectively, and even when individual propositions are taken over from the former, their significance by no means remains unchanged in their new context. The rhetorical terms are reinterpreted from the standpoint of Enlightenment semiotics; that is to say, they acquire a different valence and function within the new discursive framework.

In my remarks on Enlightenment semiotics in the first chapter, I emphasized that eighteenth-century sign theory is characterized by a strong valorization of the signified ideas and a low evaluation of the signs themselves (signifiers). Signs are mere technical aids, instruments, which – although they make possible the fixation and communication of our representations as well as the more refined operations of intellection – in themselves have neither importance nor worth. The Enlightenment can be considered as fundamentally in conflict with the sign.[59] This basic tendency shapes aesthetic semiotics also, as the following sentence by George Friedrich Meier attests: 'Signs are in general smaller and poorer objects of our cognitive capacity than the things signified.'[60] Given this fundamental view regarding the value of the sign and the material stratum of language, it would naturally be impossible to develop a doctrine of eloquence such as we find in the rhetorical treatises. On the contrary, such linguistic pyrotechnics, such virtuosity in the formation of the expression as was characteristic of courtly-aristocratic art, is adamantly rejected by the aestheticians. The essence of art is located entirely within the sphere of representations, in the experienced presence-to-mind of the represented object – in short, in a psychic immanence in relation to which the material signifier remains altogether extrinsic. When Baumgarten and Meier declare that the *vita* or life of aesthetic representations is their greatest perfection, they are merely formalizing this tendency, since this vital capacity of representations to move the soul is only achieved if the representations are grasped intuitively. For Mendelssohn, that means that the concept of intuitive cognition is a component of the definition of beauty itself, as I argued in the previous section. And, as the following chapter will amply demonstrate, the conception of the aesthetic as intuition will remain valid for Lessing as well.

The writings of this first generation of aestheticians, then, exhibit a powerful historical transformation, the withdrawal of art from the space of public performance into the immanence of the representational sphere.[61] The consequences of this transformation for the conception of poetry and poetic language are immense. With the emergence of the representational theory, poetic language use is no longer a matter of artful linguistic rendering; poetry is no longer the acme of eloquence. Rather, the task of poetry is to reach back to prelinguistic experience, to exceed the limits of language. *Poetry is no longer art in language, but language that transcends art in order to reapproach nature*.[62] In my view, aesthetic semiotics must be interpreted as the theoretical codification of the new status of poetic language. As the discipline which attends to the laws of aesthetic semiosis, it does not merely observe and describe, but draws its object within the regime of an organized body of discourse and, in so doing, transforms that object, constitutes it anew. *Aesthetic semiotics positions poetry within the field of values that is circumscribed and articulated by the Enlightenment myth of the sign.*

The theoretical structure of aesthetic semiotics is easily grasped. According to Meier, the discipline is governed from beginning to end by a single principle from which all the rules of aesthetic sign use can be derived. Meier's formulation of this principle runs as follows:

...the signs must not only be beautiful in themselves, but they must also be – as regards the beautiful thoughts which they are supposed to express – so constituted that the entire beauty of the thoughts in all its strength and beauty [sic] can be cognized from and through them.[63]

I call this the principle of transparency. Its normative force consists in the demand that the linguistic level of the poetic text, that is, the level of the signifiers, not emerge into the foreground of consciousness, that the cognition which the poetic text transmits not remain a symbolic cognition, but rather be actualized as intuition, as the experienced presence-to-mind of the represented object. For representational aesthetic theory, the poetic text is a transparent text the reading of which induces that subjective absorption in the represented world – that experience of quasi-seeing – which the age called aesthetic illusion. Poetic language is diaphanous; it presents its object to intuition.

The principle of transparency is the commanding tenet of aesthetic semiotics as developed by Meier and further elaborated by Mendelssohn. It determines all the questions raised within the discipline, the entire field of inquiry. We can conceive of this field as embracing two major theoretical tasks: (1) the determination of those semiotic-linguistic procedures which guarantee the transparency of poetic language; (2) the comparative semiotic description of the individual arts and the determination of their particular limits and possibilities of combination. The third chapter will present a detailed account of how these tasks are solved in Lessing's *Laocoon*. My intention here is merely to review the major semiotic-aesthetic claims that Meier and Mendelssohn make in order to outline the theoretical context in which Lessing's analysis is conceived.

## The semiotics of poetry

Let us consider first the question of poetic transparency, which leads quite naturally to all the basic tenets of the Enlightenment theory of poetic language. If it is true, as Mendelssohn avers, that 'words usually convey only a symbolic cognition,' and if aesthetic representations are by definition intuitive, then poetry, because it is made of words and at the same time is intended to qualify as aesthetic, poses a special problem for the discipline of aesthetic semiotics. The problem is to show by what means 'symbolic cognition could be transformed through poetry into an intuitive cognition.'[64] The easiest way to solve this problem is through proscriptive rules, rules which eliminate interference at the level of the signifier. It is here that the Enlightenment theoreticians wage their campaign against the semiotic ideal of courtly-aristocratic culture. They intrumentalize the sign, reduce it to the status of a mere vehicle, and thereby prohibit artistry at the level of the text's expressive surface. The overriding principle in this regard is clearly stated by Meier: 'One must avoid everything through which the attention is diverted from the object itself and is steered principally toward the contemplation of the signs and images in which the object is clothed.'[65] Examples of semiotic operations that interfere with intuition are the so-called 'word figures' (*figurae verborum*) of traditional rhetoric, excessive wit, puns, lengthy descriptions, and rhyme. The last provides, I think, an instructive case in point.

In 1747, the *Horatian Odes* of Samuel Gotthold Lange appeared and a foreword by Meier entitled 'On the Value of Rhymes' accompanied the volume.[66] Meier begins this attempt to analyze the aesthetic value of rhyme by distinguishing between two types of poetic beauty. 'The first type includes everything which is appealing and consists in thoughts, and the second consists in the beauties of words.'[67] The former type, as is to be expected, is the truly essential one, while the latter constitutes the 'lowest class of the poetic beauties.'[68] Given these premises, the aesthetic value of rhyme follows quite naturally:

> The expression of poetic thoughts through words is merely the clothing of the poem and everything in this expression through which the beauty of the thoughts becomes, as it were, visible is itself a beauty. To this class belong then all those beauties of words through which they become genuinely perfect signs of the thoughts, and certainly rhyme cannot be counted among these. Rhyme is not a sign of a thought, and it does not make the thoughts livelier, or more noble, or more probable, etc. Therefore rhyme is not a beauty of poetic expression.[69]

Meier does not see rhyme and the other 'beauties of words' as constituting a stage in the production of a communication, as is the case in rhetorical theory; not as the final concretization, stylization and presentation of thoughts that, for a particular communicative purpose, have been invented and arranged. Rather, he views these verbal features as a *particular level within a stratified representation*. Here we see the decisive difference between performance theory and representational theory as regards the question of text production: whereas the former theory-type depicts text production as a generative process that moves across a series of phases culminating in the finished message, representational theory models text production as the correlation of an ideational level of content and a material level of expression. What governs the evaluation of this expressive level is the principle of transparency, unmistakeably operative here in the analogy of the costume that allows the figure beneath to remain visible. This principle achieves the thoroughgoing instrumentalization of the sign or signifier that characterizes Enlightenment theory generally. Rhyme, according to Meier, violates the means–end logic that should characterize the relationship between expression and content. Rhyme is not subordinated to a thought, which, in turn, it expresses; rather, it is an excess within the signifying element itself. In rhyme, the materiality of the signifier is allowed to acquire a value of its own, apart from its function of indicating a mental representation. And for this reason, Meier concludes, rhyme is foreign to the 'essence of a poem.'[70]

More interesting than such negative rules as the proscription of rhyme, however, are the positive, prescriptive rules the aestheticians develop. These rules have principally to do with the choice of such *individual* words as are conducive to the intuitive actualization of the represented object on the part of the reader. I stress the term 'individual' here in order to emphasize a major consequence of the semantic bias in Enlightenment theory: the orientation toward the signified ideas necessarily leads to a predominance of the lexical over the syntactical component; the emphasis is on especially effective words or lexical tropes (metaphor) to the total disregard of syntactical figures. A revealing example of such poetically effective words is the proper name, a lexical class which Baumgarten considers as enhancing a poem's sensateness.[71] Proper names designate individuals, not abstract, conceptual entities, and they are therefore actualized imaginatively by the reader as a manifold of features. The proper name is only understood when its referent is made present to the mind as an intuited entity and precisely such intuitive actualization, of course, characterizes the reception of poetic texts. In this sense, proper names are only a limit case of that general class of terms that Baumgarten and his followers refer to as *emphatic* words (*emphatici, nachdrückliche Wörter*).[72] These are terms which are especially rich because they evoke a cluster of representations and therefore convey the mind immediately beyond the stage of symbolic cognition in order to evoke a quasi-perceptual experience of the object or quality they refer to. As I mentioned in the first chapter, Mendelssohn felt that these emphatic terms still bore traces of a primordial act of naming through sound imitation.[73] That is to say, the emphatic terms are those elements within language that most energetically point beyond language; they are located, as it were, at the meeting point of language and perception.

This general rule (that the more emphatic are the terms, the more sensate the poem will be) illustrates very well the *priority of designation over discourse in aesthetic theory*. Poetry is viewed primarily in terms of the act of naming, that is, the seizure of intuited experiences through linguistic designations. Just as the emphatic terms of successful poetry recall their original, mimetic institution, so too does the poetic use of language generally manifest itself in terms of language acts which are themselves secondary forms of naming. One such act is the mention of a characteristic epithet or adjective, a semiotic procedure accorded what seems today an exorbitant amount of attention by the eighteenth-century theoreticians. These epithets, which evoke an especially forceful and rich idea of the noun they modify, account for the painterly (*malerisch*) force of poetic language; they create that sense of immediacy by virtue of which language comes to function like a work of the plastic arts. Mendelssohn gives the following description of the effect such terms have in the didactic poetry of Johann Lorenz Withof (1725–89): '...he is content to show his objects from the side that enables them to effect the senses in the most lively fashion; and he leaves to his readers the pleasure of cognitively actualizing those associated ideas to which he seems to allude, as it were, with a single stroke of the brush; all his adjectives are important, emphatic and indispensible.'[74] The choice of the painterly epithet repeats the gesture of a primordial act of naming: it characterizes the whole object in terms of its single most salient feature and thereby signifies the object in such a way that the reader can imaginatively ramify the linguistic representation and attain to a full intuition of the object. As I will show in the next chapter, this doctrine of the painterly epithet, a commonplace of the century, is the basis for Lessing's notion of an optimally sensate quality.

Another especially instructive example of the priority of designation in aesthetic semiotics is provided by the theme of metaphor. With the advent of representational theory, metaphor begins to occupy the central position in poetics that it continues, to this day, to command.[75] This point emerges clearly into view if we compare the Enlightenment theory of metaphor with that of Gottsched, whose 'critical *ars poetica*' (*Critische Dichtkunst*) remains firmly anchored in rhetorical doctrine. Gottsched's discussion of metaphor displays four essential characteristics: It is *classificatory*; that is to say, metaphor is viewed as one of several 'flowers of speech' or tropic designations, which themselves form an oppositional class to the rhetorical figures. Secondly, Gottsched considers metaphor, along with the other tropes, as serving an *ornamental* function. The use of such 'flowers of speech' as metaphor establishes the differential quality of poetic speech, its greater artfulness *vis-à-vis* the other speech genres. Thirdly, Gottsched's description of metaphor is a *substitutional* account. Metaphor is for him an intra-linguistic operation, a movement from one term to another within the code. Finally, Gottsched's discussion exhibits a decidedly *instructional* character. As is inevitably the case in performance theory, the rules formulated – Gottsched lists four pertaining to the selection of metaphors – are directives for production, guidelines for the generation of accomplished poetic texts.[76]

These four characteristics of Gottsched's discussion of metaphor entertain with one another a relationship of systematic solidarity; they are part of the immanent conceptual network that constitutes the performance theory-type. For representational theory, however, the problem of metaphor presents itself in altogether different terms, a fact which can be demonstrated quite clearly with reference to an essay by Sulzer entitled 'Remarks on the Reciprocal Influence of Reason on Language, and of Language on Reason.'[77] Sulzer views metaphor as an essentially cognitive process: it is through metaphor that newly discovered or intrinsically elusive mental representations are made accessible to the community. By presenting an idea in terms of another, similar idea, the metaphor captures representations for the culture. Metaphor is the vehicle for ideational discovery, innovation and expansion. Thus, the study of etymologies reveals a history of metaphorical displacements antecedent to the notions we currently hold and a dictionary of metaphors most in use today would constitute a list of those truths 'which have been only half seen, or viewed from a distance, without being fully developed.'[78] In Sulzer's view, then – and he is typical of mid-century thinking on the subject – metaphor is not one among several ornamental linguistic devices; it is, rather, a *natural* cognitive operation that is *at the origin of linguistic invention*.

Now the point I want especially to emphasize here is that metaphor, conceived in this fashion, becomes the quintessential poetic act. Or, to put the same matter another way, both poetry and metaphor come to be identified with the frontiers of language and cognition insofar as both bring to a clear representation ideas which as such had not been intuited by most members of the community. Sulzer explicates this in the following manner:

Such a metaphor [the example he refers to is Virgil's description of bodies *fusi per herbam* (poured on the grass)] produces an effect similar to the effect of figures in geometry. Without figures, which help the intellect precisely and accurately to define ideas that otherwise would remain altogether confused and unusable, this science would still be in its infancy. Likewise, metaphor helps us to distinguish and fix ideas, which without such aid would remain agglomerated with the mass of our representations, and in this way metaphor renders visible and sensible that which seems ungraspable to the intellect. In order to conceive of the full importance of this use of metaphor one must consider that the most acute minds sense in every moment an infinite number of things which they do not distinguish from one another and that there are as a result a great many obscure representations in the intellect of man which set limits to the growth of his knowledge. Every felicitous metaphor pushes these limits further out because it draws forth one of these previously useless ideas from its obscurity.[79]

The metaphor provides an ideational schema that allows the mind to intuit what it had known only obscurely. Far from being an ornament of the message, then, metaphor is the process which makes the invention of the message possible. And it is for this reason that Sulzer can characterize the poet's entire cultural function in terms of the act of metaphorical designation. 'The philosopher increases our store of knowledge through demonstrable arguments of reason, the *bel esprit* pushes back the limits of knowledge through the invention of felicitous metaphors.'[80]

Proper names, emphatic terms, painterly epithets, and metaphors – these are some of the semiotic operations the Enlightenment theoreticians identify as evoking that presence-to-mind of the represented object that qualifies a text as poetic. It is through such operations that the symbolic cognition characterizing our normal use of language is 'transformed. . .into an intuitive cognition.'[81] Such transformation, such achievement of transparency within language, is the sole criterion that the discipline of aesthetic semiotics requires in order to define its object of study. Mendelssohn makes the point with characteristic clarity:

The means of making a discourse sensate consists in the selection of such expressions as recall to memory at once a whole set of features in order to make us feel the signified in a more lively fashion than the sign itself. Through such means our cognition is rendered intuitive. The objects are presented to our senses as if without mediation, and the lower faculties of the soul experience an illusion in that they often forget the signs and believe that they are viewing the object itself. It is in terms of this general maxim that the value of poetic images, comparisons and descriptions, and even the value of individual poetic words, must be judged.[82]

In essence, this criterion (that the object represented by the text be actualized intuitively) is a pragmatic one. We can therefore say that aesthetic semiotics starts off from a universal pragmatic category (intuition) which defines the *telos* of poetic language and from this category works backwards in order to identify the various semiotic procedures that allow for the attainment of this *telos*. Now, given this particular analytical procedure, a very interesting theoretical question emerges: to what degree do the local poetic devices identified in the course of analysis exhibit unity on another level than the pragmatic one of allowing for and encouraging the intuitive actualization of the represented object? In other words, to what degree can poetic language be characterized in terms of a single semiotic principle? This is precisely the question that Lessing raises, and answers, in his *Laocoon*. It is Lessing's argument – this much can be said in anticipation of the next chapter – that poetry can be defined as a type of language-use in which language attains to the status of a natural sign. Here we have a semiotic principle governing the correlation of expression and content which, like the pragmatic criterion of intuitive cognition, affords us a theoretically economical account of the nature of poetry.

Aesthetic semiotics can therefore be understood as establishing the theoretical context out of which Lessing's line of questioning in the *Laocoon* emerged. But it is necessary to go further than this: we must assert – contrary to the claims made in the secondary literature[83] – that in several respects Lessing's thesis regarding the naturalness of aesthetic signification is already present in the writings of the aestheticians. Thus, the 'emphatic words' so central to poetry derive their efficacy from the fact that they preserve traces of their mimetic origin, that is, of the natural signifying procedure through which they were instituted. And metaphor, which I have called the quintessential poetic act, can likewise be defined as a natural sign: 'Natural signs I understand to be words which express actual or metaphysical similarities between two objects of which the one corresponds to the proper, the other to the figural meaning of the word... To this class belong all metaphorical expressions whatsoever.'[84] It is Meier, however, who is

the first to move beyond such local examples of natural signification and to state the matter in the form of a general proposition: 'All arbitrary signs must imitate natural signs to as
great a degree as possible if they are to be truly beautiful.'[85]
The conclusion we must draw from this is that Lessing's thesis
regarding the naturalness of poetic signs is neither a product of
individual brilliance (Todorov) nor the anticipation of an
epochal change (Schröder). Rather, it is the expression of a
*structural necessity within Enlightenment culture.* Given the
conceptual array that characterizes the representational theory-
type, poetry was, as it were, predestined to be classified as a
natural sign.

Meier's principle of naturalness formulates in the terminology of Enlightenment semiotics a general rule for the use of
signs in poetry: the arbitrariness of the sign is to be overcome
and poetry is to employ to as great a degree as possible natural
signifying procedures. Two possible interpretations of this rule
presented themselves to the eighteenth-century theoreticians.
That is to say, the natural signs of poetry could be conceived
either as expressive or as iconic depending on whether they
were viewed as non-conventionalized utterances of feelings,
thoughts and attitudes or as mimetic mappings of objects and
events. In the first case, we are merely dealing with a naturalness of the second degree, a use of arbitrary linguistic signs that
is natural in the sense of 'unpremeditated, artless and direct.'
The second interpretation, however, makes the stronger claim
that poetry changes the nature of linguistic signification altogether. Lessing, as the next chapter will set out to show, argued
for this latter view. In the writings of Meier and Mendelssohn,
both types of natural signification are mentioned though only
the use of natural expressive signs is discussed at all concretely.[86]

Meier, for example, thinks of naturalness in signification as
a stylistic norm. The elegant, cultivated, avowedly artistic type
of writing such as the stylistic ideal of aristocratic art demanded
is judged from the standpoint of the enlightened bourgeois as

affected and mendacious: 'An arbitrary sign, insofar as it is very beautiful and therefore similar to natural signs to a high degree, is called *natural* insofar as this expression is opposed to *affected* [*signum coactum & affectatum*]. Affectedness in signs is always an imperfection which arises either from bad and false rules of art or from a miserable application of the rules of art.'[87] The style of the poem must not reveal any intentional working or cultivation, but rather must appear as an improvisation, a natural outgrowth of the subject matter: 'The beautiful arrangement must come into being among the beautiful thoughts themselves without one's having thought of it before and expressly having the intention to use such an arrangement.'[88] This description takes us far from the learned poet (still Gottsched's ideal) who is familiar with the rules of effective artistic performance and knows how to calculate their tactically most efficient use. The poet Meier imagines makes of his language a series of natural signs by approximating something like 'natural' – that is unaffected or even non-deliberate – speech.

The idealization of the natural in sign use is carried a step further in Mendelssohn's notion of naive expression. The concept of the naive, of course, inevitably implies naturalness and the absence of affectation. One of the interesting features of Mendelssohn's use of the term, however, is that he gives it a semiotic definition: 'When from a simple sign a signified state of affairs is cognized which for its part is important, or can have important consequences, then the signification involved is called naive.'[89] Naive expression reveals its content 'without wanting to,' or 'without a deliberate intention,' or – and this is the most telling predicate – 'without self-consciousness.'[90] The absence of rhetorical device and ornament, the brevity, the unassuming literalness of the naive expression, all those features, in short, which Mendelssohn characterizes as 'simple,' are interpreted as indicators of the naturalness of the utterance. Such naturalness means that the speaker is entirely absorbed by the idea or mental representation he attends to. Not only is he unconcerned with the possibility of deliberately working the linguistic signifiers as a means of expressing the idea more adequately; he is even unaware of the presence of an audience whose approval he might want to win. Hence the unadorned simplicity of the expression: it is an artless emanation of the signified idea itself. And since it is the signified content that stands before the speaker's mind when the naive expression is formulated, then that expression will be characterized by precisely the sort of transparency which defines the aesthetic generally. The naive is a type of sign use that makes possible the intuitive actualization of the signified content, the presence of which constitutes the universal pragmatic criterion for aesthetic texts. Mendelssohn insists precisely on this point:

Since it is apparent that in the naive the signified object strikes our senses as greater and more important than the sign, then it will likewise be felt in a more lively fashion. That is to say, we will cognize the signified *intuitively*; for we have an intuitive cognition of an object when we represent the signified to ourselves in a more lively manner than the sign. – The naive expression provides an *intuitive cognition*, which is therefore perfect, and, if it allows us to perceive a set of features simultaneously, is *sensately perfect*; for this reason the naive is entirely compatible with the purpose of the fine arts; for the essence of the fine arts consists in *perfect sensate representation*.[91]

This passage returns us to the question of poetic transparency from which we began. Naive speech, like metaphor and emphatic terms, like painterly epithets and proper names, transforms the symbolic cognition language ordinarily affords into an intuitive cognition of the represented object or idea. The capacity of poetry to accomplish this transformation derives from the fact that in poetry those natural signifying procedures predominate which are at the origin of language and culture: mimesis, naming, metaphor, expressive speech. This localization of poetry at the fringes of culture, at a point where the instruments of civilization (signs) recover their natural forcefulness and immediacy, is an event which, in decisive ways, restructures the European attitude toward poetic discourse. Since the time of the Enlightenment there has existed a radical discontinuity between the language of poetry and the other languages of culture. Enlightenment aesthetics – seeking perhaps a substitute for the lost Word of revelation – isolates poetic language as a privileged form of linguistic representation, an ideal transparency. In so doing, it ascribes to poetic semiosis a double significance, at once archaic and utopian: poetry at once recuperates the immediacy and richness of the origins of culture and anticipates the culture's ultimate goal. For it is an ideal transparency toward which, in the eighteenth-century view, all our cultural endeavors are directed. The aim of culture is an ideal language in which, according to Wolff, 'symbolic cognition is converted...into an intuitive cognition'[92] and the signs of human institution are rendered isomorphic with those of nature.

## Comparative semiotics of the arts

The second major task of aesthetic semiotics comprises the comparative description of the various arts and the determination of their limits and possibilities of combination. It is here that we move beyond exclusively poetic concerns to a genuinely aesthetic inquiry touching on all the art forms. Such a comparative aesthetic inquiry presupposes, of course, that all the art forms be considered members of a single class, bearers of a common trait; and, as we have seen, the aestheticians define this class as the set of perfect sensate representations. Essentially this is a functional definition: in order to qualify as an art work an artifact must allow for the intuitive actualization of a represented object – with the characteristic representational-conative activity and pleasure that accompany such intuitive apprehensions. Given this functional criterion, it becomes possible to classify and compare the arts as *means* for attaining (that is, evoking in the receiver) the *end* of aesthetic intuition. This is precisely the logic behind the preface to Lessing's *Laocoon*, as we shall see subsequently. For the present, I refer to this question of means and ends in aesthetic theory merely

in order to show why aesthetic semiotics assumes such importance in the comparative study of the basic art forms. The
reason is quite simple: the different 'means' which distinguish
the various arts one from another are nothing other than the
different semiotic media the arts employ. Therefore, the most
natural classification of the arts – the grid which most accurately traces the lines of demarcation isolating each art form –
will be based on semiotic criteria. Such a classification will
enable us to discern the inner affinities and mutual exclusions
that obtain among the arts and to circumscribe the proper
domain of each.

Comparison and delimitation are indeed the tasks that
Mendelssohn sets out to accomplish through his semiotic
taxonomy of the arts.[93] In order to subdivide the aesthetic field
into the various regions the arts occupy, Mendelssohn introduces a series of semiotic categories each of which allows for
two alternative determinations. In this way, the unitary field
of 'perfect sensate representations' is progressively split into
different sub-fields until all the traditional art forms have been
derived. It will prove useful, I think, if we briefly review the
steps of this derivation.

Mendelssohn begins by introducing the category of *sign type*.
The alternative determinations within this category – natural
vs. arbitrary – are those familiar to us from the general
discussion of Enlightenment semiotics. Mendelssohn formulates the distinction with his customary lucidity:

The signs by means of which an object is expressed can be either natural
or arbitrary. They are natural when the connection of the sign with the
signified object has its basis in the properties of the signified itself.
The passions are linked by virtue of their nature with certain movements
in the parts of our body as well as with certain tones and gestures.
Therefore, whoever expresses an emotion through the tones, gestures,
and movements appropriate to it is employing natural signs. By contrast,
those signs are called arbitrary which by virtue of their nature have
nothing in common with the signified object, but which are arbitrarily
accepted in its place. To this type belong the articulate tones of all
languages, alphabetical characters, the hieroglyphic signs of the ancients,

and some allegorical images which can justifiably be counted among the hieroglyphs.[94]

This opposition severs the aesthetic field into the two realms of the fine arts (natural signs) and the *belles lettres* (arbitrary signs). In the former, the content is actually mapped onto the signifier, either expressively or iconically. In the latter, the content is conveyed by conventionally accepted signs that are not directly connected with the objects they stand in for.

With this first division Mendelssohn has succeeded in isolating poetry and rhetoric, the two forms of *belles lettres* he recognizes, from the other art forms. In order to distinguish the fine arts from one another, however, further categories must be introduced. These categories specify various modalities of the material used to fashion the signifier. In other words, Mendelssohn defines the arts according to distinctive features of the material of expression. The initial category in this regard pertains to the sense organs a given sign vehicle appeals to: all artistic signs are received either through audition or through vision. This distinction separates off music, the art employing audible natural signs, from the other fine arts. The remaining visual natural signs can be further subdivided according to the arrangement of their parts, which either follow one another in time or are juxtaposed in space. Successive ordering yields what Mendelssohn terms 'the expression of beauty through movement,'[95] while simultaneous ordering characterizes the arts of form. The only visual art in which the signs follow upon one another in time is dance. Finally, the arts of form can be distinguished according to their dimensionality: spatial forms are either two or three dimensional, surfaces or bodies. Thus painting, as an art of surface forms, is isolated from sculpture and architecture, which fill all three dimensions.

In order to end with a complete list of the traditionally recognized art forms, Mendelssohn is compelled to introduce additional categories, although these do not allow for the systematic or truly generative sort of derivation that characterizes his initial distinctions. The category of content, for instance, is brought in to distinguish theatrical dance, which represents human actions and feelings, from 'common' dance, which does not. An examination of content also allows one to capture the difference between architecture, which represents such values as comfort and solidity as well as the wealth and status of the building's owner, and sculpture, which knows nothing of such values. But this contentual distinction is actually grounded in a functional difference between the two art forms. The reason architecture brings such values to expression is that it has its origin in real needs (e.g., the need for shelter) and therefore possesses an ineluctably practical moment. Sculpture, on the other hand, is designed to serve the end of pleasure alone. The same functional partition separates rhetoric from poetry since the former has persuasion as its aim whereas the latter is intended merely to please the reader or listener through the perfect sensate representations it evokes.

Mendelssohn's classification of the arts (which is schematized in Figure 3) exhibits, needless to say, definite inadequacies. Perhaps the most obvious error is the use of the category of function to distinguish between rhetoric and poetry as well as between architecture and sculpture, for it is this category which allows Mendelssohn to sort out aesthetic representations from all others in the first place: aesthetic representations *in general* serve the purpose of 'pleasing' (*gefallen*) and for this reason they can be defined as the genus of perfect sensate representations.[96] To say that there are species within this genus that have a different function is like saying some birds are insects. Rhetoric and architecture, therefore, should have been omitted from the classification altogether.[97] Another problem is that the categories which define the material features of the sign vehicle are only applied to the natural signs. A more thoroughgoing use of these categories might have revealed that certain poetic forms tend toward simultaneity and spatial juxtaposition, others toward successivity and temporal ordering. In this text at least (we shall soon see that it is not always the case),

## Figure 3

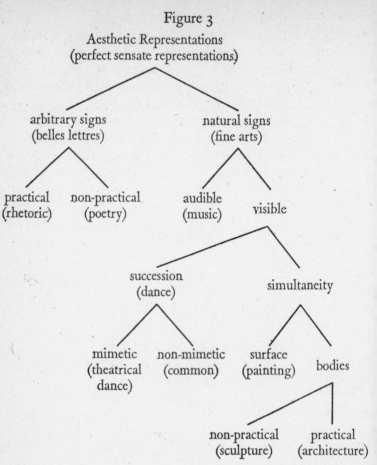

Aesthetic Representations
(perfect sensate representations)

arbitrary signs
(belles lettres)

natural signs
(fine arts)

practical
(rhetoric)

non-practical
(poetry)

audible
(music)

visible

succession
(dance)

simultaneity

mimetic
(theatrical
dance)

non-mimetic
(common)

surface
(painting)

bodies

non-practical
(sculpture)

practical
(architecture)

Mendelssohn attributes no importance to the material constitution of the linguistic sign.

But the important matter is not to criticize Mendelssohn for a lack of systematic rigor, as if he were our contemporary; it is rather to see what the classification makes possible, what its use is within the context of Enlightenment aesthetics. As I view it, Mendelssohn's classification serves to support two basic theoretical-axiological operations: the definition of the essence and intrinsic scope of each art form and the derivation of rules

governing the combination of elemental art forms into multi-
media constructs. The following paragraphs briefly review
each of these points.

Just as the arts in general have an 'essence' (*Wesen*) –
namely, perfect sensate representation – so too does each of the
individual art forms. What determines the essence of the
individual art, however, is that qualifying predicate that sets
it off from the other arts. Thus, the essence or purpose
(Mendelssohn uses these terms interchangeably) of painting
is to evoke perfect sensate representations through the use of
two-dimensional natural signs. By transforming his classificational grid into an order of essences in this manner,
Mendelssohn hypostatizes his own cultural values, as we shall
presently see concretely. What I want to insist on now,
however, is that the essential definitions generated from the
classificatory matrix enable Mendelssohn to establish a set of
rules intrinsic to each art form. In the main, these rules have
to do with the range of contents which a given art form can or
should transmit. For Mendelssohn – and for Lessing as well, as
the next chapter will attempt to show – *aesthetic rules often
take the form of restrictions on content selection derived from
the overriding aesthetic purpose of the representation as well
as from the nature of the sign vehicle a particular art form
employs*. Thus poetry, because its signs are arbitrary, can
represent 'everything for which the soul can produce a clear
representation.'[98] Since there is no necessary connection between words and what they refer to, the limits of poetic content
are marked off solely by the general requirement of sensate
intuition. (It is here, of course, that the problem of poetic
transparency has its origin.) However: 'The object of the fine
arts is more restricted.'[99] Because each art form employs a
specific type of natural sign, it cannot possibly represent certain
contents without making use of other sorts of sign than that
which defines its essence. Such transgression of essential
boundaries, Mendelssohn holds, has an aesthetically deleterious
effect.

Aesthetic rules state not only what is a possible content selection within a given art form, but also what is an optimal one. The best known and perhaps the most interesting example of such a prescription is the so-called rule of the pregnant moment.[100] The invention of this rule is usually ascribed to Lessing but in fact it was Mendelssohn who first formulated it. (Lessing's contribution was, as in so many other cases, to have given this accepted tenet of Enlightenment theory greater precision and a clearly defined systematic position.) The rule of the pregnant moment governs the representation of action in the spatial arts. Direct depiction of a successively unfolding action is precluded in these arts because their simultaneity of deployed forms does not possess the attribute of sequentiality. Therefore, painter and sculptor must select that point in the action which is most meaningful in terms of the entire course of events. The representation of this particular moment allows the imagination of the viewer to move back and forth along the suggested sequence and thereby to fill in the implied but unspecified past and future of the action. Thus the rule, as derived from the nature of the sign vehicle, might be formulated as follows: spatial signs must be used to represent a single point in time; this point should be as meaningful as possible in terms of the action leading up to and following upon it.[101] In some later (1776) remarks on Hemsterhuis' *Lettre sur la sculpture* which I have already referred to in connection with the formula for beauty, Mendelssohn pushes this analysis a step further, distinguishing between rules governing two-dimensional and rules governing three-dimensional forms. Paintings, he argues, are viewed from a single point in space, sculptures from several, so that a sculpture requires a greater span of time for reception. For this reason sculpture must represent fewer details and suggest less ongoing action. In this way the represented figures can logically remain stable throughout the temporal process of viewing the sculpture from several perspectives. 'I can contemplate beauty at rest from all sides without expecting any change.'[102] Mendelssohn's assumption here is that the perceptual conditions of reception should always be integrated into the content of the work, that the receiver adopt the position of an *onlooker*. This assumption goes to the heart of representational aesthetics: the subject is absorbed in the represented content, he does not occupy the more distant and self-conscious position of the appreciative beholder.

As both these rules (the rule of the pregnant moment and the rule of reduced activity in sculpture) illustrate, an important purpose of aesthetic semiotics is to establish for each of the arts the special conditions of possibility of aesthetic efficacy; to determine how, given the nature of the signs it employs, a particular art form can convey contentually replete, global, intuitive representations that realize the soul's full representational-conative potential. The derivation of these rules is accomplished through an examination of the distinctive features of the sign vehicle, *especially insofar as these affect the process of aesthetic reception*. Of course, such an inquiry presupposes that the structure of aesthetic reception has itself been idealized in advance or – to put the same matter another way – that certain possibilities of aesthetic reception have been excluded, others rendered normative. My brief comparison of representational theory with the performance and expression theory-types has indicated along what lines such idealization takes place: for Enlightenment aesthetics, the reception of art works simulates the structure of perception; the work is essentially a transparency allowing for that absorbing experience of the aesthetic object as virtually present which the age called aesthetic illusion. But aesthetic semiotics not only presupposes such a delimitation of aesthetic reception, it is also an active factor that contributes to the normativization of this reduced form of aesthetic experience within the culture at large. Aesthetic semiotics *at once reflects and accomplishes* the localization of art within the immanent mental sphere, the transformation of art works (both present and past) into media for the transmission of aesthetic representations. Such is the discursive efficacy of the discipline of aesthetics and of the semiotic instruments it employs.

Let us turn now to the second use Mendelssohn makes of his semiotic taxonomy of the arts, namely the development of a grammar for the combination of the elemental art forms. The prerequisite of this task is that each of the arts has been defined in its essence and that sets of rules governing aesthetic efficacy within each art form have been established. It then becomes possible to proceed in the following manner:

...and since, as we have already seen, every art has a special purpose, the artist who wants to combine arts must choose the purpose of a single art as his chief aim and subordinate the other arts to this one in such a way that they can be regarded as means to the chief end. For the sake of brevity we shall call the first the main art and the latter the auxiliary arts.

From the special purposes that define each art as a sub-species [of art in general] special rules can be deduced which are peculiar to each art *vis-à-vis* all the others. In a combination of the arts these rules can enter into conflict with one another and in such a case exceptions are unavoidable.

If such a conflict of special rules is not to be avoided, then the most minimal exception possible must be made, and this on the part of the auxiliary arts. These arts should serve in their combination merely to elevate the main art and to lend it certain beauties which it does not itself possess. For this reason, the auxiliary arts must always yield to the main art and relinquish some of the stringency of their own laws. Those rules which follow from the universal definition of the fine arts in general can never contradict one another in a combination of individual arts. However, if the special rules of the main art conflict with the general rules of the auxiliary arts in such a way that the intended combination of arts would be impossible should the special rules of the main art be completely satisfied, then to be sure the exception must occur on the part of the main art.[103]

I have quoted this lengthy passage not only because it so clearly presents Mendelssohn's analysis of the combination of art forms, but also because it illustrates so many of the points I have touched on regarding Enlightenment aesthetic theory generally. Here the theoretical structure of aesthetics as a hierarchy of rules – rules of art in general (that is, pertaining to aesthetic representation), rules following from the essence or purpose of each art, special rules that maximize aesthetic efficacy within each art – is made apparent. Here the deductive form of the argumentation and the philosophical neutrality of the writing are easily visible. Finally, we can discern here – and I especially want to emphasize this point – the true target of the analysis: as described here, the arts do not at all reflect the creative force of an individual or cultural identity, but rather the entirely impersonal rules that govern the deployment of aesthetic representations. What the theory aims for is a calculus of aesthetic efficacy.

The particular question at issue in the passage is, of course, what rules govern multi-media combinations among the arts. Mendelssohn develops his solution with such lucidity that little commentary is required. Essentially what we find here is a theory of *structural dominance*. In any combination of the arts, one of the arts *must* define the priorities of compositional selection. That is to say, the particular rules intrinsic to the dominant art form are, in all cases of conflict, to take precedence over the rules of the other arts. The rules referred to here, let us recall, guarantee optimal aesthetic efficacy within an individual art form. What the law of structural dominance requires then is that the subordinate or auxiliary arts not be realized in their intrinsically most efficacious form if such realization interferes with the attainment of perfection in the dominant art. In opera, poetry yields to the dominant art of music and remains schematic in its images, musical in diction as well as rhythm and meter. However, when music is employed to support poetic declamation, it is kept as simple as possible, reduced to a tool for creating emphasis. The only instances where the special rules of the dominant art do not take priority are those where obeying them would render the combination of the arts impossible. For example, in opera the music must be restricted by the demands of mimetic coherence and intelligibility; it must 'avoid the general confusion of emotions which can in certain places be entirely appropriate in a symphony.'[104] This reduction of complexity constitutes the sole concession required of music in such an alliance of the arts. The musician must agree to speak, as it were, according to the depth grammar of poetry and drama, to accept as binding the minimal conditions of poetic and theatrical signification.

I have tried to show that, by applying aesthetic semiotics to the comparative study of the arts, Mendelssohn achieves a twofold theoretical goal: the derivation of the set of rules proper to each art and the development of a grammar governing combinations of different art forms. These theoretical operations possess, as I indicated above, an axiological component; they serve to legitimate specific aesthetic and cultural norms. The obvious and trivial sense in which this is true is that the theoretical conclusions tend to favor particular artistic styles. For example, the insistence on logical organization and hierarchy in the theory of multi-media combinations evinces a neoclassical aesthetic bias. But a more interesting sense in which the theory is value-laden emerges when we consider how it declares a single, limited structure of aesthetic experience as the sole valid one. I alluded to this issue above when I pointed out that the formulation of the art-specific rules guaranteeing aesthetic efficacy presupposes a restriction of the possible types of aesthetic reception. Here I want to demonstrate this point in terms of a concrete example. Allegory is allowable in painting, Mendelssohn claims, so long as the correlation of the represented content and the allegorical sense is motivated, so long as the allegorical sign is natural. However: 'If a butterfly is supposed to signify the soul; . . . if a stag is supposed to signify now a troubled conscience, now I know not what; then these are merely symbolic signs, far less intuitive than the most arbitrary words. Such an expression not only departs from the essence of painting, it also denies the character of the arts in general. . .'[105] This rejection of highly conventionalized allegorical signification can be considered emblematic for Enlightenment aesthetic theory generally. What is here said to depart from the 'essence' of painting, indeed

94

from the sphere of aesthetic legitimacy altogether, is a particular mode of being of art works and the type of receptive behavior that accompanies it. Mendelssohn cannot accept as aesthetically valid a work which has the status of a *text*. He cannot accept a receptive behavior that has the structure of a *reading*, that abides in the domain of symbolic cognition and that comprehends the work/text as relating to a body of erudition. It is thus not simply one style that is being criticized here for the sake of another. Rather, art and the processing of art are being relocated and reprogrammed within the culture at large. The work no longer assumes its place within a group of texts – other works, bodies of knowledge and doctrine – but presents itself as a transparency through which the object is seen as if for the first time. This quasi-seeing, this intuitive apprehension of an imagined object, is the idealized and hence restricted version of aesthetic experience which Enlightenment theory, and more generally Enlightenment culture, produce.

The redefinition of aesthetic experience affects the reading of linguistic texts as well. We have already seen that Enlightenment theory depicts poetic language as a transparent medium and that it requires that the reception of poetic texts entails intuition. If this is the case, that is, if reading too is supposed to result in a quasi-perceptual experience, then the material features of the sign vehicles of poetry will have to be accorded the same sort of theoretical attention as those of the other arts. Indeed, to compare the relative aesthetic efficacy of the arts, as it was from Dubos to Lessing the passion of the age to do, will necessarily require that the effects exerted on the process of aesthetic reception by the material constitution of the signifiers employed in each art be scrupulously compared. This, of course, is the project of Lessing's *Laocoon*, which is a detailed semiotic analysis and comparison of poetry and the plastic arts. I want to conclude this chapter by calling attention to a text in which Mendelssohn anticipates Lessing's basic findings and in which the cultural transformation of poetic language into a medium for conveying a quasi-perceptual aesthetic experience is clearly in evidence.

In his notes on Edmund Burke's *Philosophical Inquiry into the Origin of our Ideas of the Sublime and the Beautiful* (1757), Mendelssohn takes up the question of the relative merits of painting and poetry. In doing so, he joins a debate involving several eighteenth-century theoreticians, among them Jean Baptiste Dubos, Breitinger, and of course the British author of the *Inquiry*. Rather than attempting a global and absolute evaluation of the two arts, as his predecessors had done, Mendelssohn follows a methodological tack familiar to us from his derivation of the rules intrinsic to each art form: 'It is a common mistake to compare the effects of two powers without taking into consideration that which defines each art as a special type. If poetry is to be compared with painting, then one must constantly keep the distinction in view that the former has its effect as a simultaneous order, the latter as a successive order.'[106] It is the spatial or temporal organization of the sign vehicle which Mendelssohn views as the decisive factor influencing the conditions of aesthetic reception and therefore limiting the range of objects a given art can effectively express. Thus, a poetic representation of a spatial object or configuration is bound to be less successful than a painting because a temporal process is required to understand the signs and considerable imaginative effort must be exerted to reconstitute the spatial image that is intended. The sequential structure which the sign vehicle imposes upon the process of reception conflicts with the spatial arrangement of the content.[107] However, what is a disadvantage for poetry when spatial objects are to be represented is an advantage when the artist seeks to achieve a strong emotional response on the part of the receiver. 'It is for no other reason than this [temporal order of reception], I believe, that more powerful affects are aroused through music and poetry than through painting and sculpture. The first instant discloses for us everything that can move us in a painting and one must bring reflection and a trained eye to the task if one wants to discover something new in the second instant.'[108] The sequence of poetic signs allows for the development of an emotion in the reader across a temporal experience involving expectation, surprise and discovery[109] and it is for this reason that, where the artist wishes to communicate an affective experience, the successive order of linguistic signs will be the more apposite semiotic medium. For Mendelssohn there can be no question of an absolute superiority of one art over another. Each art has its proper domain of excellence, each a range of contents which it can express most effectively.

What is important about Mendelssohn's analysis is that it takes the Enlightenment idealization of poetic language to its furthest extreme. Whereas his published treatises on aesthetics (the 'Reflections' and the 'Chief Principles') set no limits on poetic content selection because poetry employs arbitrary signs, the notes on Burke's *Inquiry* insist that *all* the arts, poetry included, are restricted by the material constitution of their signifiers. The principle which dictates the nature of this restriction can be stated as follows: *in all the arts aesthetic efficacy will be maximized if a relationship of isomorphism obtains between the perception of the sign vehicle and the internal representation of the signified content.* We have seen this principle applied in Mendelssohn's discussion of allegorical painting, where he denies aesthetic value to a painted text such as would elicit a decoding rather than a perceptually grounded reception. In the notes on Burke, the same tendency of thought exhibits itself as regards poetry: poetry is viewed as aesthetically most efficacious when it exhibits an iconic relationship between signifier and signified, that is, when it *attains to the status of a natural sign.* To be sure, Mendelssohn neither states this thesis explicitly nor describes its ramifications in detail. Above all, he fails to provide a clear definition of the contentual restrictions that accrue to poetry due to the principle of isomorphism. But, with his claim that the sequentiality of linguistic signs provides the basis for a poetic form of iconicity, he does suggest how Meier's vague requirement that poetry employ 'essential signs' might be reasonably construed. It will remain for Lessing to transform this suggestion into a systematic, concretely articulated theory.

# 3 · LESSING'S *LAOCOON*

## Preface

In a famous review from 1769, Christian Garve characterized one of the central difficulties of Lessing's *Laocoon* as follows: 'Thoughts are determined to some degree by their signs and that which would have seemed doubtful or even incorrect to us, if expressed simply or plainly, strikes us in the more appropriate and illuminating designation we have given it as true and evident. In this way, the soul is often blinded by its own light.'[1] The figure of thought is typical of the eighteenth century: Ideas, mental representations, make up the inventory of our knowledge of the world. When we think a truth, we are thinking an idea, or group of ideas, that corresponds to a real state of affairs. But because the mind is finite, it cannot think ideas alone. They are too elusive; lacking definite contours, they slip into oblivion. Therefore man marks his ideas with signs, which, being themselves easily manipulated sense ideas, allow him to recall his representations, to hold onto them, to analyze them into their constituent features and to join them in the chains of his reasoning. The link between sign and idea is arbitrary, for man has willfully chosen the sign as the vehicle for his directly intuited thought and he could have as easily selected another. By virtue of this arbitrariness, however, a distance is opened up between sign and idea, and in the space of this distance resides the possibility of error. It is possible to attend to the sign and not be aware of the thought. It is possible even that signs introduce themselves into the movement of our reasoning to such a degree that it is the logic of signs which we follow and not the logic immanent to our thoughts. The mind is led away from the truth by the very instruments which allow it to think the truth. And this, Garve suggests, is the central problem of the *Laocoon*: Lessing's incomparable style employs signs that in themselves seem so compelling that they divert attention from the ideas they mark and therefore allow falsehoods to pass for indubitable truths.

Ironically, Lessing could have used Garve's remark as an epigraph for the *Laocoon* itself, though not in order to warn the reader about the potentially deceitful formulations the work contains. Garve's statement coincides with one of Lessing's own most profound suspicions and therefore suggests his project and method. The *Laocoon* is a critique of wrong labels and false metaphors.[2] Consider in this regard the opening paragraphs of the preface, where Lessing localizes his critical procedure (IX, 3). Three nameless individuals, the amateur, the aesthetician and the critic, are introduced, and to each is attributed a specific activity. Each represents a particular perspective on the arts and to the perspective of each corresponds a definite methodology. The amateur ('Liebhaber') represents the standpoint of immediate aesthetic experience. What he does is called 'empfinden' (feeling) or 'verspüren' (sensing), a mute, preconceptual activity entirely inside the encounter with individual works. His sensitive capacity of 'Gefühl' (feeling) registers the pleasurable effect that defines the aesthetic. At the opposite pole from the amateur's feeling is the cool neutrality of philosophical reflection. The aesthetician, with whose portrait Lessing pays a deserved tribute to Mendelssohn, represents the standpoint of pure conceptualization, where individual works and experiences are left behind and the mind operates solely with universals. Both standpoints admit little possibility of error; each has a kind of evidential guarantee. For aesthetic experience this guarantee is the immediacy of feeling, incontrovertible and unmistakable. For pure conceptualization it is the rigor of the syllogism, which, when performed according to the rules of logic, cannot possibly miss the truth. But the critic, who is neither totally within aesthetic experience nor totally above it in the abstract field of concepts, who *mediates between particular works and general principles* – the critic is very likely to err. Moderation[3] and scrupulous care alone can protect him from falsifying the facts:

As regards the comments of the critic, on the other hand, everything depends on the correctness of the application to the individual case; and, since there have been fifty critics of wit for every one of acumen, it would be a miracle indeed if such application had always been made with the caution needed to balance the scale evenly between the two arts (IX, 3).

The standpoint of the critic, his field of activity, is language – not mute, immediate experience of the individual instance, nor conceptualization that subsumes all individuals beneath universals, but that difficult middle region where experience first becomes ordered, categorized, articulated. The hazard is that the critic will be too 'witzig' (witty), not 'scharfsinnig' (acute) enough; that is, according to doctrinaire rationalist psychology, that he will combine things without due attention to their differences. And the locus of such false combinations, the vehicle which hardens them into institutional truths, is metaphorical language:

The dazzling antithesis of the Greek Voltaire, that painting is a mute poetry and poetry a speaking painting, certainly never had its place in any textbook. It was a witty idea of the sort that often occurred to Simonides; its true portion is so striking that one feels compelled to overlook the unspecific and false component which accompanies it (IX, 4).

The task of the *Laocoon*, anticipated here in phrasing remarkably similar to Garve's, is to clear up the confusions engendered by such seductive metaphors as those of Simonides. The malady of modern criticism, and to an extent of artistic practice as well, derives, in Lessing's view, from the literalization of metaphors. Criticism has forgotten the differences bridged by the metaphorical equation; similarity in only one respect has hardened into identity in all. The danger of such errors crops up as soon as the critic steps out of immediate experience in order to formulate a general proposition. Winckelmann's empirical observations of the Laocoon statue, for instance, are entirely sound. The general principle to which he relates these observations, however, is muddled.[4] But the metaphor against which the entire *Laocoon* is directed, the one which has misled critics and artists alike, is 'poetisches Gemählde' (poetic painting): 'I very much wish that modern textbooks on the art of poetry had made use of this term [i.e., 'fantasy' or 'enargia'] and had avoided the word painting altogether. They would have spared us a whole set of half true rules the major justification of which is merely the correspondence of an arbitrary name' (IX, 92).

Programmatic for the *Laocoon*, then, the following fragment: 'Necessity of expressing oneself about such things as precisely as possible' (B., 399). Against the metaphorical wit of his predecessors Lessing sets the vigilance of 'Scharfsinn' (acumen), the faculty of discrimination. The *Laocoon* aims to take apart inherited equations and to reaffirm the differences between things. On the scale of critical justice each art will be accorded its own. (Cf. the quotation above, from IX, 3.) This task begins with the first sentence of the preface. If criticism has been deceived by a metaphor, then the best corrective for its errors is to return to the initial use of that metaphor in order to determine its valid meaning:

Der erste, welcher die Mahlerey und Poesie mit einander verglich, war ein Mann von feinem Gefühle, der von beyden Künsten eine ähnliche Wirkung auf sich verspürte. Beyde, empfand er, stellen uns abwesende Dinge als gegenwärtig, den Schein als Wirklichkeit vor; beyde täuschen, und beyder Täuschung gefällt. (The first person who struck a comparison between painting and poetry was a man of sensitive feeling who sensed that the two arts had a similar effect on him. Both, he felt, represent absent things to us as present, appearance as reality; both create an illusion, and the illusion in both cases pleases us (IX, 3)).

The paragraph conducts the reader back to a hypothetical instant prior to the first utterance of the suspect metaphor or comparison, back to immediate, as yet uninterpreted experience. Here we are shown the nature of things before they are named; that is, the nature of painting and poetry before any deceitful metaphor amalgamates them beyond warrant. Such a pre-significative moment is, however, impossible to describe.

Instead of exhibiting the literal truth of things as they are, the paragraph brings into play the central preconceptions of the *Laocoon* and constructs the pre-linguistic moment in the inherited idiom of eighteenth-century aesthetics. Notice that Lessing accepts the legitimacy of the comparison. On one level painting and poetry do coincide, and this level provides the *tertium comparationis* of the metaphor or simile uttered by the 'first person.' At its origin the suspect metaphor is true: it is an emotive statement that registers an immediately felt similarity of effect. All claims that Lessing strictly distinguished poetry and painting are misleading so long as they do not recall the proper level on which these arts are considered one, the level of aesthetic effect. This presumed unity of the two arts governs the entire argument of the *Laocoon*.

It is advisable to consider this unity of effect more closely. One of the earliest sketches for the *Laocoon* expresses the matter with a forthrightness that the finished text lacks.

Poetry and painting, both are imitative arts; the purpose of both is to awaken in us the liveliest, most sensate representations of their objects. They therefore have in common all the rules that follow from the concept of imitation, from this purpose.

However they make use of entirely different means for their imitations; and from the difference of these means all the specific rules for each art are to be derived.

*Painting* uses figures and colors in *space*.

*Poetry* articulates tones in *time*.

The signs of the former are *natural*. Those of the latter are *arbitrary* (B., 358–9).

According to this passage, the unity of painting and poetry is that both are mimetic arts. Both are therefore governed by those rules that derive from their shared purpose of imitating. The two arts have different rules as well though, and these stem from their respective means of imitation. Poetry uses arbitrary signs consisting of articulate sounds arranged temporally; painting employs natural signs made up of colors and figures deployed in space. If we consider this analysis as a skeleton of Lessing's aesthetics, then we can see why it was necessary for him to pay tribute to Mendelssohn in the 'Preface.' Like Mendelssohn, Lessing conceives of aesthetics as a hierarchy of rules.[5] The rules of art generate the aesthetic in general; the rules of signs account for the individual art forms. Painting and poetry are specifications of a single, aesthetic type of representation. The differences between the arts can be accounted for by formulating the rules of sign which govern each one. Poetry, for instance, will be described in terms of the rules pertinent to articulate tones, sequentially arranged and arbitrarily linked to ideas or signifieds. In other words, all the limitations of language use will be relevant to the description of poetry. Yet these rules alone would not suffice to define poetry. As I have suggested in my discussion of Mendelssohn, poetry must be defined in terms of the rules of art as well. Poetry is language used in aesthetic function, not merely any piece of discourse. Poetic language is constrained by the superior rules that account for the aesthetic in general.

The main part of this chapter attends to the differences between the arts. Here I want to sketch some of the consequences of the unity of the arts posited in the opening paragraph of Lessing's 'Preface.' In the previous chapter I argued that the common 'Endzweck'[6] (purpose) of the arts was to elicit a pleasurable, even passionate response in the receiver. The rules of art defined the type of representation which would make possible such a response, so that the aesthetic field was constituted as the field of perfect sensate representations or sensate intuitions. In Lessing's fragment, it seems, we are faced with a different rule: the concept of 'Nachahmung' (imitation) defines the aesthetic in general. Lessing's departure from Mendelssohn, however, is only apparent. Note that in the fragment quoted above the function of mimesis is defined primarily in terms of effect; an imitation evokes lively, sensate representations in the receiver. In other words, the effect of mimesis, as Lessing here describes it, approaches Mendelssohn's notion of perfect sensate representation.

It should be recalled that the notion of mimesis was not

foreign to Mendelssohn either. Mendelssohn's use of the term imitation was seen to involve two aspects, a referential and effective aspect.[7] Viewed in terms of its efficacy, an imitation functions to make present to the subject the particular object it refers to, and this evoked presence is called an illusion. An illusion is the presence-to-mind of an existentially absent object. This notion of illusion is echoed in the opening paragraph of Lessing's 'Preface.' There the common effect of the arts on the amateur is described as follows: 'Both, he felt, represent absent things to us as present, appearance as reality; both create an illusion, and the illusion in both cases pleases us' (IX, 3). For Lessing as well as for Mendelssohn, *the most fundamental rule of art prescribes that the works must provide a sensate intuition in which the value qualities of the object directly affect the beholder and thereby arouse aesthetic pleasure.* This intuition is an illusion, that is, it is an intuition of an object present-to-mind but existentially absent.

The opening paragraph of the 'Preface' establishes the framework for the remainder of the work – a contention confirmed by the retrospective summary of the *Laocoon*'s central thesis, which Lessing provides in the second of his *Antiquarische Briefe (Antiquarian Letters,* 1768). There he says his task in the earlier work was to show how poet and painter both undertake ' . . . to arrive at the same goal of illusion by entirely different paths. . . ' (X, 237). The formulation epitomizes the tension between sameness and difference that characterizes the emotive metaphor of the amateur and governs the entire argument of the *Laocoon.* The differences between poetry and the plastic arts are differences of method, means, technique ('Wege'); their unity is their shared aim ('Ziel'). Lessing distinguishes the arts in order to insist on their proper unity. As regards the *telos* of the arts, Lessing still holds to the dictum he is so often said to have rejected: *ut pictura poesis.*

From the central concept of illusion several far-reaching consequences result. For instance, if both poems and works of plastic art render absent objects present-to-mind, then they must both appeal to the imagination. Art works are two-tiered. They have a sensible stratum, in which the work is materially given, and a non-sensible or immaterial stratum, where the genuine aesthetic object is rendered imaginatively present-to-mind. The non-sensible, imaginative stratum presents us with those illusionary objects, the value qualities of which afford aesthetic pleasure. The sensible stratum is the stratum of signs (signifiers), which awaken the images of absent things in the mind. Aesthetic reception passes through or beyond the sensible stratum of signs in order to reach the non-sensible stratum where the imagination actualizes the aesthetic object: '. . . what we find beautiful in a work of art is not found beautiful by the eye, but rather by the imagination through the eye. If, therefore, the same image is excited anew in our imagination through either arbitrary or natural signs, in each case the same pleasure must arise anew, although not to the same degree' (IX, 45).

The imagination constitutes objects not immediately given to sense. It elevates man beyond mere sensation and therefore beyond animality: 'Animal eyes are harder to deceive than human eyes; they see nothing but what they see; we, on the other hand, are seduced by the imagination so that we believe we see even what we don't see' (B., 447). Lessing is adamant in his insistence that the imaginative field of illusionary objects is the true locus of aesthetic experience. An experience which abides on the level of sensation, by contrast, is not aesthetic at all. Examples abound. The long discussion of Sophocles' *Philoctetes* in the fourth chapter attempts to demonstrate how the protagonist's cries do not remain on the level of actually perceived screams but conduce to and are integrated within the imaginative construct of the drama.[8] To violate the rule of the pregnant moment '. . . means to bind the wings of fantasy and to force it – because it cannot go beyond the sense impression – to busy itself beneath it with weaker images beyond which it sees the visual fullness of the expression as its own limit' (IX, 19). Ugliness is inadmissible in the plastic arts because it necessarily asserts itself on the level of sensation; it is 'allezeit Natur, niemals Nachahmung' ('always nature, never imitation').[9]

The role of the imagination in a particular work provides a criterion of aesthetic excellence: 'Dolce admires therein [i.e., in a description by Ariosto] the extensive knowledge of corporeal beauty which the poet exhibits; I, however, look solely at the effect which this knowledge, expressed in words, can have on my imagination' (IX, 125). The imaginary object must have complete autonomy. Where it is a vehicle for theoretical knowledge (as in the above passage) or for allusions to extra-artistic persons and events (as in Virgil's description of Aeneas' shield [IX, 111–14]), Lessing will inevitably condemn the work.[10] The free use of the imagination is also the guarantee of artistic creativity. Lessing's analysis of the Virgil imitation in Petronius' *Satyricon* demonstrates this point very well. The Petronius poem reveals a predominance of 'Gedächtniß' (memory) over 'Einbildung' (imagination); that is, the poet's reduplicative faculty of memory clings to the stratum of individual words in the precursor poem, preventing him from attaining to an imaginative vision of the aesthetic object. 'It is hard to believe that he would have succumbed to this impropriety if he had merely produced the work out of his own imagination without an original in front of him which he wanted to copy but did not want to betray having copied' (IX, 38). The same rule holds for inter-artistic borrowings. If the artist transforms the art work of his predecessor into an object of his imagination and expresses it in his own medium, then he is an 'Original.' Should he, however, adopt his predecessor's means of imitation, should he, in other words, attend primarily to the sensible stratum of the work, then he is a mere 'Copist' (IX, 51).

This is not to say that Lessing evaluated art in terms of the subjective force or genius involved in the act of creation. He is – herein unique for his age – highly suspicious of 'den schwanken, nichts lehrenden Ausdrücken von Erhitzung der

Einbildungskraft, von Begeisterung...' ('such wavering, empty expressions of excitement of the imagination, of inspiration...' X, 237). Art, for Lessing, is curiously impersonal. This is one reason for his disagreement with Winckelmann: whereas for Winckelmann the beauty of the Laocoon statue derives from the assimilated cultural wisdom of the artist and the statue is an expression of this wisdom, for Lessing the statue is artistically successful because it conforms to the superindividual rules of beauty. The wisdom of the artists, in Lessing's view, is that they willingly submit their subjectivity to the objective laws of beauty governing art in general and the specific, but no less objective laws governing the individual art forms.[11] 'Milton says regarding Pandamonium: some praised the work, others the master who had produced it. Praise of one is therefore not always praise of the other as well' (IX, 125).

Fundamental to all the specific issues involved in the *Laocoon* is Lessing's insistence on the autonomous nature of the imagined object. In this object alone reside the value qualities which affect the receiver. The imaginary, aesthetic object rendered present-to-mind in the moment of illusion is autonomous in the sense that it serves no other function than that of presenting itself in its own intrinsic beauty. Such extraneous functions as truth to life or expressiveness, communicative ends, the transmission or demonstration of knowledge, flattery or other sorts of appeal to the audience, disqualify a representation from the aesthetic.[12] The value qualities apprehended in the intuition of the represented object alone determine the worth of the art work and alone provide the source of aesthetic pleasure. The different formulations in the *Laocoon* characterizing the aim of art – *Vergnügen*, *Nachahmung*, *Täuschung* (pleasure, imitation, illusion) – are not contradictory. They merely emphasize different aspects of the representational relation that defines the aesthetic for Lessing.

The same rule of autonomy applies to the individual art

forms. 'The proper definition of an art form can only be that which it is capable of producing without the aid of another art form' (B., 440). Just as art in general must constitute itself without relying on extra-aesthetic functions, so too must each art form work within its allotted portion of the aesthetic field without drawing on the resources or techniques specific to another art form. That which accords each of the arts its identity, as we know from Mendelssohn's classification of the arts, is the type of sign it employs to evoke ideas of its aesthetic objects. The task of circumscribing the 'proper definition of an art form,' then, falls to aesthetic semiotics, the discipline which describes the rules and restrictions of each variety of aesthetic sign. Here critical 'acumen' is employed to determine what is proper ('eigentlich') to each art form, to delineate 'die Grenzen der Mahlerey und Poesie' ('the limits of painting and poetry' (X, 1). This critical work of differentiation is the locus of Lessing's most important achievements and the second section of this chapter attempts to evaluate these achievements by retracing the limits of the arts as Lessing described them. In the third section I will return to the question of the unity of the arts, an issue present from the beginning of Lessing's preface.

## A global model of aesthetic signification

### Method

Lessing's *Laocoon* is a far more complicated text than I can account for here: it interweaves various intentions and codes, bringing together, for example, contingent polemical aims, archaeological and art-historical opinion, aesthetic norms, an anthropology, cultural prejudices, an idiosyncratic will to self-justification often deserving the label vanity, an incomparable stylistic élan, and other important as well as trivial elements. In view of this complexity – which invites a stimulating but disordered essayism[13] – and in view of my restricted concerns,

I shall discuss the *Laocoon* from a single perspective. I shall treat it as if it presented a global theory of aesthetic signification. This 'as if' is fictional, to be sure, but no more so than any working hypothesis. Whether it is arbitrary, or justified by the subject matter, will be determined by its degree of descriptive force, its capability of organizing various statements made in the *Laocoon* and accounting for the relations which obtain between them.

In the description of Baumgarten's, Meier's and Mendelssohn's theories of aesthetic signification the terms signifier and signified, or sign and thought, were sufficient to account for the theoretical models and corresponded to the terminology of the writers themselves. This is no longer the case with Lessing, whose attention to the interrelated aspects of aesthetic signification is scrupulous and detailed. I have therefore found it necessary to expand the two-sided model of the sign in such a way that this greater detail can be dealt with unambiguously. Where I spoke before of sign (signifier) and thought (signified), I will here use the terms expression and content (or the planes of expression and content). These terms are borrowed from Louis Hjelmslev's *Prolegomena to a Theory of Language*.[14] I follow Hjelmslev[15] further in isolating three aspects of each of these two functions related by the sign function: purport (for which I use the term material), substance, and form. Thus, in discussing Lessing's global model of the aesthetic sign, I will use terms comparable to Hjelmslev's denotative semiotic:

|              |           |
|--------------|-----------|
|              | material  |
| content:     | substance |
|              | form      |
|              | form      |
| expression:  | substance |
|              | material  |

These six terms, then, will be applied descriptively, allowing me to say, for instance, that, where Lessing speaks of the 'opening of the mouth' in a painting as a 'blotch' (IX, 17), the first phrase refers to the content substance, the second to the expression substance.

I must emphasize that my argument does *not* entail an exact correspondence between Hjelmslev's notions and those operative in the *Laocoon*. What is involved, rather, is the use of Hjelmslev's terms in a general sense, rendering them more broadly applicable than their strict glossematic meaning allows. The following definitions can serve as a prospective guide to the discussion: The material of expression is the sensuous stuff out of which the expression is formed. The form of expression consists of the rules according to which the material is divided, shaped and arranged in combinations. The formed material, the instantiated expression resulting from the interaction of expression form and expression material, will be referred to as the substance of expression (or expression token). On the plane of content, the material is the undifferentiated semantic mass. The form of content includes the principles of content selection and organization which, when projected onto the content material, yield a content unit or group of content units, the content substance of the work. While glossematics is concerned solely with expression form and content form, Lessing's general semiotic approach (comparing poetry with the plastic arts) attends to all six components of the global sign function. Furthermore, since it is a question in the *Laocoon* of aesthetic signification, the signs analyzed are subject to aesthetic constraints as well as purely semiotic constraints.

The reason I choose to employ Hjelmslev's model of the sign function is not, as I said, because Lessing's analysis corresponds exactly to the glossematic notion of the sign, but because I feel there are sufficient similarities to warrant the descriptive use of glossematic terms. These similarities pertain primarily to the relation between form and material. For Hjelmslev form is an abstract system which is projected onto the undifferentiated material. The classical example of this projection is the division of the color spectrum accomplished by the content form underlying the color terms of a language. Analogous to this content form in Lessing are the rules of content selection and organization that govern the plastic arts as well as those governing poetry. Thus, the notion of the 'pregnant moment' in the *Laocoon* does not refer to individual contents of paintings or sculptures but is a rule for the selection of content. It describes a normative-aesthetic principle followed by the successful artist when a single phase of a visible action is isolated for representation. The analogous rule for poetry prescribes that the most sensate quality be selected from all the visible-experiential features clustered about a person or thing and that this quality alone be linguistically designated. In both cases we have an unorganized mass of semantic material (here a totality of visual ideas) that is divided and organized according to general rules. It is interesting to note (I shall return to the point in greater detail) that the reception of the work constituted through the organization of material by form does not abide at the resulting content substance. Rather, as every reader of the *Laocoon* knows, the imaginative actualization of the content reaches beyond the single, painted moment or the single, designated quality into the content material itself. In fact, both principles of content form that I have mentioned are chosen by Lessing in order to guarantee that such imaginative actualization of content material is possible in the course of reception (aesthetic experience).

I will attend to each of these points later in greater detail and have introduced them here only in order to provide examples of my use of terms. It is not merely the notions of pregnant moment or sensate quality that I consider describable with this terminology, but the entire aesthetic sign as Lessing conceives it. My thesis is that *Lessing's comparison of poetry and the plastic arts is organized according to a global model of aesthetic signification*. The schematization in Table 2 illustrates the basic components of this model. The left-hand column gives Hjelmslev's terms (with 'material' substituted for 'purport'). The second column translates these terms into

## Table 2

| | | Totality of visible aspects | Totality of imagined, |
|---|---|---|---|
| Material | Semantic/ ideational material | Totality of visible aspects | historical, legendary, etc. aspects |
| Substance | Content Units | Bodies (as images or ideas sponsored by the imagination) | Actions (global content substance) Functional units (individual content units) |
| Form | Rules of selection and arrangement | 1. fully determined entities<br>2. equal ontological status of all entities<br>3. choice of beautiful contents<br>4. harmony of spatial parts<br>5. perceptual logic and habits<br>6. selection of pregnant moment<br>7. form strongly determined by material | 1. abstract entities<br>2. various ontological regions<br>3. choice of functional contents<br>4. unity of action<br>5. narrative logic (logic of action)<br>6. selection of most sensate quality<br>7. supremacy of form over material |
| Form | Rules of arrangement (syntax) | Dense syntax<br>Spatial deployment | Discrete syntax<br>Temporal deployment |
| Substance | Work in its physical embodiment | Statue or painting as physical object | Spoken text in its physical manifestation |
| Material | Sensuous stuff | 'Matter' (strongly material) | 'articulate tones' ('weakly material) |

the broader, but more vague sense in which I employ them here. The third column gives the corresponding terms operative in the *Laocoon* as applied to painting and sculpture, the fourth column as applied to poetry.

The entire diagram is presented here less as a finished product than as a general orientation for the ensuing discussion. In a sense, the diagram is misleading insofar as it suggests a taxonomical mode of thought that is in fact alien to Lessing's writing. While he accepts and adapts a good deal of the classificatory procedure of his predecessors and contemporaries, especially Mendelssohn, Lessing also introduces a dialectical[16] tendency into aesthetic theory. This tendency – almost palpable in the sententiousness of Lessing's formulations – can be brought to the fore only by interpreting the precise description of the various components of the aesthetic sign. Another misleading aspect of the diagram is that it does not account for several important factors in the comparison of the arts, for instance, the correlation between expression and content planes in each type of sign. Despite these shortcomings, however, it seems to me that the notion of a global model of aesthetic signification with explicitly distinguished components has the advantage of providing a framework within which the status of Lessing's examples and conclusions can be unequivocally determined.

## The plane of expression

### Material of expression

What is the material of expression of painting? of sculpture? How do they differ from one another and from the expression material of poetry?

At first reading Lessing seems to pay little attention to the first two of these questions. The *Laocoon* contains no extensive discussion of the aesthetically relevant qualities of paint or stone, which, after all, are not the same thing. In fact, Lessing recognizes no differences between the two materials which would be pertinent to his line of inquiry: 'I want to remind [the reader] that I use the term painting to embrace the plastic arts in general...' (IX, 5–6). He abstracts from the differences between paint and stone in order to arrive at a generic notion of expression material applicable to both painting and sculpture.

One of the fragments related to the published text of the *Laocoon* lists three oppositions definitive of the 'Verschiedenheit der Zeichen' (the difference of signs): signs are 'natürlich' (natural) or 'willkührlich' (arbitrary), 'nebeneinandergeordnet' (ordered next to one another) or 'auf einander folgend' (following upon one another), 'sichtbar' (visible) or 'hörbar' (audible) (B, 433). The first opposition applies to the correlation of expression and content, but the second two tell us something about the expression material. The plastic arts are characterized by an expression material that is visible and spatial. 'Figuren und Farben im Raume' (figures and colors in space) is how the sixteenth chapter classifies the plane of expression. These two features of the expression material, however, do not have equal status for Lessing. It seems, rather, that the spatiality of the plastic arts is less important than their visibility. The concept of space is tailored to the concept of vision: it is a purely Euclidean space; that is, space as seen. For this reason it is possible for Lessing to subsume both painting and sculpture under the same heading, as if there were no essential differences between them.

I think that the implicit reduction of spatiality to visible space – a tacitly performed operation of no little consequence for the entire *Laocoon* – can be grasped very well by contrasting Lessing's position with that of Herder. In the fourth of his *Kritische Wälder* (*Critical Sylvae*, 1769)[17] Herder develops a theory of sculpture that is consciously directed against the facile equation of painting and sculpture in the *Laocoon*. For Herder the corporeal products of sculpture do not define the surface of a tableau, but rather seize their own territory, assert their own position and thereby establish their singularity. From its material, sculpture carves out shapes that are irreducible to the uniformity of vision. In its density and thickness the material itself, the ineluctable occupant of the space its shape calls into being, emerges as the definitive moment of the aesthetic experience. The spatiality of sculpture is not the form of vision constituted from a standpoint external to the representation. In Herder's conception the subject stands within the space of the sculpture and that space is experienced in the energetic movement of *tactile* differentiation that identifies the bodies of both subject and statue. The spatiality of sculpture is the dynamic space of labor where hand and matter meet.

For Lessing, space is the simultaneity of things within a synoptic view, the homogeneous form of vision. Spatial things are 'Was das Auge mit einmal übersiehet...' or 'was in der Natur mit eins gesehen wird' ('What the eye surveys at once...' or 'what is seen in nature at once' IX, 102–3). Space is the unity of things inside a slice of time, their coexistence within a momentary vision. Despite the fame of Lessing's distinction between the spatial and the temporal arts it must be said that the concept of space does not come into its own in the *Laocoon*.

The reduction of space to the form of visibility is merely one aspect of a fundamental tendency of the *Laocoon* – the attempt to elide the materiality of the art work.[18] Even in the description of the expression material normative aesthetic judgements are at work. What Lessing repeatedly urges for art is the transformation of matter into the immateriality of a mental representation, the elimination of every material residue which could burden or limit the movement of the imagination. In this tendency he is a rationalist, a student of Leibniz, for whom matter was only the limitation, the boundary, of finite thought.[19] Thus, even within the visible (itself already an intellectualization of matter and an internalization of the space it occupies) Lessing betrays a preference for the intelligible visibility of form over the non-articulate visibility of color. He even goes so far as to suggest – herein similar to Kant[20] – that the arts might have been better off had oil painting never been invented.[21]

Yet this tendency, which reduces the full dimensions of a

material-filled space to the frame of a theoretical regard and which is concerned only with the formal and intelligible within the visible – this tendency presupposes that the concept of matter is playing a role in Lessing's discourse. Again and again Lessing speaks of the 'materiellen Künste' (material arts) meaning the plastic arts. Equally as often he calls attention to the 'materiellen Schranken' (material confines) of painting and sculpture. *Lessing does recognize a degree of materiality in the plastic arts and he sees in it the determining factor of their limitations.* Some relevant passages:

1. Ich glaube, der einzige Augenblick, an den die materiellen Schranken der Kunst alle ihre Nachahmungen binden, wird auf dergleichen Betrachtungen leiten.

   (I believe that the single moment to which the material confines of art bind all its imitations will lead to such considerations) (IX, 19).

2. Und nur dieses scheinbare Unabläßliche in der materiellen Nachahmung der Kunst ist es, was sein Schreyen zu weibischem Unvermögen, zu kindischer Unleidlichkeit machen würde.

   (And it is only this apparently unceasing quality in the material imitation of art which would make of his screaming feminine weakness, a childish inability to bear suffering) (IX, 20).

3. ...die Dinge selbst, oder die natürlichen Zeichen derselben in den engen Schranken des Raumes oder der Zeit...

   (...things themselves, or their natural signs within the narrow confines of space and time...) (IX, 44-5).

4. Ob uns schon der Dichter die Göttin ebenfalls unter einer menschlichen Figur denken lässt, so hat er doch alle Begriffe eines groben und schweren Stoffes davon entfernet, und ihren menschenähnlichen Körper mit einer Kraft belebt, die ihn von den Gesetzen unserer Bewegung ausnimt.

   (Although the poet likewise makes us think of the goddess as a human figure, he has nevertheless removed all ideas of course and heavy matter and he has enlivened her body with a force which exempts it from the laws of human locomotion (IX, 55)).

5. ...denn die Kunst kann nicht mehr thun, als die Natur selbst, und das schönste Gesicht in der Natur selbst, wird nicht aller Menschen Beyfall in einerley Grade haben. Homers Helena ist und bleibet die einzige, an der niemand etwas auszusetzen findet, die alle Menschen gleich stark entzücket.

   (...for the plastic arts can do no better than nature herself, and the

most beautiful face in nature will not find everyone's approval to the
same degree. Homer's Helen is and remains the sole beauty in whom
no one finds anything to criticize and who delights everyone with
equal force (B., 381)).

Only when we grasp the systematic function of the concept
matter (and the related concept 'Natur') in the *Laocoon* can
we account for the preference, for instance, of outline over
color otherwise than by referring to Lessing's personal taste.[22]
The plastic arts are materially anchored. Because they have a
real, material object as their material of expression, they
possess an ontic basis which gives them the determinateness of
things in nature. This natural, existential element contributes a
self-assertiveness, a flagrancy, to their expression plane, which
means that the imaginary presentation of the aesthetic object
(the rendering present of the absent object that is the content
of the work of art) is impeded. The play of the imagination is
delimited by the imposing presence of the material. Thus, a
painting of Helen cannot attain to universal, ideal beauty
because the painting, as an instance of a material art, holds the
imagination to the contours of a determinate natural object (5).
The plastic arts introduce into the aesthetic experience some of
the heaviness and coarseness of things themselves and this
thingness cannot be altogether left behind in the movement
from perception of the expression (of the expression substance)
to imaginative constitution of the content unit signified (3, 4).
The materiality of the expression material (the phrase is not
redundant for Lessing, as I will try to show) *exerts a restrictive
influence on the entire aesthetic sign* (1).

The flagrancy of the expression plane takes the form of an
accentuation of space. I have said that Lessing's impulse is to
reduce space to the form of a momentary vision. What resists
this impulse is the materiality of the expression plane. The
material substratum of the plastic arts causes momentariness
to perdure, so that the 'Augenblick' (moment, but literally:
look of an eye) that defines space is frozen (1, 2). Lessing's
famous theory of the pregnant moment (which pertains to the

form of content) can be read as a reaction to the threat of mortification that the plastic arts bear within them. In effect, all the plastic arts are dangerously close to 'still life,' what the French call 'nature morte.' Frozen or petrified by the materiality of their expression plane, the plastic arts bring to the fore a spatiality which resists assumption into the temporal movement of the imagination.

Thus, Lessing does acknowledge, though begrudgingly, the constitutive role of material in the plastic arts. Because of their material anchorage, their ineluctable thingness, the plastic arts possess an element that is other than thought, alien and therefore threatening to the free play of the imagination. To be sure, the role of this material and the perduring space it constitutes is acknowledged only to be subsequently effaced. Artistic accomplishment in the plastic arts consists in great part for Lessing in the masking of materiality and spatiality so that the imaginative aesthetic experience can unfold in time. Artistic failure ensues when the perduring spatiality of the expression material enters into an antagonistic relation with the imagination's temporal flow:

Since it is the case that this single moment acquires in art an unchanging perdurance, then art must express nothing which cannot be thought of otherwise than as transitory. All phenomena which, according to our conception of them, are essentially defined by the fact that they suddenly break out and suddenly disappear, that they can only be what they are for a moment – all such phenomena, be they pleasant or frightening, acquire through their prolongation in art such an unnatural appearance that the artistic impression becomes weaker with each successive viewing until we finally sense revulsion or horror at the entire object (IX, 20).

This argument concerns the plane of content, in particular the form of content, which, in the plastic arts, is determined by habits of perception. But it is relevant to my purposes here insofar as it is a special case of the general problem of space and material in the plastic arts. In ordinary perception space is the form of a momentary vision. If we observe an action unfolding in time, then we see a succession of configurations.

Space is taken up into time without interference; each phase of the event is merely a momentary arrangement of coexistent things. The same holds for our experience of an enduring object: the vista beheld presents the same configuration in each of the successive phases, but the successivity of the experience is in no way troubled. In art, however, spatiality comes to the fore as something other than a moment within a temporal flow. The space of the representation holds the imagination in place, forcing it to abide within a single moment (on the level of content). The space of painting or sculpture is a frozen space which can assert itself to such a degree as to resist being taken up into the movement of subjective experience. Lessing's example in the passage quoted illustrates, in a pronounced way, *a conflict that is always liminally present in the material arts* – a conflict between the temporal movement of soul and imagination on the one hand and the flagrant spatiality and materiality of things on the other. The 'Grauen' (horror) which the subject senses once this conflict becomes manifest is the terror (in English we speak of being 'petrified') that life knows when met with its antithesis. When regarding a painting, the subject sees his imagination, or the products of his imagination, in an externalized and reified form. A second example: 'Had the arms been pressed close to the body by the rings of the snakes, it would have spread coldness and death over the entire group' (IX, 40). The represented figure (on the level of content) is suggestive of death because its immobility removes the possibility of any temporal development. Stripped of every before and after, the human figure becomes mere body, that is, material without soul and life. Static, purely material space – on which the plastic arts are necessarily dependent – is the death of time, the medium of the imagination's play.[23] There is a level of Lessing's discourse where the apparent formalism of his semiotic investigation coincides with psychological-mythological configurations.[24]

A fundamental ambiguity permeates Lessing's treatment of the plastic arts, an ambiguity which can be resolved only by considering the evaluative context within which individual characterizations of the arts take place. When it is a matter of the positive evaluation of the arts, then Lessing will inevitably emphasize their thrust toward the immaterial. Space and matter are aesthetically pertinent insofar as they are visible. The visible is valuable as form and outline rather than as color, and form and outline, finally, contribute to the imaginative vision of something not given in the material work, be this the prior and subsequent stages of an action (as in the theory of the pregnant moment) or an ethical-religious ideal:

Ideal of corporeal beauty. What is it? It consists principally in the ideal of form, but also includes the ideal of complexion and of permanent expression (B., 339).

The expression of corporeal beauty is what defines painting.

The highest form of corporeal beauty, then, defines its highest realization.

The highest form of corporeal beauty exists only in the human being, and even in the human being only by virtue of the ideal (B., 440).

When, however, it is a question of comparing painting and poetry, then Lessing will emphasize the limitations of the former, limitations which derive from the material nature of the sign vehicle in the plastic arts. Such is the burden that the arts bear. To take one example, everything in the plastic arts is visible, asserts itself as visible, and thus confines the movement of the imagination. This is the sense of Lessing's challenge to Klotz in the *Antiquarian Letters*: ' . . . instruct me just a little how to look at a painting in such a way that that, which one sees, is meant not to be seen' (X, 239). Or, as a second example, the material basis becomes a source of interference because of its perdurance (as when transitory events are represented). Or the determinateness of the material over-specifies the aesthetic object (the content unit) with accidental properties: a painted Helen must be thick or thin. The *Laocoon* is a study of the 'limits of painting and poetry.' The limits prescribed for the plastic arts are in essence the perimeters within which the artist must work in order to reduce interference on the level of the sign vehicle, that is, in order to prevent the material of expression from emerging into the foreground. This point will be confined at every level of the aesthetic sign.

It seems, however, that I have involved myself in a contradiction. The result of the foregoing is that the expression material of the plastic arts, the sensuous stuff out of which the aesthetic signs are fashioned, is classified as visible, spatial and material. My claim is that, despite its redundancy, this statement makes sense for Lessing. The materiality of the plastic arts' expression material is a legitimate distinctive feature of these arts from a comparative semiotic perspective if it is presumed that the expression material of poetry is immaterial, if poetry forms its signs in a material that is absolutely proximate to thought, spirit, or imagination.[25] The assumption that makes possible the locutions 'material arts' and 'material confines of the arts' is precisely this: poetry has already left the materiality of things behind; its medium – voiced sounds – is much closer to the imagination than the material medium of the plastic arts. The statement is never made explicitly in the *Laocoon*, but its consequences are everywhere in evidence: the expression material of poetry is qualified as audible, temporal and (apparently) immaterial.[26]

According to Lessing, poetry fashions its signs from 'artikulirte[n] Töne[n] in der Zeit' ('articulate tones in time' IX, 94). This, of course, does not conform to the contemporary semiotic view nor to the glossematic definition of expression material. From the standpoint of contemporary theory, Lessing's articulate tones are already expression substance defined as the imposition of expression form (the phonological system described in terms of distinctive features) upon the undifferentiated sound continuum producible by the organs of speech. The conflict does not concern me since I am using glossematic terminology in an extended sense and since Lessing's agreement or disagreement with modern theory is not at stake here. For Lessing the articulate sounds are the expression material and are combined or arranged (according to the form of expression) to yield words and word chains (the substance of expression). What is important about these sounds when compared to the expression plane in the plastic arts is that they are not extended in space, they do not perdure in time, they are not as 'material' as the material of the plastic arts. The sounds of poetry are perceived (heard) but this perception does not remain in the foreground and has no flagrancy. The sounds disappear as soon as they are uttered, giving way to an imaginative experience of the content they are arranged to signify.

### Form of expression: the plastic arts

The differences between painting and poetry, as regards this decisive issue of materiality, emerge more distinctly when we consider Lessing's account of the expression form. I use the notion of expression form, of course, in a general sense. The term designates the arrangement and combination of *figurae*[27] (non-significant elements such as lines, colors, or 'articulate sounds') as well as sub-signs (natural signs of particular things that enter into combination in a painting, words combined in a poem). We are dealing, then, with the abstract system organizing the expression, what I shall call, following Charles Morris, the syntax of painting and poetry.[28]

If one were to look for statements about the expression form in a semiotic-aesthetic theory of the plastic arts, one might well begin by gathering prescriptions for the rules of visual harmony or of perspective. William Hogarth's *Analysis of Beauty* (1753), a text which had considerable resonance in Germany, would be an important source for an eighteenth-century account of the first sort of rules. In the *Laocoon* Lessing is not concerned with such questions. To be sure, he is aware of their importance for the plastic arts. For instance, his judgement that the sculptors of the Laocoon statue had to keep the snakes lower than Laocoon himself (whereby 'snakes' and 'Laocoon himself' refer to the sign vehicles in their spatial disposition) alludes to the importance of compositional rules: 'The same number of coils about the neck of the figure would have spoiled that pyramidal triangulation of the group which is so pleasing to the eye; and the pointed heads of the serpents jutting out of this bulging mass would have produced such a sudden break in proportionality that the form of the entire composition would have been rendered most repulsive' (IX, 41). The plastic arts are compelled to apply rules of proportion to the formation of the expression – a factor which, as the quotation shows, proscribes the signification of certain contents.

But Lessing's attempt to illuminate the generic differences between poetry and the plastic arts (rather than all painting-specific rules) tends to avoid discussion of such compositional principles as the previous example refers to. Instead, the theory of the arts presented in the *Laocoon* defines the most general combinational rules, those definitive of every painting or sculpture. One could speak here of the principle underlying and constituting the syntax of the plastic arts. In its most general form this principle states that the signs, and the elements beneath the level of signs, are arranged spatially: 'Mahlerey' (painting) uses signs, 'die sie nur im Raume verbinden kann' ('which it can only combine in space' IX, 94). The consequences of this are explicated in the following passage:

Bey dem Dichter ist ein Gewand kein Gewand; es verdeckt nichts; unsere Einbildungskraft sieht überall hindurch. Laokoon habe es bey dem Virgil, oder habe es nicht, sein Leiden ist ihr an jedem Theile seines Körpers einmal so sichtbar, wie das andere. Die Stirne ist mit der priesterlichen Binde für sie umbunden, aber nicht umhüllet. Ja, sie hindert nicht allein nicht, diese Binde; sie verstärkt auch noch den Begriff, den wir uns von dem Unglücke des Leidenden machen.

*Perfusus sanie vittas atroque veneno.*

Nichts hilft ihm seine priesterliche Würde; selbst das Zeichen derselben, das ihm überall Ansehen und Verehrung verschaft, wird von dem giftigen Geifer durchnetzt und entheiliget.

Aber diesen Nebenbegriff mußte der Artist aufgeben, wenn das Hauptwerk nicht leiden sollte. Hätte er dem Laokoon auch nur diese Binde gelassen, so würde er den Ausdruck um ein grosses geschwächt haben. Die Stirne wäre zum Theil verdeckt worden, und die Stirne ist der Sitz des Ausdruckes.

For the poet a cloak is not a cloak; it covers nothing; our imagination sees through everywhere. Whether Virgil's Laocoon wears one or not, his suffering is in either case visible to the imagination in every part of his body. For the imagination, his brow is wrapped with the priestly band, but not concealed. Indeed, this band not only does not hinder us; it even strengthens the idea we form for ourselves of the victim's misfortune.

*Perfusus sanie vittas atroque veneno.*

His priestly dignity is of no avail; even its sign, which everywhere earns him reverence and honor, is soaked and desecrated by the poisonous venom.

But the artist had to abandon this accessory idea if his chief work was not to be diminished. If he had left just this band about the brow of Laocoon, he would have considerably weakened the expressiveness. The brow would have been partially covered, and the brow is the seat of expression (IX, 43).

At issue here is whether the sculptor should represent Laocoon clothed or not, with a band around his head or without one. Essentially this is a question of content form, that is, of the rules of selection that prevail in the choice of content. Lessing opts for a "naked Laocoon" as the signified of the sculpture rather than a "clothed Laocoon" because the body possesses greater intrinsic value (higher value qualities) than clothing, 'das Werk sklavischer Hände.' ('the work of enslaved hands' IX, 43). It is not the truth-value of the representation which determines the artist's choice, but the intrinsic value of the imaginary, aesthetic object (Cf. above, sec. 1). But why is it that this alternative appears at all? The reason is – and this is the thrust of Lessing's argument here – that the form of expression constitutive of the plastic arts precludes the appearance of both content units (i.e., both "clothing" and "body"). The passage shows how the syntax of the plastic arts restricts their semantics. The text describes a sign and its terms are therefore semiotic terms[29] – a fact of which Lessing is

sufficiently aware to exploit its potential for apparent para-
doxes. In this sentence: 'For the poet a cloak is not a cloak; it
covers nothing;...' the first 'cloak' refers to the entire sign
(expression and content), while the second is a syntactic term,
naming the relation in which the expression token /cloak/
stands to another, implied expression token /body/.[30] The syntactic relation (in a sculpture) between /cloak/ and /body/ is
equivalent to the relation between cloak and body in the
world. The former *covers* the latter. The verb 'cover' in the
second clause is also a syntactic term, equivalent to the second
'cloak' of the first clause.

Lessing's argument can be paraphrased as follows. Given the
content units "clothing" and "body," what is the syntax that
conjoins their respective expression tokens? In the plastic arts
the expression tokens are in a real, dynamic relation to one
another, competing, as it were, for the same space. The
expression tokens of the plastic arts can only be combined
within this single space. Therefore, they displace and obscure
one another. The syntactic relation between the expression
tokens /clothing/ and /body/ is one of covering. At this point
a second constraint on the plastic arts must be considered.
The relation between expression and content in painting and
sculpture is one of similarity; globally considered, paintings
and sculptures are natural signs. This implies, among other
things, that the imaginative actualization of the content unit is
strongly determined by the perception of the expression
substance. (The arbitrariness of the *individual* signs of poetry,
by contrast, loosens this determination of the imaginative
content actualization by the perceptual apprehension of the
expression.) If /cloak/ covers /body/ on the expression plane
of the plastic arts, then /body/ is no longer perceptible, and
therefore the content unit "body" cannot be actualized in the
imagination of the beholder. *The two content units "cloak"
and "body" are mutually exclusive in the plastic arts because
of the syntactical relation of covering that their respective expression tokens entertain.* The same rule holds for the content

units "band" and "brow." By virtue of the syntax of painting, designation of the former precludes designation of the latter.

Swift describes a group of scholars who, disgusted with the problems and ambiguities of language, decide to replace discourse with the actual display of the things to which their words refer.[31] Each is compelled to carry with him samples of whatever things he wishes to "speak" about and so each is burdened by an enormous sack of real things, a kind of material lexicon. For Lessing, the plastic arts are similarly burdened by the heaviness and density of things. This is true on several levels (for instance as regards the question of abstraction), but especially so on the level of syntax. The expression tokens that together make up a painting or sculpture (itself a global expression token) relate to one another as would the real items which they denote. Their relation is dynamic, existential. That is not to say that the expression tokens are identical to the things themselves in nature, nor that all the relations that obtain between things in nature determine the expression tokens as well. A /robe/ does not keep a /body/ warm. Only those relations between things which are relations for vision are transposed to the art work. These are essentially spatial relations. Thus, while a sculpted robe is not a real robe it nevertheless possesses something of the existential nature of the real robe. Like the real robe the expression token is material (but not the same material) and occupies space. It stands in front of or envelops the expression token /body/. 'For the poet a cloak is not a cloak.' For the sculptor it is; not entirely, but insofar as the expression token / cloak / is material and occupies space. *The syntax of the plastic arts is the set of spatial relations between real things*.

Thus, the syntax of the plastic arts is strongly determined by the materiality of the expression material. The plastic arts are constituted by an abstraction from reality so that of all those determinations which define things in reality only those pertinent to vision remain. Despite this abstraction, however, an element of worldliness continues to inhabit the art works.

The individual expression tokens in painting or sculpture can be deployed only within the range of possible spatial arrangements of things in nature. In the plastic arts the imaginative play of artist and audience is circumscribed by this worldliness and exteriority.

## *Form of expression: poetry*

The greater imaginative freedom attainable through poetry is not attributable merely to syntax. Other factors, such as the arbitrary (unmotivated) correlation of expression and content planes as well as the abstraction that language has always already performed, are extremely important in this regard and I will deal with them subsequently in detail. For the present I will attend merely to the question of poetic syntax. Before approaching even this issue, however, I want to suggest a general hypothesis regarding Lessing's comparison of the arts, a hypothesis already hinted at on several occasions. This will help orient the present discussion and prove relevant to later considerations as well. Above all, it will make explicit the general pattern of thought that I have been ascribing to Lessing all along.

Implied in Lessing's discourse is a vague notion of reality as the actuality of the present instant in which things mutually affect one another causally and are fully determined by the nexus of relations they bear to other things. Human beings are locked into this world of pure present actuality by sensation and perception (between which Lessing probably wouldn't distinguish except perhaps by calling sensation an obscure representation and perception a clear representation). Mind can disengage itself from the world, acquiring prospect and retrospect, concepts, laws, freedom, and ideals, through *a progressive process of semiosis*. Now Lessing nowhere uses this term, but I think it appropriate. Let me merely recall that the progress from immediate sense intuition through conceptualization to philosophical mastery, as Wolff describes it, is accompanied stage for stage by a refinement of sign use. Aesthetic theory sought to halt this progressive semiosis, which it interpreted as a loss of metaphysical repleteness, a disintegration of global representations, and an impoverishment of subjective experience. One need only recall Baumgarten's statement that the semiotic refinements of language in comparison to painting are of no consequence for aesthetic theory, which is concerned solely with sensate representations.[32] Furthermore, the ideal content of aesthetic representations for Baumgarten was the fully determined object which semiosis leaves behind. Lessing stands very much in the tradition of Baumgarten, Meier and Mendelssohn, but he also departs from them (especially the former two) insofar as he positively evaluates semiosis as a process which opens up new and wider aesthetic horizons. Central to this reevaluation is the notion of freedom.

Consider the plastic arts: here the process of semiosis has begun (the arts use natural signs), but remains in a rudimentary state. It is still dependent on and burdened by the materiality and spatiality of things, and a degree of worldliness which, for instance, governs the syntax of the arts and commits aesthetic experience to the perimeters of perception. Regarding the freedom of the imagination the consequence is this: in the plastic arts the imagination is not entirely itself, has not yet established itself in its autonomy. Rather, it remains outside itself, entangled in and restricted by actual things in their existential nature. Insofar as the imagination achieves an actualization of content units only via the spatiality defining the syntax of the plastic arts, it is not entirely free. Its play is delimited by the possible deployment in space of actual things. This is not the case in poetry. Poetry is an aesthetic use of language and as such can take advantage of the advanced stage of semiosis which language occupies. Language, by virtue of its syntax, the arbitrariness of its signs, its abstractness, its introduction of categories other than sense-related ones, has already carried the process of semiosis to a high degree of refinement by the time poetry begins. Again and again, as I will show, Lessing points out the advantages that accrue to poetry by virtue of the semiotic advancements language has already made. Eventually I will argue that poetry, in Lessing's view, reverses the direction of semiosis, turning it back toward worldliness, and thereby recovers, on its own level of development, the immediacy which language left behind. For the present, though, it is important to emphasize that in Lessing's view poetry takes advantage of the freedom from actuality that language has attained for mind.

In part (but only in part) the freedom from contingency that poetry affords the imagination is due to its syntax. As far as I can discern, Lessing makes only one remark about linguistic syntax in the *Laocoon* (IX, 110), and I will attend to it in another context. What is important here is the general notion of syntax that allows us to see the difference between the plastic arts and poetry, whatever natural language it is composed in. A passage I have already quoted in part provides a good starting point. Lessing is arguing that the accepted rule according to which every good poetic representation can be translated into a painting deserves to be limited:

Man ist geneigt diese Einschränkung zu vermuthen, noch ehe man sie durch Beyspiele erhärtet sieht; blos aus Erwägung der weitern Sphäre der Poesie, aus dem unendlichen Felde unserer Einbildungskraft, aus der Geistigkeit ihrer Bilder, die in größter Menge und Mannigfaltigkeit neben einander stehen können, ohne daß eines das andere deckt oder schändet, wie es wohl die Dinge selbst, oder die natürlichen Zeichen der selben in den engen Schranken des Raumes oder der Zeit thun würden.

One is inclined to suppose that such a limitation is necessary even before one sees it corroborated by examples; merely by taking into consideration the wider sphere of poetry, the infinite field of the imagination, the spirituality of its images which can be ranged beside each other in the greatest number and variety without covering or damaging one another as things themselves, or their natural signs, would within the narrow confines of space and time (IX, 44–5).

The images of poetry are, in my terms, content units. They are characterized by 'spirituality,' a term which stands in opposition here to materiality. The content units of the plastic arts are not material, but they are supported by expression tokens which are. These tokens stand in such a (syntactic) relation to one another that they 'cover' and 'damage' one another, as I have shown. This covering on the level of expression is carried over onto the level of content. The same syntax, however, does not constrain poetic signification. In a poem (in language) both the content units "cloak" and "body" – to stay with our prior example – can appear, because their expression tokens do not obscure one another. In a poem, a sentence like /Laocoon's body was twisted in pain beneath his sacred robes / is entirely possible. In a painting or sculpture it is not.[33] The 'spirituality' of the poetic images derives from their indepen- dence of the material conditions in which actual things are found. The imagination is free to deploy both content units "clothing" and "body" in the play through which it actu- alizes the global content of the poem. As Lessing says in the passage I quoted previously, the imagination 'sees through everywhere.' The freedom of the imagination to deploy these more spiritual images almost as it pleases is attained by *the dissolution of the material-spatial nexus of natural signs into a series of discrete expression tokens*. Poetic images do not cover one another because their expression tokens are conjoined in an articulate syntax. Rather than competing for the same space, as do the expression tokens of the plastic arts, the sounds and words combined by poetry are discrete units that never cover, contaminate or merge with one another. *The plastic arts are characterized by a dense syntax, the arrangement of material things within the same space; poetry possesses a discrete syntax so that its expression tokens are isolated from one another and therefore are rendered freely deployable.*

In the plastic arts the imagination still operates with images of material things (bodies of stone, masses of color) within the confines of a single space. The poetic imagination, however, takes advantage of the economy of language which substitutes for the manifold and interlocking qualities of things a set of easily manipulated discrete elements.[34] Wolff had already pointed out that this economy reduces the expenditure of imaginative energy and therefore increases imaginative freedom and inventiveness.[35] Lessing pursues this thought in his comparison of poetry and the plastic arts by showing how poetry takes advantage of the economy of language to achieve effects unavailable to painting or sculpture. It is no longer a question of returning from language to another type of representation, as it was for Baumgarten. In Lessing's view, poetry should exploit and render aesthetically profitable the independence from worldliness that the advancement of semiosis from natural signs to verbal language has achieved.

Closely linked to the discreteness of poetic signs is another distinguishing characteristic of poetic syntax which is of far-reaching importance for the entire *Laocoon*. The discrete expression tokens combined in poetry follow one another in time. Opposed to the dense, spatial syntax of painting is the discrete and temporal syntax of poetry. These two characteristics are inseparable: the discreteness of the expression tokens is guaranteed by the fact that they depart as soon as they are uttered or heard. The movement of time erases each expression token, relegating it to memory, and delivers up a new one before the mind. 'For the eye, the parts it has attended to remain constantly present; it can go over them again and again: for the ear, however, the parts it has heard are lost if they do not remain in memory' (IX, 102). The successivity of poetic expression is also related to poetry's freedom from the constraints of worldliness and to the autonomy of the poetic imagination. In effect, the interlocking of things and of qualities in the dense syntax of the plastic arts is overcome in poetry by dissolving space into time.[36] The temporal movement of thought negates space, takes apart the confused simultaneity of things, and, by virtue of this negation, attains to mastery over the manifold impingements imposed by the world in its brute presence. I have already pointed to this pattern in Wolff, for whom thought (distinct cognition) begins as the successive unfolding in reflection of what is presented at once to clear cognition. The 'enunciables' discriminated by reflection are then marked by arbitrary signs, the successivity of which corresponds point-for-point with the successivity of thought.[37] It was precisely this step into successivity and symbolic cognition which aesthetic theory tried to reverse in order to regain a global, intuitive apprehension of the object. Lessing, however, regards the successivity of symbolic cognition as a potential source of aesthetic effect. For Lessing, the negation of worldliness accomplished by the successivity and discreteness of linguistic signs allows the imagination to return to itself from its exile in space and exteriority. Because it deploys its expression tokens in time, poetry is characterized by a syntax that conforms to the movement and life of the imagination.

## Summary

Lessing's description of the expression plane, as I have interpreted it here, illustrates what I hold to be the central issue of the *Laocoon*. The differences between poetry and the plastic arts are not merely classified, but are related to one another in terms of a teleology. Poetry approaches more closely than does painting or sculpture the end of autonomous imaginative activity. By virtue of its immateriality and its discrete and temporal syntax, poetry detaches the mind and imagination from the sensible, the material, the external – all moments definitive of the plastic arts. In poetry the aesthetic object is purely a product of the imagination; it has passed through or been processed by mind. The plastic arts themselves are artistically successful only insofar as they induce an imaginative movement that leaves the material work behind. This can only be a relative and partial success, however, because, due to the worldliness they preserve within them, the plastic arts can never attain to the spirituality ('Geistigkeit') that characterizes the poetic imagination. It is a conservative success, achieved by avoiding those sorts of contents which would thrust the expression substance into the foreground. An example: 'The wide opening of the mouth alone – ignoring for the moment how brutally and repulsively the other parts of the face would be distorted and displaced – is in painting a blotch and in sculpture an indentation which has a most repulsive effect' (IX, 17).

The decisive issue in the comparison of the arts in terms of imaginative autonomy is the question of presence and absence. The paradigm of presence for Baumgarten and Meier was the sensate presence of the object in direct perception, a fact which accounts for the suspicion of symbolic cognition that motivates Baumgarten's intuitionist aesthetics. For Lessing, however, as already for Mendelssohn, the question becomes more complicated. Art is located between presence and absence; it is the imaginative presence-to-mind of an existentially absent object. This accounts for the reevaluation of linguistic representation or symbolic cognition: *the advantage of poetry is that the task of rendering the object existentially absent has already been accomplished by language.* The plastic arts, however, are necessarily troubled by the brute, existential presence that characterizes their material plane of expression. In other words, Lessing's analysis shows how the sensuous presence of the expression substance in a work of the plastic arts brings about a non-presence-to-mind of the imaginary object.

The synoptic view, in which the represented object is seized in a global intuition, is not the rule for the plastic arts, but an ideal case. In fact, the plastic arts always bear elements within themselves which could disrupt the ideal intelligibility of visible form. The previously cited examples of /blotch/ and /indentation/, for instance, compel the beholder to abide at the level of sensation. The materiality of the arts also threatens to deaden the life of the imagination by asserting itself as something foreign to the imagination's vital movement. Non-presence-to-mind can also come about because of the obscurities, distractions and dispersements that characterize sense experience, in which things cover one another, or compete for our attention, or are spread out in space.[38]

Language negates worldliness, rendering empirical objects existentially absent, so that the mind can imaginatively attend to its contents without material interference. Whereas the sensuously visible is always shot through with elements of invisibility (the opacity of things, for instance), the contents of poetry are *elevated to the status of imaginative visibility* where the restrictions of sense no longer hold sway. All content units are imaginatively present to mind regardless of the contingencies of existential position. Things appear in an ideal transparency: 'our imagination sees through everywhere.' In poetry, the mind does not pass through a medium other than itself but directly views its own products. In the succession of present moments that characterizes the experience of a poem, each content unit is attended to separately as the object of a unique instant of imaginative activity. Raised by language to the level of concepts, the things of the world are more perfectly present-to-mind and the mind is more perfectly present-to-itself than mere sensuous presence could allow.

## Content plane

### Introduction

My reading of the *Laocoon* attempts to hold together two strands of argument: on the one hand the static, classificatory comparison of the arts, on the other hand, the comparison of the arts in terms of a teleology. The differences between the plastic arts and poetry, which the classificatory procedure of the *Laocoon* registers, lose their merely descriptive function and become criteria of evaluation as soon as the teleological moment asserts itself. The *Laocoon* is not neutral *vis-à-vis* its subject matter;[39] rather, it evaluates poetry and the plastic arts in terms of the norm of autonomous imaginative activity.

From the point of view of this norm the arts are not synchronous despite the fact that they exist together in any given historical moment. In the progressive detachment of mind from worldliness poetry occupies both a 'later' and a 'higher' stage than do painting and sculpture. Poetry is located at a more advanced level in the progress of semiosis by which mind liberates itself from actuality. The arts are articulated in the *Laocoon* according to an ideal history, a logical, rather than a chronological progress:

| Worldliness | Painting - - - →<br>Natural signs | ← - - - Poetry<br>Language | Mind/God |
|---|---|---|---|

(progressive semiosis)

Painting, given in the form of natural signs, is less purified than poetry. It occupies a more primitive stage of semiosis, it is more world-bound, than its sister art. Artistic achievement in painting is measured by the degree to which the limitations of this worldliness are transcended. As it were, a successful painting points forward to a more advanced stage of semiosis. The parallel argument for poetry is more complex and I have not yet developed the themes in the *Laocoon* which are required for an account of the issues involved. Here I will suggest very generally that poetry is successful insofar as it reintroduces immediacy at its own level of semiosis; in other words, insofar as it transforms its arbitrary, individual signs (words) into natural signs. Poetry and painting, then, ideally converge and Lessing's most important theoretical writing after the *Laocoon*, the *Hamburgische Dramaturgie* (1767) describes the locus of this convergence: 'The art of the actor occupies a middle position between the plastic arts and poetry' (IX, 204).

Though we are dealing here, as I said, with an ideal history, it would require little effort to imagine the logical scheme of progressive semiosis projected onto the succession of human events. Such a projection, I believe, occurs in the *Erziehung des Menschengeschlechts* (*On the Education of Mankind*, 1780) which describes man's progress toward God and the truth of revelation as a progress from 'Bild' (image) to 'Begriff' (concept). Jürgen Schröder has recently suggested such

an interpretation of the *Erziehung*: 'And at the end of this
infinite path of the history of language – where the language
of man, who is finally absolved from sin and has therefore
achieved pure likeness to God, is taken up in the language of
God – there beckons an idiom in which image and word
coincide with concept and meaning, and revelation coincides
with reason. An imageless and wordless language of pure
knowledge.'[40] Rather than emphasizing the novelty of this
conception, however, as Schröder does, I choose to insist on the
traditional aspects: as my first chapter attempted to show, there
is operative in Wolff's discussion of language, and in Enlightenment semiotics generally, a notion of a progressive
semiosis moving from the pre-linguistic, intuitive encounter
with things in perception through distinct cognition supported
by arbitrary signs to a perfect philosophical language in which
the semiotic character of knowledge is shed and the world is
represented quasi-intuitively and at the same time perfectly
clearly and distinctly. This philosophical language corresponds
to divine cognition which is intuitive and perfectly distinct,
'an imageless and wordless language of pure knowledge.'

As we investigate Lessing's account of the content plane of
poetry and the plastic arts, we shall find ample evidence of the
semiotic advancement of the former in comparison with the
latter. Just as the relative immateriality of poetry's expression
plane and the discrete and temporal nature of its syntax provided a lever, so to speak, by which the spirit and imagination
could lift themselves out of the restrictions of worldliness, so
too will the poetic-linguistic formation of content prove to be a
guarantee of greater spiritual-imaginative freedom.

### Material of content

The material of content is the undifferentiated semantic mass,
a relatively inchoate cluster of ideas. From this material each
art form, each mode of aesthetic signification, selects and
organizes more or less discrete units. The rules for this selection

and organization comprise the form of content and the content units resulting from the projection of form onto material are the content substance of the individual art works. Lessing's method in the *Laocoon* is two-sided. At times he attends to individual works in order to arrive at the rules underlying their composition; that is, he moves inductively from content substance to content form. At other times he begins with content form in order to deduce the range of potential content substances.[41] In either case the form of content occupies the center of interest and it is there where the differences between poetry and the plastic arts are articulated. The material of content, by contrast, is essentially pre-artistic. Nevertheless, Lessing does offer some considerations regarding the content material which are worth examining because they have consequences for the entire *Laocoon*.

Poetry selects from a field of potential contents which is broader than, and includes, the field available to the plastic arts:

> However, if the smaller cannot embrace the larger it is possible that the smaller be contained in the larger. I mean to say: although not every trait which the painterly poet uses can have the same positive effect on canvas or in marble, might not every trait which the artist employs be equally effective in the work of the poet? Without question; for what we find beautiful in an artwork is not found beautiful by the eye, but rather by the imagination through the eye. If, therefore, the same image is excited anew in our imagination through either arbitrary or natural signs, in each case the same pleasure must arise anew, although not to the same degree (IX, 45).

The range of contents available to poetry includes the visible world plus a good deal more. The plastic arts are restricted to the visible. Poetry has greater scope because its signs are arbitrary, and because arbitrary signs, ' . . . precisely because they are arbitrary, can express all possible things in all their possible combinations. . . ' (B., 433).

At first this distinction seems evident enough, and indeed it was a commonplace of the age.[42] It becomes problematic, however, when other statements in the *Laocoon* are considered.

In Chapter twenty, for instance, Lessing argues that painting (that is, the plastic arts), and painting alone, can imitate corporeal beauty.[43] This implies, though, that the plastic arts represent contents which fall outside the scope of poetry. The contradiction is only apparent, and the *Laocoon* provides the distinctions necessary for its resolution. In my terms, it is a matter of discriminating between the content material and the global content substance of art works. (A second distinction between global content substance and individual content substances – content units – is also required here, and will be drawn shortly.) It is entirely possible that physical beauty be a component of the content material of a poem (e.g. Helen's beauty in the *Iliad*[44]); it is not possible, however, that physical beauty appear as the global content substance of a poem.

A fragment leading to the core of Lessing's disagreement with Caylus allows us to develop this distinction between material and substance in Lessing's own terms:

Caylus' calculation of the paintings in the epic poets provides a standard of the *usefulness* of each *for the painter*, but not a standard of the *positive quality* of the poets themselves.

At least not of their quality in the *painterly portion* of their work. Rather: if indeed this greater usefulness for the painter is supposed to be a positive quality, then it must be said that this quality has its origin in the richness and variousness of the action, which is the content of the poem: but this is a positive quality which the poet can often share with the most miserable writer of histories.

For example, Christ's Passion is described in the New Testament very sparely and miserably. Nevertheless, it has provided material enough for the most superb paintings (B., 373).

Lessing is quite willing to accept Caylus' contention that a poem can supply visual ideas which can in turn be rendered in paintings. He objects, though, to the equation of the poem with the painting in all respects. If the poem provides visual ideas, then this simply means that a large portion of the 'Stoff,' the content material, is drawn from the visual realm. This 'material' is there before the poet sets to work, and, while it is implied in his work, it is not the aesthetic object (the global content substance) of his poem. The 'material' includes all the aspects of content which could be rendered in an historical, prose narrative, the entire argument implied, but not necessarily represented, in the plot. Lessing contrasts the 'Stoff' with the 'mahlerischen Theil' (painterly portion) of the poem. The word 'mahlerisch' is applied to whatever is rendered in an illusionary presence to the receiver, what is presented to the reader's imagination. This aspect of the content is not the visual 'Stoff,' nor is it even a visible totality of coexistent parts. Rather, it is the uniquely poetic content substance resulting from the formative processes governed by the interacting rules of art and language. Poet and painter can share the same material, the raw data of the history, but each forms that material according to different rules and the artistic labor of each yields a totally different content substance. Another fragment expresses this in terms similar to my own: 'Folglich liegt es nicht an dem vorzüglichen Genie des Homers, daß bey ihm alles zu mahlen ist; sondern lediglich an der Wahl der Materie.' ('As a result, it is not due to Homer's excellent genius that in his work everything can be painted, but rather simply to his choice of material' B., 401).

This last quotation has the advantage of severity and shows clearly that Lessing discriminated between the poetically rendered content substance (Homer's 'genius' is his mastery of poetic, formative principles, not some idiosyncratic force) and the content material. Having insisted on this point, however, I am compelled to modify it somewhat. When the poet chooses (he need not do so) to orient his work toward a visual content material, *individual* content units (content substances) result that are very close to the content units of the plastic arts. The entire sixth chapter, which attempts to prove that Virgil did not imitate the Laocoon statue, rests on this possibility. For instance, *à propos* of the arrangement of the snakes in the statue, Lessing remarks: 'So sehr dem Auge diese Vertheilung gefällt, so lebhaft ist das Bild, welches in der Einbildung davon zurück bleibt. Es ist so deutlich und rein, daß es sich durch Worte nicht viel schwächer darstellen läßt, als durch natürliche Zeichen.' ('The image of this arrangement which remains in the imagination is lively to the same degree as it pleases the eye. It is so distinct and clean that it can be presented to the imagination with words hardly more weakly than with natural signs' IX, 49). And from this observation he concludes that Virgil would have been entirely capable of conveying the image, '...wenn ein sichtbares Vorbild seine Phantasie befeuert *hätte*...' ('...if a visual object had inspired his fantasy...' IX, 49). Here we are dealing with a convergence of poetry and painting that involves more than the unformed content material designatable in a prosaic historical narrative. In this hypothetical case (for Virgil did not – that is Lessing's point – so represent Laocoon), the content substance attended to by the imagination would be nearly identical in both poem and sculpture, the only difference being in the degree of vividness.

The orientation of the poet toward a visual content material, then, yields a content substance which is imaginatively concretized in a primarily visual manner. Here, as so often, Lessing remains very close to the visual paradigm of aesthetic reception common to the early eighteenth century. Yet, it is important to emphasize that this is only one possibility of poetic reception and creation. A series of fragments, the line of thought of which was strongly influenced by Mendelssohn's comments on the first *Laocoon* sketch,[45] makes this clear. The fragments culminate in a contrast of two poetic styles, the Homeric and the Miltonic, the former being more strongly oriented toward the visual:

As a result, poetry represents bodies in terms of just one or two traits. Difficulty that painting sometimes meets with in painting in the other traits. Distinction between poetic paintings where the traits can easily and successfully be painted in and those where they can't. The former are the Homeric paintings, the latter the Miltonic and Klopstockian (B., 395).

Homer has only a few Miltonic images. They are striking, but they don't attach. And it's precisely for this reason that Homer remains the greatest painter. He thought each image completely and neatly. And even in ordering exhibited a painter's eye. Note on the groups which in his works never exceed three persons (B., 395–6).

These fragments allow us to draw together the issues touched upon thus far. We recall first that the range of potential content material of poetry is greater than, and includes, that of the plastic arts. In Fig. 4 below this is represented by the inclusion of the box PA (plastic arts) within the box P (poetry). An individual poet can choose to select his content more or less from the area (PA) common to the two arts, that is, from the field of visible images. This choice generates either a Homeric style (the circle H) or a Miltonic style (the circle M).

Figure 4

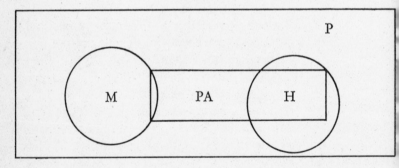

A Homeric style conveys individual content units which are translatable into works of plastic art, so that poet and painter create similar aesthetic objects; that is, they present a similar, highly visual image. Still, poem and painting must be held apart. Note the opening of the first of the two fragments: 'As a result, poetry represents bodies in terms of just one or two traits.' This passage requires us to make a further distinction – between the linguistic content substance and the aesthetic content substance. From the wealth of content material, the poet selects one or two visual traits for linguistic designation; these constitute the linguistic content substance. These traits, however, suggest a totality of visual features which the painter can realize through a process of 'ausmahlen' (painting in). The painter executes the visual representation suggested by the linguistically designated traits. This completion or filling-in of a linguistic schema is not unique to the painter. The reader himself *imaginatively* 'paints in' the details omitted, but hinted at, by the schema. The Homeric style, then, selects its linguistic content substance in such a manner as to *provoke an imaginative process of concretization* that reaches into the content material, transforming the linguistic content substance into a total, quasi-visual image. This image is, in my terms, the aesthetic substance.

It is therefore not only orientation toward a visual content material which generates a Homeric style. Aspects of content form are involved as well. Homer selected those traits explicitly marked in the language of his poems with visual images in mind. 'He thought each image completely and neatly.' The Homeric poems are so formed that they elicit a visual-imaginative concretization. Not every poem, however, aims for such a response. Virgil, for instance, had he imitated the Laocoon statue, would have had before him an image ' . . . so distinct and clean that it can be presented with words hardly more weakly than with natural signs.' That is, an image that could have been painted in imaginatively on the basis of a few suggestive traits. What Virgil offers us instead is not at all designed for a totalized, quasi-visual concretization:

Diese Züge füllen unsere Einbildungskraft allerdings; aber sie muß nicht dabey verweilen, sie muß sie nicht aufs reine zu bringen suchen, sie muß itzt nur die Schlangen, itzt nur den Laokoon sehen, sie muß sich nicht vorstellen wollen, welche Figur beyde zusammen machen. Sobald sie hierauf verfällt, fängt ihr das Virgilsche Bild an zu mißfallen, und sie findet es höchst unmahlerisch.

These traits fill our imagination, to be sure; however the imagination must not abide there, it must not try to make them complete, it must see now only the snakes, now only Laocoon, it must not want to represent to itself what sort of figure the two make together. As soon as it begins to do this, the Virgilian image begins to displease and the imagination finds it most unpainterly (IX, 49).

The aesthetic substance intended by Virgil is not an integral, totalized image, but a rapid sequence of ideas that remain fairly schematic, fairly close to linguistic substance. Virgil exploits the rapid tempo of alternating ideas (traits) rather than attending to the visual completeness of the images he evokes.

Let me summarize the distinctions made thus far: The material of content is the wealth of ideational stuff, both visual and not, which is segmented and arranged to yield a content substance. It is possible that poet and painter share a good deal of the content material and the painter can draw on the content material implied in a poem in order to get subjects for his painting. At times, though, poet and painter share more than material. The Homeric style instigates a process of concretization that engenders relatively totalized visual images. The aesthetic substance of the poem is, in such a case, very similar to that of a painting. Even here, however, there exists a fundamental difference between the two art forms. The aesthetic substance of the Homeric poem is only implicit; it is only potentially there in the poem itself, and a process of concretization, of 'painting-in,' is required in order to actualize imaginatively the totalized image. What the poem offers is a linguistic substance, a schema consisting of a few suggestive traits. This schema, in the case of the Homeric style, provokes and steers the imaginative concretization. The role of imaginative activity in the reception of a painting is, by comparison, considerably reduced. The painting has already 'painted-in' the details; the painting presents not a schema, but a particular image, not a potential image, but an actual one. This is important: the painting is closer to the material of content than the poem is; the active, creative role of the imagination in reception is therefore reduced. Ultimately this adherence to the material of content derives from the materiality of the expression plane in the plastic arts. Because its expression tokens are particular, fully determined material things, the content substance must likewise be fully determined, completely 'painted-in.'

The poet need not evoke an aesthetic content substance that is flushed out with visual detail. He can choose, as Virgil did in his Laocoon narrative, to keep the aesthetic substance close to the linguistic substance so that the imaginative experience is rapidly paced and schematic or he can pursue a Miltonic style that is oriented hardly at all toward the sphere of visual content material. Lessing insists on both these possibilities. Still, there can be little doubt that Lessing preferred the Homeric style which, because it elicits a predominantly visual-imaginative response, is more proximate to painting. The Miltonic images, says Lessing, following Mendelssohn almost verbatim,[46] 'are striking, but they don't attach. And it's precisely for this reason that Homer remains the greatest painter.' This value judgement provides some problems for my argument regarding progressive semiosis. If Lessing evaluates Homer as greater than Milton, and if Homer's art is more proximate to painting than the purely linguistic art (i.e., aesthetic substance and linguistic substance coincide) of Milton, doesn't this imply that Lessing did not want to see art move forward along the advancing line of semiotic progress? There are several arguments involved here, and I must attend to them further on. Let me merely suggest two points: First, Homer's medial position between Miltonic poetry and painting – a position which corresponds, by the way, to the position of drama as described in the *Hamburgische Dramaturgie* – is not bought with a sacrifice of imaginative freedom. Homer at once takes advantage of the imaginative freedom afforded by language *and* introduces into poetry the vividness of immediate experience. Second, the advancement of semiosis introduces, as it progresses, new difficulties, no less serious than those of natural signs. Language threatens to render the world absent not only existentially, but absent from the imagination as well.

The proximity of Homer to painting is one aspect of a development that poetry must take. Poetry must achieve its own type of natural signification, it must transform the arbitrary signs of language into natural signs.

One final point remains to be made here. I have said that in the Homeric style the aesthetic content substance coincides with that of painting. Before this statement can be accepted altogether though, a distinction between individual content substance and global content substance is required. The images evoked by the Homeric style are instances of the former. These individual content substances are arranged according to formative rules that yield a global content substance unique to poetry. The global content substance is the action represented by the entire poem or by a stretch of narrative contained in the poem. As it were, a poem can contain several paintings, that is, painting-like aesthetic substances, but it cannot be equivalent to just one painting. The points of coincidence between poetic content substance and painterly content substance occur, within the poem, on a micro-level. It is usually a matter of a few words.

The region shared by painting and poetry in the Homeric style is the focus of Lessing's interest from Chapter fifteen on: 'I want to remain now with the paintings of merely visual objects which poet and painter have in common. Why is it that some poetic paintings of this type can't be used by the painter at all and that, on the other hand, some actual paintings lose the greatest part of their effect when rendered by the poet?' (IX, 93). Attending to the Homeric style in its relation to painting is a methodological restriction designed to foreground the differences between painting and poetry even where the two arts seem to overlap. The results of this investigation are well known: 'Es bleibt dabey: die Zeitfolge ist das Gebiete des Dichters, so wie der Raum das Gebiete des Mahlers.' ('It's settled: temporal sequence is the territory of the poet just as space is the territory of the painter' IX, 107). This distinction – the purport of which I will attend to later – pertains to the global content substance of the two arts, the manner in which it is formed, and the mode of its reception.

### Content form: semiotic rules of selection

It is useful to begin the discussion of content form with a synopsis of the issues involved. I have said that the material of content embraces the entire field of ideas that can be mentioned in a prose account. Painting is limited to the visual sector of this field. The substance of content, what appears before the imagination in the illusionary presence evoked by the art work, derives from the projection of form onto material. When I speak of content form in relation to Lessing's theory, I am using the term to designate the group of principles according to which aspects of the content material are selected and arranged. The form of content, then, includes the rules governing the operations of selection and arrangement which yield the content substances of works of art. In general, the operation of selection produces the individual content substances and arrangement produces the global content substance. While there is *some* overlapping as regards the individual content substances of painting and poetry, the global content substance of each art is considerably different. Thus, arrangement is primarily what distinguishes poetry from the plastic arts. Furthermore, the characteristic arrangement of each of the two art forms dictates the mode of reception characteristic of each. If the aesthetic experience of a painting is significantly different from that of a poem, this difference is due to the difference in content form, especially that part of content form that governs arrangement.

The rules of content form are of two sorts, semiotic and aesthetic. The semiotic rules derive from the type of sign used and define the operations of selection and arrangement possible within each medium. The aesthetic rules further limit the set of formative operations to those which yield an aesthetic effect; not everything which can be signified (according to the semiotic restrictions) can be aesthetically signified. The arts are generated by the interaction of the rules of art and the rules of signs. The content form is thus determined by two basic pragmatic interests: a communicative interest (the painting or poem must use its signs so as to yield an intelligible message) and an aesthetic interest (the communicated message must have an aesthetic effect).

This general scaffold can be filled in somewhat by considering a particular example:

Poetry shows us bodies only in terms of a single aspect, only in a single position, only according to a single property, and leaves everything else regarding them indeterminate.

Painting cannot do this. In painting, one part or one property pulls all the others along with it; painting must make everything determinate.

For this reason, a trait can be very sensate or painterly in a poem, but cease to be so in a painting because it is weakened, or even contradicted, by all the other determinations that accompany it.

For example, Hercules
– *rabidi cum colla minantia monstri*
*Angeret, et tumidos animam angustaret in artus,*
is an excellent image. I see the full strength of the hero; I see the raging lion in its terror as it swells with its throttled breath. But just order the painter or sculptor to execute this. Now the lion has jaws, it has claws that it can strike with, indeed that it would have to strike with given the resistance it offers its vanquisher; and Hercules is now undefeatable, but no longer invulnerable. And so now I see him simultaneously suffer where I should only see him in victory (B., 371–2).

The material of content in this case embraces all the particulars involved in the encounter between Hercules and the lion. To render this material in an aesthetic representation it is necessary to select from this potentially infinite mass of particulars. The operation of selection yields the content substance. The point of the passage is that the poet has a greater freedom of selection than the painter. This freedom is, as Lessing says in a related fragment, the 'Vorzug der poetischen Mahlerey vor der wirklichen...' ('advantage that poetic painting has over actual painting...' B., 427). The poet can abstract from all the particulars involved in the episode, focusing solely on the single aspect, position or quality he wishes to present to the reader's imagination. The selected aspects can then be mobilized to evoke, in this case, the heroic strength which is the central idea he wants to communicate. The purity of this idea – it alone stands before the reader's mind – is achieved by the selective operation involved in content formation. The painter, however, cannot attain such purity. There is no such thing as a single quality in a painting, but rather any content unit represented is inevitably linked with others. The poet operates with single ideas, leaving indeterminate the related aspects of the content material, but the painter is compelled to represent fully determined objects. The idea of heroic strength, which the poet can foreground so well, appears in the painting within a matrix of features, some of which weaken the idea, some of which even contradict it.

Content form, viewed as a selective operation, is like a filter through which the material of content is passed in order to produce content substance. The selective filtering performed by the painter is a relatively crude operation. Large pieces of the content material, blocks of several interlocking features, reappear on the level of content substance. This observation allows us to grasp the specific relation between form, substance and material that characterizes the plastic arts. Because the plastic arts must represent, along with each chosen quality, numerous other, perhaps aesthetically unpropitious ones, because they are compelled to reproduce the full determinateness of things in reality, the selective operation (form) characteristic of the plastic arts is limited to gross, large-scale choices. This means that, having made one of these broad choices, the painter must abandon the selective process and follow the dictates inherent in the block of content material to which he has committed himself. The choice of "lion," for instance, is also a choice of the content units "claw," "teeth," "mane," "tail," etc. In painting, content form is narrowly circumscribed by the material coherence of things as we know them in reality. In other words, in painting the material of content exerts a dominating influence, even over form. The artist is required to execute the painting according to the material logic, as it were, of his chosen subject matter.[47] It is on account of the restricted role of form that material of content and content substance coincide to such a degree in the plastic arts.

Artistic creativity and imaginative freedom manifest themselves principally on the level of form, that is, in the operations of selection and arrangement that produce the content substance, the aesthetic object. At least as regards the selection of content units the painter's imaginative freedom is curtailed. The creative imagination must follow the dictates immanent to the large block of content material selected. The wound which the lion strikes in Hercules' loin is not selected by the artist's will, but is determined by the material of content itself. This predominance of material over form on the level of content corresponds to the predominance of material on the level of expression. The materiality, which characterizes the expression plane of the plastic arts, asserts itself on the level of content. The sign vehicle /lion/ is a fully determined, material object. Since a relation of similarity exists between the expression and content levels of the plastic arts, the determinateness of the expression token is carried over onto the content plane. The passage on Hercules and the lion quoted above, then, demonstrates a semiotic rule of content selection: by virtue of the type of sign he employs the painter is highly restricted in the content selections he makes. The materiality of the expression plane requires that the content substance be a fully determined object (or at least fully determined in its spatial and visual qualities), which is to say that the content substance must coincide with the content material to a very great extent. Both on the level of expression and on the level of content the plastic arts remain entangled in worldliness.

Compare with this state of affairs the selective operation in poetry. Here a single, marked aspect does not bring with it a set of other, interconnected aspects. The content unit "lion" is determined only by those features which the poet chooses to make explicit. Therefore, the poet can – to maintain my earlier metaphor – filter out all those features which weaken or contradict his intended aesthetic effect. The "heroic strength" of Hercules emerges, precisely on account of this selective filtering, on the level of content substance without the impurities of other features. In poetry, the selective process is free enough to be able to leave the features "claws," "teeth," "wound," etc. behind. To be sure, these features may be implied by the poem, but they are only implied; that is, they are only content material and the content material does not assert itself as content substance, as is the case with the plastic arts.

The greater freedom of selection (and therefore the greater imaginative freedom) available to the poet is attributable to the semiotic medium he works with. His ability to select single aspects and features derives from the fact that language has provided him with a repertoire of discrete content units. While the painter operates with gross perceptual blocks, the poet draws his selections from the sets of linguistic meanings made available in the paradigms of his language. Thus the material of content comes to the poet already formed. Language has already performed a process of filtering on the interlocking ideas of reality that constitute the content material insofar as it has isolated these ideas one from another. Language delivers to the poet a segmented reality, a set of positive meanings or ideas, from which he can then select those meanings that will best contribute to the achievement of his intended aesthetic effect. This is why I distinguished between linguistic content substance and aesthetic content substance in my discussion of the Homeric style. The formative operation of selection in poetry produces first of all a linguistic content substance, the meaning of the word selected. This linguistic substance may be concretized, that is, imaginatively ramified so as to encompass other, implicit traits, or it may itself serve as the aesthetic content substance, as in the Virgil example or in the lines on Hercules by Statius quoted above. The type and extent of concretization is a stylistic variable dependent on the poet's choice. As such it only underlines the greater freedom of selection characterizing the content form of poetry.

Notice how far Lessing has moved from Baumgarten and Meier and yet how close he remains to them. Baumgarten's insistence on the fully determined object with its metaphysical truth and repleteness is completely abandoned by Lessing. For Lessing, perception of the fully determined object cannot attain to the truth of poetry but is burdened with inconsistencies and inner contradictions. The abstraction brought about by the unfolding of the con-fused features in symbolic cognition is reevaluated by Lessing as the very source of imaginative freedom and of the purity of aesthetic effect: 'Es ist wahr, der Zug des Dichters muß sich zeichnen, muß sich sichtbar darstellen laßen können; aber der Dichter braucht für die Wirkung nicht gut zu seyn, die er in der materiellen Ausbildung des Künstlers thut, der nothwendig andere Züge damit verbinden mußte, von welchen das Auge nicht abstrahiren kann, von welchen aber wohl die Einbildungskraft bey dem Dichter abstrahiren konnte.' ('It is true that the trait selected by the poet must be such that it can be drawn or visually represented; but the poet need not be concerned with the effect which this trait has in the developed material image of the painter who of necessity combines it with other traits which the eye cannot abstract away, but which the imagination, in the case of the poem, can' B., 372). The attenuation of reality through abstraction, to which Baumgarten and Meier reacted almost allergically, has become here the signature of imaginative freedom. And yet the experience afforded by poetry is still conceived by Lessing as a quasi-perception, as direct intuition, a kind of imaginative seeing. The existentially absent object appears as present-to-mind and is directly attended to as an intuited idea: 'I see the full strength of the hero.' The perceptual model of reception is not abandoned but is relocated on the level of spirit and imagination. The reason for this is that Lessing is still operating within the representational paradigm, for which, as I insisted in the first chapter, all cognition is essentially specular.

The operation of selection which in part constitutes the content form is determined, then, by the semiotic medium. The artist who works with visible natural signs is limited to large-scale choices and, beyond these, must conform to the dictates of his content material. The poet has a greater freedom of selection because language has already segmented the nexus of features of perceptual reality into groups of discrete meanings from which he can choose those most conducive to his aesthetic aims. A passage from the eighth chapter of the *Laocoon* approaches this same issue from a slightly different point of view:

Gods and spiritual beings, as represented by the artist, are not completely identical with those which the poet makes use of. For the artist, they are personified abstractions which must constantly maintain the same set of characteristics if they are to be recognizable. For the poet, however, they are actual, acting beings with properties and affects that fall outside their general character and that can predominate over that character according to circumstances. For the sculptor, Venus is 'Love,' and nothing more; he must therefore endow her with all the pure and modest beauty and all the graceful charms which delight us in the objects of our love. The slightest deviation from this ideal causes us to interpret the image incorrectly. Beauty, but with more majesty than modesty, is no longer a Venus, but a Juno.... For the poet, however, Venus is indeed 'Love,' but as the goddess of love who, in addition to her general character, has her own individuality and is therefore just as capable of the impulses of aversion as she is of those of affection. What wonder, then, if in a poem she burns with anger and fury, especially if it is injured love itself that causes her to do so? (IX, 63).

At first reading this example seems to make the opposite point as the previous one (Hercules). There it was a matter of the abstractness of poetry in contrast to the full determinateness of the plastic arts, while here the moment of abstractness seems to belong to painting and sculpture and the content substance of poetry is defined as concrete ('actual, acting beings'). In fact, however, the greater concreteness of poetry, its ability to thematize the individuality of the goddess according to the particularities of circumstance, derives from the abstract, conceptual nature of its content units, from its greater freedom of selection. Poetry's ability to say more stems from its ability to say less.

Venus, the goddess of love, is to appear as the content substance. For the sculptor she will appear as a visible human figure, and as such she must be recognizable as Venus. Because the sculptor's freedom of selection is limited, the figure will be fully determined (visually and spatially at least); that is, furnished with such content units as particular gestures, physiognomy and stance. Each of these content units bears a potential threat to the intelligibility of the statue, for, in a sculpture, there is no distinction between essence and accidental qualities. "Venus" appears in a matrix of accidental features and is inseparable from these. This is why the sculptor must represent the goddess so abstractly: he must insure that every accidental feature can be subsumed beneath the concept "love." Because the content form is dominated by material, the plastic arts are limited to an abstract concept of love (e.g. beauty, modesty, charm). In the plastic arts full determination and abstractness coincide.

Poetry attains to a concreteness of content substance which avoids both particularity and empty abstraction. The reason for this is that the poet can select the essence of the goddess merely by employing the content unit "Venus." This content unit is discrete and it remains self-identical no matter what accidental qualities are combined with it. In every environment of accidental features "Venus" remains the same. She has 'her own individuality' which is present and communicable to the reader across a broad spectrum of different accidental contexts. In the poet's representation, then, "Venus" is not merely "Venus as beautiful, modest and charming" but also "Venus as jealous, as raging." It is language that affords the poet this possibility. Through the segmentation of the world which language has accomplished, essence has been isolated from accidental features, has been abstracted from the particularities of individual occasions. Language provides the poet with the content unit "Venus" (or "love"), enabling him to deploy it in a variety of contexts. This point is never explicitly formulated in the *Laocoon*, but in *Wie die Alten den Tod gebildet* (*How the Ancients Represented Death*, 1769) Lessing forthrightly states what in the *Laocoon* is only tacitly assumed:

Der Dichter hingegen, der seinen personifirten abstrakten Begriff in die Classe handelnder Wesen erhebt, kann ihn gewissermaassen wider diesen Begriff selbst handeln lassen, und ihn in allen den Modificationen einführen, die ihm irgend ein einzelner Fall giebt, ohne daß wir im geringsten die eigentliche Natur desselben darüber aus den Augen verlieren.... Fur ihn [den Dichter] *hat die Sprache bereits selbst die abstrakten Begriffe zu selbständigen Wesen erhoben; und das nehmliche Wort hört nie auf, die nehmliche Idee zu erwecken*, so viel mit ihm streitende Zufälligkeiten er auch immer damit verbindet.

The poet, however, who elevates his personified abstract concept to the class of acting beings, can to some degree allow that personification to act in contradiction with the concept and can introduce it into a poem in all the modified states that any particular case brings forth in it without the slightest chance that we lose track of its genuine nature.... For the poet, *language has already elevated even abstract concepts to the status of independent beings; and the same word never ceases to awaken the same idea* no matter how many conflicting accidental features the poet might combine with it. (IX, 39–40, my emphasis).

The poet does not encounter the world as a nexus of qualities given in perception. The perceived world has already been segmented and conceptualized for him by language. Language provides him with a repertoire of discrete content units (meanings, ideas) supported by discrete expression tokens. From this he can select those content units which best serve his particular aesthetic aim.

In the case of both Hercules and Venus, the visual presence of the content introduces an element of opacity into the aesthetic representation. The idea, be it "heroic strength" or "love," is encumbered by the multitude of visual features that necessarily appear on the level of content substance. The painting or sculpture cannot attain to univocal meaning and therefore cannot present the intended idea directly and unambiguously. The close relation between content material and content substance in the plastic arts implies that the infinite, unmasterable complexity and confusion of features that characterizes reality interferes with the intelligibility of the painting or sculpture. The advantage of poetry is that it reduces this complexity by abstraction. In poetry the idea is presented in the word that signifies it and can be directly attended to by the reader. The word negates reality in its particularity, in its existential presence, and renders the world imaginatively present in the form of a univocal idea. Whereas the painting presents Hercules in an ambiguous spatial simultaneity that contains both activity and passivity, strength and vulnerability, the poem presents a sequence of discrete ideas, each of which is intelligible in its uniqueness.

### Selection and imaginative freedom

The examples of Hercules and Venus show how certain advantages accrue to poetry by virtue of the greater range and freedom of selection possible within its characteristic semiotic medium. The application of critical 'acumen' to determine the differences between the arts has brought results that point to the superiority of poetry over the material arts. For this reason, the attempt to use painting as a standard for poetry is for Lessing not merely a misuse of categories, but a threat to the highest form of artistic achievement. When Spence, for instance, inquires why poets so seldom represent the muses with all the attributes that the painters give them, then Lessing's semiotic distinctions between the arts provide a ready answer: 'To the poets, Urania is the muse of astronomy; we recognize her office from her name and from what she does' (IX, 72). Language supplies the content unit "muse of astronomy" and the signifier /Urania/ is all that is needed to introduce this content unit in a recognizable fashion. But

Spence's question means more to Lessing than a conceptual mistake: 'Wouldn't it be as if a human being, who is capable of speaking out loud and permitted to as well, were simultaneously to make use of the signs which the mutes in the Turkish seraglio, lacking a voice, have invented among themselves?' (IX, 72). To suggest that poetry should follow painting in the representation of allegorical attributes is to rob poetry of its proper language, to enslave poetry in a more primitive semiotic medium, the 'mute language of the painters' (IX, 72).

The freedom of selection made available to poetry by language is imaginative freedom as well, both for the poet and for the reader. This becomes especially clear when the content substance is drawn from the non-visible field. Consider first an example that seems to fall between the visible and the non-visible, Homer's representation of Thetis being elevated up to Olympus.[48] When the painter chooses to represent a human figure, that figure will be fully determined spatially and visually, as the previous examples illustrated. In his discussion of the Thetis example, Lessing further defines the type of determination that limits the plastic arts: the painter is compelled to represent his figures as conforming to the laws of gravity and movement that hold in our empirical experience. Because the viewer must reconstitute the imaginary content of the painting through perception, the world of the painting must not disturb the viewer's ordinary perceptual expectations. The representation of the ascending figure makes real something which the viewer cannot accept as real because it runs counter to his perceptual habits. The figure becomes, as Lessing says in the same passage, a perceptual 'Ungereimtheit' (absurdity), and the content, which must be imaginatively concretized as if it were a perception, is therefore rendered unintelligible. Not only is the painter limited to large-scale selections regarding his individual figures, he also is limited to contents which are consonant with our perceptual habits and expectations.

Because the human figure is represented to perception, the content unit "Thetis" necessarily contains the semantic markers "heavy" and "material" – 'all the concepts of a course and heavy material.' These markers must be present if the painting is to be intelligible; that is, they must be evident in the perceptual-imaginative actualization of the content substance. If they are not, then the painting is semantically aberrant, an 'absurdity' equivalent to a logical contradiction. *The content plane of the plastic arts is governed by the logic of our perceptual expectations.* This is not the case, however, for poetry. The poet can select a content unit "human figure" which is not determined by the semantic markers "heavy" and "material." He can therefore put together a world which, though entirely intelligible to the reader, does not conform to the perceptual logic of our ordinary experience.

The restrictions imposed upon the imagination by the plastic arts become all the more apparent when strictly non-visible contents are considered. Though one might expect a careful consideration of Milton (or perhaps Klopstock) to be the focal point in the discussion of this particular issue, Lessing's attention is primarily directed toward Homer: 'Homer deals with two species of beings and actions; visible and invisible. Painting cannot indicate this distinction; in painting, everything is visible, and visible in the same way' (IX, 81). Lessing's method is to construct hypothetical translations of Homeric events into paintings in order to exemplify what semantic features are lost or added by virtue of the change in semiotic medium.[49] The thrust of his argument is that every content unit in a painting is marked as "visible." That is to say, each content unit in a painting carries a semantic marker which dictates that that content unit be imaginatively concretized as something actually seen. This aspect of the content plane in the plastic arts gives painting a certain advantage in representing contents which necessarily are semantically determined in this way. For instance,. "corporeal beauty" is a content which prescribes a visual concretization. The very notion of beauty for Lessing is, as I shall show, inseparable from a visual concretization. Thus, painting has the advantage of being able to introduce beauty as content substance because every content unit of painting is represented "as seen." This advantage, however, becomes a disadvantage as soon as the artistic intention requires that a distinction be drawn between the visible and the non-visible. Like the "ascending goddess," the non-visible is a semantic contradiction in the plastic arts precisely because any content unit "X" necessarily becomes "X as actually seen." Painting reduces the various ontological levels of the Homeric world to the homogeneous world of visual experience. 'Grandeur, strength, speed – all of which Homer attributes to his gods in a higher, more miraculous degree than even to his most excellent heroes – must in a painting sink to the common measure of mankind, and Jupiter and Agamemnon, Apollo and Achilles, Ajax and Mars, all become beings of the same sort, indistinguishable from one another except for certain conventional, external properties' (IX, 84–5).

Translation into painting necessarily performs a leveling of the multi-dimensioned Homeric world, a reduction to the common semantic denominator "visible." To limit the poet to what could be painted, then, is to restrict his imaginative freedom – and the reader's – precisely at those points where the imagination exercises itself most expansively:

...so gehet bey dem Dichter dieser ganze Kampf unsichtbar vor, und diese Unsichtbarkeit erlaubet der Einbildungskraft die Scene zu erweitern, und läßt ihr freyes Spiel, sich die Personen der Götter und ihre Handlungen so groß, und über das gemeine Menschliche so weit erhaben zu denken, als sie nur immer will.

...thus this entire battle occurs in the poem invisibly, and this invisibility allows the imagination to expand the scene, it gives the imagination free play to think of the characters of the gods and their actions however grandly, however much transcending common human measure, it wishes (IX, 82).

Lessing's point deserves to be underlined: language, the semiotic medium of poetry, allows for a freedom of imaginative play which is unattainable in the plastic arts. The plastic arts are limited first of all by the logic of perceptual expectations so that, for example, the content unit "human body" is necessarily represented as "heavy." The poet can eliminate the semantic marker "heavy" simply by formulating the sentence, "Thetis rose upward toward the clouds." Furthermore, the plastic arts necessarily present their content units as "visible"; the "invisible" lies outside the semantic universe of painting and sculpture. The poet, however, can represent content units which need not, indeed cannot, be imaginatively actualized "as seen." The imagination of poet and reader leaves the narrowly circumscribed world of the visible behind in order to attend to figures and events that far exceed the dimensions of ordinarily perceived things. In so doing, the imagination attains to an optimal degree of freedom.

The example of the Homeric gods can close my discussion of the semiotic rules governing content selection. In brief, I have insisted on the following points. Freedom of selection is much greater in poetry than in the plastic arts because, whereas the artist is limited to gross perceptual blocks of interlocking features, the poet can select discrete content units abstracted from their worldly context. The poet's freedom in this regard derives from the work of segmentation and abstraction performed by language: 'For the poet, language has already elevated even abstract concepts to the status of independent beings; and the same word never ceases to awaken the same idea . . . ' The advantages afforded the poet by this greater freedom of selection are several: purity of aesthetic content substance (Hercules example); ability to render concepts concrete by using them in a variety of contexts (Venus example); freedom to represent worlds other than our ordinarily perceived world (Thetis example); freedom to represent worlds with various ontological levels (example of the Homeric gods). Freedom of selection is equivalent to imaginative freedom. The world the poet evokes is more the work of his own formative abilities than is the world of the painter. Lessing's

discussion of the selection process involved in content formation shows how the advanced stage of semiosis (language)
which poetry takes as its point of departure provides a greater
freedom from worldliness, a greater autonomy of the imagination, than is available in the more rudimentary medium of
natural signs.[50] Gombrich's remark is entirely accurate: 'The
more one reads the *Laokoon*, the stronger becomes the impression that it is not so much a book about as against the visual
arts.'[51] The reason for this, however, is not merely Lessing's
resistance to the neo-classical style, as Gombrich argues, but is
ultimately Lessing's commitment to the ideal of imaginative
freedom and autonomy and his assumption of a progressive
process of semiosis as the vehicle by which the spirit liberates
itself from the entanglements of worldliness.

### Aesthetic rules of selection in the plastic arts

The semiotic rules of content selection do not suffice to distinguish each art form. They must be supplemented by
aesthetic rules, which further constrain the selective operation
and guarantee that the signification achieved will have an
aesthetic effect. It is a matter of distinguishing between that
which each semiotic medium can signify and that which each
can signify aesthetically.[52]

Thus far I have argued that the plastic arts, insofar as they
employ natural signs, are characterized by the following
features: (1) The materiality of the expression plane introduces
a high degree of flagrancy on the level of expression. The
expression asserts itself as an object of sensation. (2) Again by
virtue of the materiality of the expression plane, the plastic
arts are characterized by a dense syntax in which things cover
one another and obscure one another from view. (3) On the
level of content the artist must select large-scale blocks of interlocking features, fully determined things. (4) The world
represented by natural signs is *unidimensional* in an ontological
sense. It is exclusively a visible world and its intelligibility is

determined by our normal perceptual expectations. (5) Because the signification of natural signs is based on the similarity of content and expression, the imaginative content is necessarily actualized as if it were an object of vision. The illusion afforded by natural signs is always a visual illusion. We do not read a painting, we see it.

These five aspects of natural signs provide the conditions within which the artist must work and they determine the sphere of his possible aesthetic achievement. The question of the aesthetic rules of content selection, then, can be answered by determining what sorts of choices the artist must make if he is to achieve an aesthetic representation within the restrictions imposed by natural signs. What choices are open to him within the perimeters established by his medium? An aesthetic representation affords pleasure by presenting to intuition an imaginary object endowed with value qualities (perfections or imperfections). The highest perfection which can be so presented to the imagination within the boundaries of the material arts is physical beauty. 'Der Ausdruck körperlicher Schönheit ist die Bestimmung der Mahlerey.' ('The expression of corporeal beauty is what defines painting' B., 440). In making his content selections, the artist is limited to the physically beautiful. His purpose is to present physical beauty to the imagination in an illusionary presence.

More accurately formulated: the presentation of beauty is the artist's *primary* aim. Given two, equally beautiful figures (stances, gestures, etc.), he will select the most expressive one, that is, the one where the inner, emotional state of the figure is most clearly legible in its surface contours. And finally, where two possible choices are equal in terms of both beauty and expressiveness, the artist will select the one closest to conventional decorum. Content selection in the plastic arts is calculated according to a descending hierarchy of values – *Schönheit, Ausdruck, das Uebliche* (beauty, expression, decorum).[53] The first part of the *Laocoon* illustrates how this calculative procedure of content selection was at work, even if only unconsciously, in the formation of the Laocoon statue. Chapter five, in particular, shows very clearly how the choice of such expressive features as the free arms, the exposed torso and the naked brow of the statue is dictated by the syntax of visual natural signs and by the role of perceptual habits in the actualization of the content. Since Virgil's representation of the Laocoon material is used as a point of comparison, it is easy to see how the sculptor's aesthetic options are limited due to his semiotic medium. In the second chapter Lessing demonstrates that the extremes of emotion, though their visual manifestation is highly expressive, are avoided by the artist so that his figures maintain beauty in appearance. Because the argument regarding the supreme value of beauty in the plastic arts does not seem to be tied up with the question of semiotic constraints, I wish to attend to it in some detail.

That physical beauty is, in Lessing's view, the 'höchste Bestimmung' ('highest calling,' IX, 43) of the plastic arts is a fact well known. Less often recognized is the theoretical status of this claim. It is, as I see it, an aesthetic rule of content selection which is deduced from the dual requirement that the arts should yield pleasure by presenting an imaginary object to intuition and that they should (and can) achieve this end only within the restrictions established by the type of sign they employ. From this perspective, Lessing's insistence on the supremacy of beauty in the plastic arts must be interpreted not as enthusiasm for the beautiful but as a complaint that physical beauty is all that the arts can achieve. The fact that the value of beauty guides the artist's content selections militates against the ultimate value of the arts themselves. Unmistakable is Lessing's conviction that the restriction of the plastic arts to beautiful objects marks them with a superficiality that is nearly contemptible.[54] The painter's eye is amoral. It judges the world according to external beauty and ugliness and is unable to penetrate to the inner qualities of man. If the good and the beautiful coincide for the painter, then this very fact condemns painting morally. Here another aspect of Lessing's disagreement with Winckelmann is perceptible: Winckelmann's error, ascribing the quietude of the statue to qualities of the Greek soul, is tantamount, for Lessing, to an aesthetization, in the modern, pejorative sense, of the passionate and compassionate Greek humanity. Winckelmann takes the physical beauty of the statue out of its properly aesthetic sphere and transforms it, under the terms noble simplicity and quiet grandeur, into a norm of spiritual attitude. Lessing cannot accept this move because physical beauty is for him a supreme value only within the narrowly circumscribed limits of the plastic arts. Far from being a human ideal for Lessing, the beautiful appearance of the statue is merely the best that the plastic arts can do.

The moral problem inhabiting the very center of the plastic arts is that we all judge amorally, with a painter's eye, as soon as we encounter a painting or sculpture:

Der Meister arbeitete auf die höchste Schönheit, unter den angenommenen Umständen des körperlichen Schmerzes. Dieser, in aller seiner entstellenden Heftigkeit, war mit jener nicht zu verbinden. Er mußte ihn also herab setzen; er mußte Schreyen in Seufzen mildern; nicht weil das Schreyen eine unedle Seele verräth, sondern weil es das Gesicht auf eine ekelhafte Weise verstellet. Denn man reisse dem Laokoon in Gedanken nur den Mund auf, und urtheile. Man lasse ihn schreyen, und sehe. Es wan eine Bildung, die Mitleid einflößte, weil sie Schönheit und Schmerz zugleich zeigte; nun ist es eine häßliche, eine abscheuliche Bildung geworden, von der man gern sein Gesicht verwendet, weil der Anblick des Schmerzes Unlust erregt, ohne daß die Schönheit des leidenden Gegenstandes diese Unlust in das süsse Gefühl des Mitleids verwandeln kann.

The master artist aimed for the highest beauty possible within the assumed situation of bodily pain. This pain, in all its distorting intensity, could not be combined with beauty. The artist therefore had to diminish it; he had to soften the screaming into sighing; not because screaming betrays an ignoble soul, but because it distorts the face in a repulsive manner. For just think of Laocoon with his mouth torn open and then judge! Imagine him screaming and then look! It was a form which awakened pity because it revealed beauty and pain at once; now it has become an ugly, repulsive form from which we eagerly turn our eyes because the sight of pain excites displeasure and the beauty of the suffering figure can no longer transform this displeasure into the sweet feeling of pity (IX, 17).

The analysis of this passage must begin with the notion of 'Mitleid' (pity). As Lessing conceives it,[55] 'pity' is the quasi-affect that emerges when we view the suffering of another and share that suffering without being immediately struck by its cause. The protagonist on the stage, for instance, experiences fear before an impending catastrophe. This catastrophe does not immediately affect us as spectators but we nevertheless share the protagonist's emotion. The fear that we experience as spectators, however, is not actual fear since it is without an object (i.e., we are safe from the imminent calamity). It is not an ordinary affect (real fear), then, but a second-order affect. As an activation of our affective capacities achieved in the absence of an immediate, efficacious cause (object of fear), pity includes a self-reflexive component: we are reflectively aware of our affective activity, of our heightened state of emotion, in a way we couldn't be if we were actually afraid. The form in which this reflexivity manifests itself is pleasure. Pity is an objectless quasi-affect that is intrinsically self-reflexive and pleasurable. It is apparent, then, that the precondition of pity is distance: the impending catastrophe cannot be our own; we cannot be existentially implicated in the tragic event. Such distance is guaranteed in a poem by the imaginary status of the tragic event: as mimesis, the poem makes present an action which is existentially absent.[56]

The situation in the plastic arts is somewhat different. As viewers of a statue, we encounter the work primarily on the existential level of sensation. Even the imaginary object which we concretize in view of the expression substance has only a perceptual intelligibility. Thus, if the first-order affect of the hero (e.g., Laocoon's pain) is represented with maximal expressiveness, we experience his face as distorted – 'in a repulsive manner.' As viewers, we are primarily concerned with what we see and what we see is the external, physical manifestation of the hero's pain. We are repelled not by the pain itself, or by the idea of pain, but merely by the visual manifestation of that pain and agony. Our relationship to the statue is immediate, an existential relationship on the level of sensation. Where we should feel pity, we in fact experience our own first-order affect – disgust or repulsion. The ugly statue is all-too-present and we are compelled to turn away.

The function of beauty is to ameliorate the brute, existential presence characteristic of the plastic arts. Because Laocoon is represented as beautiful, the first-order affect of repulsion does not set in and we are able to move beyond the sensuous presence of the work and imaginatively concretize the priest's agony. Laocoon's suffering is thus present-to-mind though existentially absent and we have achieved the distance necessary to feel pity. Beauty is the supreme value in the plastic arts not because it is intrinsically of great worth, but because it is the only form of the sensuously present that does not overwhelm us on the existential level of sensation. In order to conduct us to the moral sense of pity, the sculptor must first appeal to our amoral painter's eye. The selection of beautiful figures in the plastic arts appears from this perspective to be the only available compensation for the characteristic flagrancy of their expression plane.

Because the imaginative experience afforded by the plastic arts is primarily visual, closely adhering to what we actually perceive in the expression substance, and because the intelligibility of the content is solely a perceptual intelligibility, the flagrancy of the expression plane is preserved on the level of content. Even the thought of Laocoon with his mouth wide open repels us, since it is a visual thought. Therefore, visible beauty must be the value quality which, both on the level of expression and the level of content, affords the initial and primary pleasure in the plastic arts. Beauty provides an atmosphere, as it were, in which the imagination can abide and from which it can move on to the sympathetic actualization of Laocoon's agony. Physical beauty is not an absolute value for Lessing, not an end in itself. Rather, it is a supreme value only

for the artist who is limited to the confines of the visible as the
sphere within which he can present value qualities to the
intuition of the viewer.

In addition to the aesthetic rule of content selection pre-
scribing the choice of beautiful objects, Lessing formulates a
second rule of selection having primarily to do with the
viewer's imaginative concretization of the work. This is the
famous rule of the pregnant moment: 'Die Mahlerey kann
in ihren coexistirenden Compositionen nur einen einzigen
Augenblick der Handlung nutzen, und muß daher den
prägnantesten wählen, aus welchem das Vorhergehende und
Folgende am begreiflichsten wird.' ('In its coexistant com-
positions, painting can only make use of a single moment and
must therefore select the most pregnant one, the one in terms
of which the prior and succeeding phases of the action are best
understood' IX, 95). The third chapter defines this moment as
'fruchtbar' (fecund):

Kann der Künstler von der immer veränderlichen Natur nie mehr als
einen einzigen Augenblick, und der Mahler insbesondere diesen einzigen
Augenblick nur aus einem einzigen Gesichtspunkte, brauchen; sind aber
ihre Werke gemacht, nicht bloß erblickt, sondern betrachtet zu werden,
lange und wiederhohlter maassen betrachtet zu werden: so ist es gewiß,
daß jener einzige Augenblick und einzige Gesichtspunkt...nicht
fruchtbar genug gewählet werden kann.

If the artist can never select more than a single moment out of ever
changing nature, and if the painter especially can only make use of this
single moment from a single point of view; if, however, their works are
made not merely to be glanced at, but to be contemplated, contemplated
long and repeatedly: then it is certain that the single moment and single
point of view selected cannot be too fecund (IX, 19).

Often discussed in terms of its applicability and often compared to aesthetic principles established by Lessing's successors,[57] the principle of the pregnant moment is seldom
analyzed in terms of its systematic function in the *Laocoon*
itself. The genealogy of the principle provides, I think, a clue
to this function. Mendelssohn, of course, had clearly stated the

principle in his 'Reflections' of 1758. But the notion also seems to me to be present in the work of Baumgarten and Meier, though not in the specific form it assumes for Lessing and Mendelssohn. I am referring to Baumgarten's category of *ubertas*, translated by Meier as *Reichtum* or *Fruchtbarkeit* (richness or fecundity).[58] Aesthetic thoughts are rich and fecund insofar as they contain or imply many other thoughts. A particular example of this fecundity is furnished in Baumgarten's description of 'pregnant ideas,'[59] those ideas evoked by emphatic terms which do not merely represent an object through an abstract concept but stimulate a quasi-perceptual actualization of the object on the part of the reader. In short, for Baumgarten and Meier the fecundity or pregnancy of ideas is linked to the process of imaginative actualization insofar as it exceeds the schematic quality of conceptual representations and recovers some of the plenitude of perceptual experience. In the *Laocoon*, the notion of a pregnant idea reappears in the poetic rule of content selection according to which the most sensate quality of an object should be chosen for explicit designation. This rule of poetic content selection has as its counterpart for the plastic arts the rule of the pregnant moment. Since the plastic arts are unable to select single traits, and since they always provide a totalized image, the painter or sculptor need not be concerned with choosing the one trait which most effectively evokes a global image of the object. In the plastic arts, imaginative fulfilment does not occur in the direction of visual detail, but in the direction of the before and after of the implied action.

The rule of the pregnant moment prescribes that the artist select a specific moment from the visual action continuum which is his content material. The choice of the pregnant moment guarantees that the viewer's imagination can transcend the represented content substance and can itself select aspects of the remaining content material – the rest of the action – for concretization. What is important here is that, as a result of the suggestiveness of the representation, the viewer's imagination acquires a freedom of production that exceeds the perimeters of the painted content. The viewer himself engenders the images of the prior and subsequent phases of the action without relying on or being limited by the determinate material representation provided by the painting or sculpture. The purpose of the rule of the pregnant moment is to insure this imaginative freedom: 'Dasjenige aber nur allein ist fruchtbar, was der Einbildungskraft freyes Spiel läßt.' ('That alone is fecund which allows the imagination free play' IX, 19). Lessing is suspicious of the sensuous presence characteristic of the plastic arts precisely because it tends to thwart creative imaginative activity. If the high point of the action is represented, then imaginative activity is compelled to remain secondary within the entire aesthetic experience. This emerges very clearly from a passage I have already cited: 'To show the eye the most extreme point means to bind the wings of fantasy and to force it – because it cannot go beyond the sense impression – to busy itself beneath it with weaker images beyond which it sees the visual fullness of the expression as its own limit' (IX, 19). The most interesting moment must be solely the product of the imagination. Lessing's complaint about illustrations in the essay 'Ueber eine zeitige Aufgabe' ('On a Timely Question,' 1776) applies in principle to all works of the plastic arts insofar as their determinate representations threaten to limit creative imaginative play: 'Sie helfen der Einbildung des Lesers nicht allein nicht; sie fesseln sie, sie irren sie.' ('They not only do not aid the imagination of the reader; they fetter it and lead it astray' XVI, 296).

Selection of the pregnant moment guarantees that the viewer can leave the painting or sculpture behind in order to make repeated imaginative sorties into the content material. From the sensuous presence of the single painted moment the imagination moves backward and forward, unfolding, as it does so, an unwritten narrative. The spatial content of the painting or sculpture is imaginatively transformed into a temporal content. Thus, the optimal concretization of the work, which the rule of the pregnant moment is designed to insure, moves in the direction of poetry. By selecting the pregnant moment, the artist transcends the material limits of his semiotic medium and approaches the type of representation possible in verbal language.

## Aesthetic rules of selection in poetry

The form of content embraces the semiotic and aesthetic rules that govern the operations of selection and arrangement in the different arts. Thus far I have discussed the selective operation in poetry and the plastic arts insofar as it is determined by the semiotic medium of each. In addition, I have accounted for the two aesthetic rules of selection – the rules of beauty and of the pregnant moment – that define an aesthetic use of natural signs and constitute the plastic arts as genuinely artistic. The next, logical step would be, of course, to attend to the aesthetic rules of selection in poetry, and from there to move on to both the semiotic and the aesthetic rules of arrangement that prevail in each art. The aesthetic rules of content selection in poetry, however, cannot be discussed without first mentioning some aspects of the problem of content arrangement.

Let me begin with Lessing's account of the plastic arts. I have shown that the artist, by virtue of his medium, cannot select discrete content units, that every choice implies a set of other choices. 'In painting, one part or one property pulls all the others along with it; painting must make everything determinate' (B., 371). This means that the definition of content selection in the plastic arts provides us at the same time with a definition of content arrangement. The several, inter-locking features, which the artist is compelled to select in large-scale blocks, are pre-arranged in spatial configurations. Because the artist works with visual natural signs, he must select bodies as his large-scale content units, and bodies are pre-given in their specific spatial array. Where the selection of discrete content units is impossible, there can be little distinction between selection and arrangement. The artist's choice is always global; it provides him with an entire work.

The same qualification applies to the aesthetic rule of content selection as well: the requirement that beauty be the supreme value in content selection at the same time dictates the aesthetic rule of arrangement. Beauty is a category that refers to an arrangement of parts: 'Körperliche Schönheit entspringt aus der übereinstimmenden Wirkung mannigfaltiger Theile, die sich auf einmal übersehen lassen.' ('Corporeal beauty has its origin in the harmonious effect of manifold parts that can be surveyed at once' IX, 120). To say that the artist must select beautiful forms is also to say that he must organize the parts in such a way that they inter-relate harmoniously in space.[60]

I will not devote, therefore, a special section to the rules of arrangement in the plastic arts because they are already contained in the rules of selection. By virtue of his medium, visual natural signs, the artist can arrange his content only in spatial configurations: 'So können neben einander geordnete Zeichen, auch nur Gegenstände, die neben einander, oder deren Theile neben einander existiren,...ausdrücken...' (Thus, signs which are ordered next to one another can only express objects which exist next to one another, or the parts of which do' IX, 94). Such objects are called bodies. 'Folglich sind Körper mit ihren sichtbaren Eigenschaften, die eigentlichen Gegenstände der Mahlerey.' ('As a result, bodies, with their visible qualities, are the proper objects of painting' IX, 94). An aesthetic use of natural signs does not merely represent what can be expressed, but what can be expressed with aesthetic effect. Therefore, superimposed upon the semiotic rule of content arrangement is the aesthetic rule of arrangement which requires that the contiguous parts interact harmoniously, that the bodies represented by the artwork be beautiful.

To be sure, it might be desirable to modify somewhat the asserted identity between selection and arrangement in the plastic arts, since the artist does have the freedom to make local selections. For instance, the artist can choose to represent "Bacchus" with or without "horns" and will inevitably opt for the latter possibility in order to preserve the overall beauty of the represented figure (IX, 61). But this choice is merely a secondary decision. The primary decision is the choice of Bacchus as a human figure including, in their specific arrangement, all the visual features that a human figure ordinarily possesses. In fact, even the choice of "Bacchus' horns" is illustrative of my point, for the artist cannot select the undetermined content unit "horns" but must inevitably realize that content unit as a specific arrangement of visual features. The "horns" must necessarily appear as a visually determined content substance, with a certain length, shape, position, and, in painting, color. In this particular visual manifestation, the "horns" violate, in themselves, the rule of beauty.

In the case of poetry, the process of selection yields discrete content units, not whole blocks of features. The "horns of Bacchus", for example, remain undetermined in terms of shape, size and position and do not constitute a specific visual image. Thus, the selective operation cannot produce an entire work as an arrangement of parts, as is the case with the artist's selection of a beautiful human figure. In poetry, the operations of selection and arrangement differ considerably: selection provides the individual content units which arrangement then combines to produce the global content substance of the work. In order to discuss the aesthetic rules of content selection proper to poetry, it is necessary to gain an overview of both selection and arrangement, for, while they are relatively distinguishable, they always operate in interaction.

The following fragment provides the sort of long perspective I require:

Da jede nachahmende Kunst vornehmlich durch die eigene Trefflichkeit des nachgeahmten Gegenstandes gefallen und rühren soll; da Körper der eigentliche Vorwurf der Mahlerey sind, und der mahlerische Werth der Körper in ihrer Schönheit bestehet: so ist es offenbar, daß die Mahlerey ihre Körper nicht schön genug wählen kann. Daher das *Idealische Schöne*...Zwar gehet auch der Dichter einem idealischen

Schönen nach; aber sein idealisches Schöne erfordert keine Ruhe; sondern grade das Gegentheil von Ruhe. Denn er mahlt Handlungen und nicht Körper; und Handlungen sind um so viel vollkommner, je mehrere, je verschiedenere, und wider einander selbst arbeitende Triebfedern darinn wirksam sind.

Since every imitative art is supposed to please and move us primarily through the excellence of the imitated object; and since bodies are the proper object of painting and the painterly value of bodies consists in their beauty: then it is apparent that painting cannot select bodies beautiful enough. Hence what is called *ideal beauty* ... To be sure, the poet also pursues an ideal beauty; but his ideal beauty does not require repose; rather, the exact opposite of repose. For he paints actions and not bodies; and actions are all the more perfect, the more, and the more diverse are the drive springs which, working against one another, effect the action itself (B., 370).

The central opposition here is that between bodies and actions as the imitated objects respectively of the plastic arts and of poetry. An imitated object is not merely something in the world, but rather is that which is rendered present to the imagination (i.e., the content substance). Once again Lessing insists that the intrinsic value of that aesthetic object provides the source of pleasure in the arts. The plastic arts select bodies as their imitated objects and beauty is the value quality proper to bodies as visually imagined. But beauty is a value that applies to bodies as a whole; it is the harmony of the various parts in their spatial arrangement. The selection of beautiful objects, then, provides the type of unity characteristic of the plastic arts. The poet also, according to the passage, pursues a kind of beauty, but, applied to a poem, the term no longer refers to the unity of diverse spatial parts. The unity of the poem stems from the overall action that is its global content substance. *Poetry arranges its parts according to the logic of action*. The fragment shows us, even before we have attended to the semiotic rules of content arrangement, what the aesthetic rule of content arrangement in poetry is. The poet arranges his individual content units in such a way that they follow one another in time and combine to yield a unified action.

Selection in poetry is the choice of the individual content units which are involved in the action. Because language – with its discrete arbitrary signs – is the poet's semiotic medium, he has a great deal of freedom to determine which content units he will introduce into the action that makes up the global content substance of the poem. For instance, he can choose, as Virgil did in his narration of the Laocoon story, to introduce a man screaming. The content unit is not necessarily attached to the image of an open mouth; it is not even necessarily a visual image. 'When Virgil's Laocoon screams, to whom would it ever occur that a gaping mouth is a necessary component of screaming and that this gaping mouth is ugly?' IX, 22). Our reception of the content unit does not move toward a visual concretization of the figure, but relates the "scream" – *according to the narrative logic of cause and effect* – to the suffering which is the central idea of the action. 'We do not relate this screaming to his character, but simply to his unbearable suffering' (IX, 23).

I want to leave the notions of action and logic of action relatively undefined for the moment in order to focus on the aesthetic rules of selection in poetry. I have established that the poet has the freedom to select abstract meaning units as supplied in the repertoire of signs of his language. Which of these meanings should he select? As I see it, the aesthetic rules of selection in poetry are essentially two: (1) Those elements should be selected which are functional within the overall action and which serve to heighten the action. (2) Those elements should be selected which stimulate an imaginative concretization of several, unmentioned aspects of the actors involved in the action.

It is clear that the first rule especially is related to arrangement. Elements are selected in view of their role in the whole work, that is, in terms of the overall action which the poet projects. With the contours of the action in mind, the poet selects those content units which will best serve the function of propelling the action. The last sentence of the fragment quoted above offers a sketch of this process: '... and actions are all the more perfect, the more, and the more diverse are the drive springs which, working against one another, effect the action itself.' The 'drive springs' are elements which are functional within the overall action, causes and effects, efforts and resistances, that evoke the energetic 'Anstrengung' ('exertion,' B., 371). Lessing felt to be the aesthetically most efficacious quality of action. The elements the poet selects, then, are these 'drive springs working against one another,' and his overall work will be all the more perfect, the more, and the more various, these elements are.

Fortunately, the *Laocoon* contains several illustrations of this selection of 'drive springs.' In Chapter five Lessing remarks that the snakes, in Virgil's depiction, are wrapped about Laocoon's torso and neck. Immediately after quoting the lines in the *Aeneid* where this is stated, he writes: 'Dieses Bild füllet unsere Einbildungskraft vortrefflich; die edelsten Theile sind bis zum Ersticken gepreßt, und das Gift gehet gerade nach dem Gesichte.' ('This image fills our imagination most excellently; the noblest parts of the body are squeezed to the point of suffocation and the poison is sent right at the face' IX, 40). Lessing's method here is noteworthy. The comment begins with the general statement that the Virgilian image – which is not a visual image – fills the imagination, that is, instigates considerable imaginative activity. The next two clauses demonstrate this assertion by citing, as it were, some of the associations that are evoked by the image and brought into the imagination's play. It is not merely "torso and neck" that the imagination attends to, but the "most noble parts" of the priest's body. That is to say, the poetic-linguistic representation introduces as a factor within the action the quasi-ethical value hierarchy ("noble" vs. "ignoble") that the culture associates with various parts of the body. Whereas in the plastic arts content units are primarily physical and perceptual in nature, in poetry the content units are drawn from a repertoire of cultural values. The decisive factor, however, is that these values are affectively charged and it is for this reason that they can function as 'drive springs working against one another.' Thus, in this particular narrative moment, the conflict is especially poignant because it is precisely the "noble" parts of the priest's body that receive the snakes' (cultural value: "vile") attack. The conflict is heightened and the degradation rendered yet more abject by the fact that the poison 'is sent right at the face.' Lessing's description, in short, demonstrates the lines' efficacy by tracing possible associative paths followed out in the course of reception. The analysis shows how an instance of poetic content selection brings several conflicting 'drive springs' into play. These drive springs are to be understood as effectively charged units of meaning.

The function of the "band" which Laocoon wears in the Virgilian scene is analyzed by Lessing in much the same way. This content unit, Lessing suggests, '...even strengthens the idea we form for ourselves of the victim's misfortune' (IX, 43). This general description of efficacy is once again followed by an evocation of the imaginative experience stimulated by Virgil's lines: 'His priestly dignity is of no avail; even its sign [i.e., the band], which everywhere earns him reverence and honor, is soaked and desecrated by the poisonous venom' (IX, 43). The "band" worn by the priest draws into the action all the associated dignity of his sacred office. It is not merely Laocoon's suffering that the imagination attends to, but the defeat of all that he stands for: the spitting of the snakes is also an act of desecration. Compare this function with the role of the "band" in a hypothetical statue. There aesthetic effect is primarily limited to what is seen, so that the "band" functions only in its material and visual positivity. It is nothing more than what appears to the eye. In the poem, however, the "band" is a meaning unit without visual and material specification. In its *ideality*, it functions as a collecting point of associations, which are then drawn into the action in the course of the reader's imaginative actualization of the poem. In this way it multiplies the 'drive springs' of the represented action.

One final example of an aesthetically felicitous content selection: 'Virgil giebt sich Mühe, die Grösse der Schlangen recht sichtbar zu machen, weil von dieser Grösse die Wahrscheinlichkeit der folgenden Erscheinung abhängt; das Geräusche, welches sie verursachen, ist nur eine Nebenidee, und bestimmt, den Begriff der Grösse auch dadurch lebhafter zu machen.' ('Virgil endeavors to make the size of the snakes quite visible because the verisimilitude of the event which follows depends on this size; the sound the snakes make is merely an accessory idea which is designed to make the idea of size all the more lively' IX, 38). The tremendous size of the snakes must be introduced as an element within the action not because size is a value in itself but because the probability of the central event – the snakes seize and strangle at once Laocoon and his sons – presupposes that the snakes be understood as possessing great length. The "size of the snakes" functions to motivate, that is, to provide a sufficient cause of, the ensuing event. It is a properly narrative element, the meaning of which derives from its causal relation to a later element. In part, the success of a narrative, or, in Lessing's terms, the perfection of an action, stems from the causal saturation of the event: nothing happens randomly; everything is comprehensible in terms of an explicitly mentioned cause.[61]

If such causal saturation is to be attained, the motivating elements must be present to the reader's mind so that the causal sequence unfolds, and is immediately comprehended, as if it were real. Thus, Virgil endeavors to render this content unit 'quite visible,' immediately present to the reader with all the conviction and evidence of an immediately perceived phenomenon. This rendering present is in part accomplished by a second motivating content unit, the "sound" caused by the snakes as they pursue their course toward the beach. The hissing of the sea demonstrates the size of the snakes, and thereby brings the important content unit "size" into imaginative focus. Note the hierarchization of the narrative elements: The "sound" is merely a secondary idea, the function of which is to support the idea of size. In itself, the "sound" plays no role in the central action. Therefore, it is imperative that the imagination move immediately to the idea of size without attending to the sound of the snakes for too long. 'Petron hingegen macht diese Nebenidee zur Hauptsache, beschreibt das Geräusch mit aller möglichen Ueppigkeit, und vergißt die Schilderung der Grösse so sehr, dass wir sie nur fast aus dem Geräusche schliessen müssen.' ('Petronius, on the other hand, makes this accessory idea into the main focus, he describes the sound as sumptuously as possible and in doing so forgets the size so much that we almost have to draw our inferences from the sound alone' IX, 38). Petronius' imitation of Virgil destroys the unity of action by expanding the subaltern idea to such a degree that it displaces the central idea of size required to motivate the overall action. *The choice of elements, their relative importance, and their expansion or explicitness are determined by the motivational logic of the main action, which is the global aesthetic content substance of the episode.* One could say, using my earlier terminology, that the poem is so composed as to leave the content unit "sound" at the level of linguistic substance; that is, it remains a schematic idea or linguistic meaning, while the reader is encouraged to concretize a fuller idea of the "size of the snakes," since it is an element serving a central function within the narrated action.

The second aesthetic rule of content selection requires that elements should be selected which stimulate an imaginative concretization of several, unmentioned aspects of the actors involved in the action. In Lessing's formulation: 'Eben so kann auch die Poesie in ihren fortschreitenden Nachahmungen nur eine einzige Eigenschaft der Körper nutzen, und muss daher diejenige wählen, welche das sinnlichste Bild des Körpers von der Seite erwecket, von welcher sie ihn braucht.' ('Likewise, poetry, in its successive imitations, can only make use of one property of bodies and it must therefore select that one which excites the most sensate image of the body from the perspective useful to the poem' IX, 95). Why poetry can only utilize one quality and not several is an issue I will deal with in the following section, where I discuss Lessing's conception of poetry as a natural sign. Here I want to attend solely to the function of these sensate qualities within the poetic text. The term 'sensate' ('sinnlich'), of course, belongs to the vocabulary of Baumgarten, Meier and Mendelssohn and applies to those sorts of representations which provide a global, intuitive, quasi-perceptual apprehension of the object. As perfect sensate representation, poetry provides a global representation of the object such that the value qualities inherent in the object simultaneously affect the reader. In this way poetic representation recovers the efficacy of perception; the poem provides a sensate intuition of the object. In the work of Lessing's predecessors – with the possible exception of Mendelssohn – the possibility of achieving such a representation through language remained unproblematic. In his formulation of the rule of the sensate quality, Lessing specifies to what degree and by what means a global, quasi-perceptual intuition of the object can be communicated in the semiotic medium proper to poetry.

The previous example of the snakes indicates what Lessing had in mind. The "sound" – a quality of the snakes as they swim toward shore – is '. . . designed to make the idea of size all the more lively.' An idea is 'lively' when it contains and makes present a variety of features in the simultaneity of a global apprehension. The term corresponds to the 'extensive clarity' of Baumgarten. The "sound," then, is a sensate quality not because it is in itself present to the reader's imagination, but because the mention of this quality induces the reader to concretize an image of the snakes in which they are rendered present-to-mind in a quasi-perceptual form.

The choice of certain sensate qualities can affect the correspondence between *individual* content substances of a poem and global content substances of paintings that is characteristic of the Homeric style. 'Homer seldom paints these [i.e., visible objects] with more than a single adjective because a single property of a visual object is sufficient to recall the others for us at once since we have them all together daily before our eyes' (B., 443). The selection of the single characteristic induces a process of concretization in which the linguistic schema is imaginatively filled in, yielding a simulated perceptual experience of the object. Here the symmetry of the rule of the pregnant moment and the rule of the sensate quality becomes apparent: both are aesthetic rules of selection the purpose of which is to induce an imaginative concretization of what is only hinted at in the work so that the receiver himself is encouraged to draw unmentioned aspects of the content material into the aesthetic experience. By virtue of the pregnant moment, the imaginative experience moves from a given painting toward poetry. By virtue of the sensate quality, the imagination moves toward painting insofar as the reader is encouraged to actualize totalized visual images that present a manifold of visual features 'at once.' The aesthetic substance thus attended to exceeds the schematic nature of the linguistic substance and attains to the status of a quasi-perception.

With the notion of sensate quality a turn in Lessing's argument – at least as I have described it – begins to show itself. Whereas all the points made thus far illustrate the advantages that poetry draws from the advanced stage of semiosis it starts off from, as regards the concept of sensate quality a certain suspicion *vis-à-vis* linguistic representation announces itself. The sensate quality provides the poet with a means to exceed his semiotic medium and recover some of the immediacy and fullness of perceptual experience. To be sure, the quasi-perception that results from the mention of a sensate quality is purely a product of the reader's imagination. No material representation fetters the imagination and therefore each reader has the freedom to concretize the image as he wishes. It is therefore not a matter of leaving language behind, but of infusing linguistic communication with richness and immediacy. Nevertheless, there is operative in the very notion of sensate quality a concept of language as a secondary and derivative mode of representation, impoverished by virtue of its schematicity, its abstractness. Here we see the dual perspective that informs Lessing's view of poetry: on the one hand, poetry is the superior art because of the freedom afforded the imagination in language; on the other hand, poetry is not truly poetry, not truly aesthetic, unless it is more than language. In order to achieve the status of poetry, the linguistic representation must not abide on the level of symbolic cognition, but must be so fashioned that the reader moves beyond the level of signs to an intuitive cognition of the represented object. Only when this condition is met is the illusionary presence of the existentially absent object – the presence-to-mind which is definitive of the aesthetic in general – guaranteed.

The Homeric style employs sensate qualities in such a way that the reader easily fills in the linguistic schema and imaginatively constitutes a quasi-visual image. Mendelssohn, who influenced Lessing on this point as on so many others, saw the possibility of such imaginative fulfillment as a criterion of poetic excellence: 'But the poet is all the more perfect, the more determinate his images are and *the easier it is for the imagination to fill in the omitted traits* and to form for itself clean and extensive ideas of the fictional entities.'[62] Several of Lessing's fragments, some of which I quoted above, show that he shared this opinion.[63] The reason is that the Homeric style, as described by Mendelssohn and Lessing, does not provide a merely symbolic cognition, but affords an intuitive apprehension of the actors involved in the narrated story.

Such an intuitive apprehension is definitive of all poetry: 'Ein poetisches Gemählde ist nicht nothwendig das, was in ein materielles Gemählde zu verwandeln ist; sondern jeder Zug, jede Verbindung mehrerer Züge, durch die uns der Dichter seinen Gegenstand so sinnlich macht, daß wir uns dieses Gegenstandes deutlicher bewußt werden, als seiner Worte, heißt mahlerisch, heißt ein Gemählde, weil es uns dem Grade der Illusion näher bringt, dessen das materielle Gemählde besonders fähig ist, der sich von dem materiellen Gemählde am ersten und leichtesten abstrahiren lassen.' ('A poetic painting is not necessarily one which can be transformed into a material painting; rather, every trait and every combination of traits, through which the poet forms his object so sensately for us that we are more distinctly conscious of that object than of his words, is called painterly, is called a painting, because it brings us closer to that degree of illusion of which painting especially is capable and which can be most immediately and easily conceptualized in terms of a material painting' IX, 92). This passage, which provides a general definition of the poetic, requires that I modify my previous interpretation of the notion sensate quality. The quasi-perception, which is instigated by the employment of sensate qualities in the Homeric style, is only an extreme case – the most successful case, perhaps – of the intuitive apprehension characteristic of poetry generally. It is not necessary that the poem lead to a quasi-visual experience in every instance. In fact, this is often impossible, as shown by Milton's poetry, for example. What is required is that the representation be sensate ('sinnlich') in the general sense that the reader believes himself in the presence of those objects designated in the words of the poem. This presence-to-mind is intuitive cognition, an awareness in which the signs withdraw from the foreground of consciousness and the ideas themselves are directly attended to. Poetry is discourse rendered transparent to the things it represents. The aesthetic illusion is achieved when the reader forgets he is reading or listening to words and feels as if he were in the presence of the represented objects. This notion of illusion as the effacement of symbolic cognition is a generalization of the experience peculiar to painting, as the final two clauses indicate. It is not painting altogether which poetic language approaches, but the experience of immediacy, of direct intuition that is common but not exclusive to painting.

Sensateness, then, is a quality of all poetic discourse. At times it is achieved by the use of sensate qualities in the narrow sense; that is, content units which provoke a quasi-perceptual (usually visual) fulfillment of the linguistic schema. At other times, even though such quasi-perceptions are not attained, the sensateness of the poem is equivalent to the intuitive character of the reader's cognitive experience. In both cases poetry coincides with painting – not in terms of specific contents nor even in terms of the type of imaginative concretization, but in terms of what might be called *the idea of painting*. This idea is intuitive immediacy. Only when such intuitive immediacy is attained does poetry reach the 'goal of illusion' which it shares with the plastic arts. The final section of this chapter will show that the poet achieves this goal by converting the arbitrary signs of ordinary language into natural signs.

### The poetic rule of content arrangement

I want to conclude my description of Lessing's global model of aesthetic signification with an account of the poetic rule of content arrangement. Arrangement is the operation which yields whole works, global content substances which themselves are the aesthetic objects attended to by the imagination. If the wholeness, which is definitive of a work, is to be achieved, then arrangement must be more than a mere joining of parts. It must join and integrate; it must operate according to a principle of unity. The plastic arts illustrate this very well: By virtue of the medium he employs, the artist must arrange his contents in space. Beauty is the principle according to which the artist makes his arrangement, for beauty is the unity of diverse spatial parts. Let us recall Lessing's definition: 'Corporeal beauty has its origin in the harmonious effect of manifold parts that can be surveyed at once.'

It is important, I think, to keep in mind that beauty is a type of arrangement, a particular principle of integration, and not something outside the work which the artist tries to copy. To be sure, there may be objects in the world which are beautiful and the artist may indeed use them as his patterns, but these objects themselves are beautiful only insofar as they manifest a harmonious arrangement of parts. The mimesis characteristic of the plastic arts is first and foremost an effective mimesis: beauty must be present as the unity of the global content substance which stands before the viewer's imagination. It is also important to realize that, as a particular type of arrangement, beauty demands a particular type of apprehension. The viewer himself must be capable of accomplishing the integrating operation which the artist has accomplished before him. Therefore, beauty can be apprehended as a perfection only in visual perception or, more exactly, in an imaginative experience which has the form of a visual perception. The viewer's synoptic view grasps at once – this 'at once' conforms to the unity of the content – the coexistent spatial parts. Beauty is a perfection of content arrangement that is tailored to, and can only be grasped in, visual or visual-imaginative experience. The same holds for the opposite of beauty. Just as the perfection of arrangement must show itself to vision, so too imperfection, visual dissonance, lack of integration: 'Auch die Häßlichkeit erfodert mehrere unschickliche Theile, die wir ebenfalls auf einmal müssen übersehen können, wenn wir dabey das Gegentheil von dem empfinden sollen, was uns die Schönheit empfinden lässt.' ('Ugliness too requires several unfitting parts which we likewise must be able to survey at once if we are to feel in doing so the opposite of what beauty makes us feel' IX, 139).

Where the synoptic view of visual perception is no longer at hand, where the spatial cohesion of the parts is dissolved into temporal succession, beauty cannot emerge as the apparent unity of the global content substance: 'Der Dichter der die Elemente der Schönheit nur nach einander zeigen könnte, enthält sich daher der Schilderung körperlicher Schönheit, als Schönheit, gänzlich. Er fühlt es, daß diese Elemente nach einander geordnet, unmöglich die Wirkung haben können, die sie, neben einander geordnet, haben; daß der concentrirende Blick, den wir nach ihrer Enumeration auf sie zugleich zurück senden wollen, uns doch kein übereinstimmendes Bild gewähret;...' ('The poet, who would only be able to show the elements of beauty in succession, entirely foregoes for this reason the depiction of beauty as beauty. He feels that these elements, ordered sequentially, could not possibly have the effect which they have when ordered spatially; that the concentrating regard which we want to cast back on these elements after they have been enumerated can still not provide us with an harmonious image;...' IX, 120–1). I want to concentrate on the phrase 'depiction of beauty as beauty.' To say that the poet cannot represent beauty as beauty is to affirm that beauty, as a perfection of content arrangement, cannot be achieved in poetry. To be sure, beauty can be an aspect of the poem's content material. The poet can refer to the beauty of his characters, he can designate beauty, but he cannot make beauty the principle according to which his individual content units are arranged and integrated into a global content substance. For this reason, poetry and painting, even in the case of the Homeric style, coincide only on a micro-level. The individual content units, which, like the sign vehicles that mark them, succeed one another in time, cannot be grasped at once and therefore cannot manifest the unity of diverse spatial parts that characterizes beauty as a perfection and principle of arrangement. The same applies to ugliness: 'In der Poesie, wie ich angemerket, verlieret die Häßlichkeit der Form, durch die Veränderung ihrer coexistirenden Theile in successive, ihre widrige Wirkung fast gänzlich; sie höret von dieser Seite gleichsam auf, Häßlichkeit zu sein...' ('In poetry, as I have noted, ugliness of form almost entirely loses its repulsive effect due to the change of its coexistent parts into successive ones; in this regard, it ceases, as it were, to be ugliness...' IX, 145). The poet can take an ugly object as content material, but this object cannot appear, in its ugliness, as content substance.[64] The specific type of arrangement that makes an object ugly does not govern the content units delivered in succession by the poem.

Beauty is not the content of painting, but the principle and perfection of its content arrangement. If a poet attempts to present physical beauty, he destroys the organizational unity that makes beauty possible and at the same time fails to provide an alternative principle of arrangement. The result is that his signs and the individual content units they communicate form no work at all. To create a genuine poetic work – genuine in the sense that it is a whole – poetry must adhere to a principle of content arrangement that provides unity not of coexistent spatial parts but of successive content units. As I have already indicated, Lessing sought this principle in the notion of action.

Mere succession does not constitute an action. Action requires that the successive parts be organized according to a principle of unity. The decisive definition already appears in Lessing's 'Von dem Wesen der Fabel' ('On the Essence of the Fable,' 1759) where 'Bild' and 'Handlung' (image and action) are distinguished in a manner that anticipates central arguments of the *Laocoon*:

> I call an *action a series of changes that together constitute a whole.*
> This *unity of the whole* is based on the *agreement of all the parts in contributing to a single purpose* (VII, 429).

A fragment, which may or may not have preceded the publication of the *Laocoon*,[65] offers a similar definition:

> *Poetry* depicts movements and, by allusion through movements, bodies.
> A series of movements which are directed toward a single purpose is called an *action* (B., 444).

The terms 'change' and 'movement' in the two definitions can be considered equivalent; both indicate a succession. The succession becomes an 'action' only when the parts are subsumed beneath a unifying principle, which Lessing defines here as the purpose of the action. With this definition in mind, let us consider the formulation in the sixteenth chapter of the *Laocoon*: 'Gegenstände, die auf einander, oder deren Theile auf einander folgen, heissen überhaupt Handlungen. Folglich sind Handlungen der eigentliche Gegenstand der Poesie.'

('Objects which follow one another, or the parts of which follow one another, are generally called actions. Therefore, actions are the object proper to poetry' IX, 94–5). Viewed in terms of the two definitions cited above, this statement must be interpreted as follows: Poetry represents actions as its proper content substance because an action is the unity of successive parts. (In the following section, I will examine the status of these parts more closely.) Another principle of unity, such as beauty, would be incapable of governing the successivity characteristic of poetry. No principle of unity would leave us without wholeness; the poem would be no poem at all, but merely a sequence of ideas. An action is a unity of temporally diverse parts and therefore action alone meets the dual stipulation of being successive and possessing wholeness.

With the introduction of a teleological principle ('Endzweck'), the disorder of mere sequence is transformed into a totality of functional parts. Furthermore, part and function are indistinguishable: the individual content unit is selected – as I argued earlier – precisely because it plays a role in the overall action. The content units of the poem are not positive entities only contingently involved in the plot. On the contrary, their very being in the poem is their function; they appear as content substance only insofar as they motivate and are motivated by other elements. 'Homer mahlet nichts als fortschreitende Handlungen, und alle Körper, alle einzelne Dinge mahlet er nur durch ihren Antheil an diesen Handlungen, gemeiniglich mit nur Einem Zuge.' ('Homer only paints successive actions and he paints all bodies, all individual things, only in terms of their participation in the action, typically with just one trait' IX, 95–6). I would argue that Lessing be understood very strictly here: only through their participation in the action do the individual content units acquire access to the poem.

Action, like beauty in the plastic arts, should be considered primarily as a global content substance resulting from a principle of content arrangement and not as something outside the poem. Indeed, reality is full of actions and the poet, in Lessing's view, is undoubtedly oriented toward this reality. But between real action and action as the global content substance of a poem there is this difference: the actions that occur in the world are never pure, they are never thoroughly organized according to a single purpose. The treatise on the fable anticipates this distinction:

A bit of history occurs; a fable is invented. For the fable, therefore, one must be able to indicate the reason why it was invented, whereas for the bit of history I am obliged neither to indicate nor to know the reason why it occurred (VII, 430).

The 'bit of history' might be termed a mimesis of action as it appears in reality; that is, of events, series of changes, that lack a single purpose. Lessing calls such real actions 'Begebenheiten' (VII, 430), occurrences that merely take place, and opposes this term to 'Handlung.' In contrast to the historical account, the fable is 'invented.' It is formed in view of and according to a single 'Grund' ('reason'), a purpose or final cause. Thus, the action brought before the imagination by the fable is more perfectly intelligible than the real event precisely because each of its elements has a reason for being, serves a function, and is comprehensible in terms of that function. The perfection of the action is a thoroughgoing functionality: 'Only in this way does it become a *perfect* fable; which it wouldn't be if it contained a single trait more or less than is necessary in order to present the moral principle intuitively' (VII, 436). Perfection of the fable is perfection of the action. Every content unit functions optimally to fulfill the governing purpose.

All actions, however, are not equally compelling. Just as beauty is the more perfect the greater the manifold of visual-spatial features it unifies, the richer its harmony, so too is an action more interesting according to the complexity and variousness of the functions it integrates within its single purpose. Recall, in this regard, the first poetic rule of selection: '...and actions are all the more perfect, the more, and the more diverse are the drive springs which, working against one another, effect the action itself' (B., 370). Selection enriches the action by drawing into it a multitude of motivating factors, while arrangement organizes these factors in the unity and consequentiality of a single action. The ideal action combines the economy of a single purpose and thoroughgoing functionalization with the diversity and intensity of such motivating elements as arouse the reader's interest and emotion: 'The ideal of actions consists: (1) in the compression of time, (2) in the intensification of the drive springs and the exclusion of accidental factors, (3) in the arousal of affects' (B., 394).

## Summary

In this discussion I have attempted to maintain a certain methodological restraint. Whereas the secondary literature on the *Laocoon* has usually regarded the semiotic notions employed by Lessing as contingent or accidental and has tended to concentrate on the ethical, political, anthropological and religious aspects of the work, I have chosen to focus entirely on the theory of aesthetic signification that underlies Lessing's comparison of the arts. From this perspective, the *Laocoon* proves to contain a fairly complex semiotic theory of the arts. The theory is not without vested interest. The classification of the arts in terms of the signs they employ and the investigation of the capabilities that each art has by virtue of these signs allows Lessing to demonstrate the advancements of poetry over the plastic arts. Because its semiotic medium provides for a greater detachment from worldliness, the aesthetic experience afforded by poetry is judged to be more valuable than that available through painting or sculpture. Language negates the brute, sensuous presence of things; the con-fused interlocking of qualities in perceived reality is dissolved into series of discrete content units from which selections can be freely made providing optimal intelligibility and purity of representation. The word, without thrusting itself into the foreground of attention, delivers directly to the imagination the ideal entities, the meanings, which in the plastic arts are encumbered and occluded by a host of other features. The reader's imagination is granted the freedom to fill in the linguistic schema as it pleases, without being limited by the full determinateness of things. At the same time, the arbitrary relation between individual sign and meaning allows for unlimited semantic scope. Whereas the plastic arts can represent only what is visible and must conform to our ordinary perceptual expectations, poetry can represent 'bloße Wesen der Einbildung' ('mere beings of the imagination,' B., 372), and can project worlds with various ontological levels. Language is the vehicle through which the contents of our experience are *elevated* to the status of freely deployable, ideal entities. Poetry, as art in language, is therefore the sphere in which the imagination exercises itself with optimal freedom, in total independence from actual sense experience.

The differences between poetry and the plastic arts, however, cannot be pressed too far. My discussion of the 'Preface' argued that for Lessing there exists a fundamental unity of the two art forms, a unity of purpose, which underlies their differences in means. Lessing's preference for the Homeric style, the poetic style most proximate to painting, likewise points to a profound identity between poetry and painting. Finally, the doctrine of the optimally sensate quality – a poetic rule of content selection – suggests, even in its most general interpretation, that poetry is perfected when linguistic representation attains to the 'idea of painting.' Thus, while Lessing's critical 'acumen' elaborates the differences between the arts and accords to each its proper domain, there are also motifs in the *Laocoon* which point toward a reintegration of these severed realms. And only when such a reunification is accomplished, only when it is shown how the arbitrary signs of language are converted into natural signs, will poetry be completely described. The final section of this chapter attends to this turn in Lessing's theory.

## Poetry as natural sign

### Chapter sixteen and the notion of natural sign

The previous section emphasized the differences between poetry and painting that result from the differences in the signs employed by each. As I emphasized in my discussion of the 'Preface,' however, these differences involve only the means or media through which the two arts seek to achieve a common aim, the aesthetic pleasure engendered by the intuited value qualities of the imaginary aesthetic object. Only when this end is reached does a signification in either natural or arbitrary signs qualify as an aesthetic signification. While poetry possesses certain advantages over the plastic arts by virtue of its semiotic medium, it nevertheless shares with painting and sculpture the goal of illusionary presentation.

In view of this goal the arbitrary signs employed by the poet introduce severe handicaps. A particular visual image, for instance, may be evoked by both painter and poet since both natural and arbitrary signs function to call forth imaginary entities. In either case the image will inspire the same aesthetic pleasure – except for a difference in degree. 'If, therefore, the same image is excited anew in our imagination through either arbitrary or natural signs, in each case the same pleasure must arise anew, although not to the same degree' (IX, 45). The pleasure, which the image conveyed through arbitrary signs affords, is mitigated by the arbitrariness of the sign relation. The arbitrariness of the linguistic sign precludes the appearance of the image in the fullness and immediacy that is attained by a natural sign of the same imaginary object. In a similar vein, Lessing notes that landscape poetry such as that of Thompson provides not a fully present image of a landscape, but merely the ' . . . schwanken und schwachen Vorstellungen willkührlicher Zeichen.' (' . . . the wavering and weak representations of arbitrary signs' IX, 78). Arbitrary signs, because of the distance between signifier and signified, cannot communicate their ideas with the same efficacy as natural signs. Instead of a full and present image, they deliver vague, ineffective ideas. 'Since figures and colors are natural signs but words, through which we express figures and colors are not, then the effects of an art which uses the former must be infinitely more rapid and more lively than those of an art which must content itself with the latter' (B., 355). Arbitrary signs open a gap between signifier and signified, a gap which interferes with the efficacy of the representation. And yet the efficacy of a representation is its most important quality insofar as it is intended as aesthetic. Therefore, poetry seems to be at a disadvantage *vis-à-vis* painting: 'The fact that painting employs natural signs must indeed offer it a great advantage over poetry, which can only make use of arbitrary signs' (B., 430).

The central problem is that, where arbitrary signs are employed, the resulting cognition will be merely a symbolic cognition. Rather than attaining to an intuitive apprehension of the signified, the receiver attends primarily to the signifier and his awareness of the signified content is vague. This issue is raised repeatedly in Lessing's writings. Already in 'On the Essence of the Fable' Lessing saw the essential function of the fable as the transformation of a general moral proposition, which as such can be represented only in symbolic cognition, into a particular instance graspable in intuitive cognition. By virtue of this transformation, the reader attends to the moral principle in a cognition that is 'clear in and of itself' and that has 'a much greater influence on the will' than symbolic cognition (VII, 443). The issue returns in the *Hamburgische Dramaturgie*, where Lessing discusses the best means of enunciating moral principles on the stage. As a general proposition ('allgemeiner Satz'), a moral principle is always separated from the immediate occasion of its utterance: '...due to its universality, it [the proposition] becomes to some degree alien to the matter at hand, it becomes a digression, and its relationship to the present situation is either not noticed or not understood by the less attentive or less acute listener' (IX, 199). Represented in symbolic cognition, the proposition is estranged from the action the viewer sees before him on the stage. For this reason, Lessing seeks a device, '...to bring the symbolic nature of the moral back to the intuitive level...' (IX, 199) so that the viewer can intuitively seize the truth of the principle as it is instantiated in the dramatic situation. This is the function of the actor's gestures, which, '...as natural signs of things, help lend truth and life to the conventional signs of the voice' (IX, 198). As natural signs, the supporting gestures help convert the merely symbolic cognition, which the enunciation of the moral principle ordinarily conveys, into vivid intuitive cognition eliciting a strong affective response.

In the case of both fable and dramatic gesture, then, Lessing insists on the transformation of symbolic cognition into intuitive cognition. In the former case, this occurs through the representation of an individual instance which, when imaginatively attended to by the reader, immediately manifests the moral truth in question. In the case of the drama, intuitive cognition is achieved by accompanying the arbitrary signs expressing the moral truth with natural gestural signs. A third solution is hinted at in the second *Anti-Goeze* (1778), where Lessing suggests that intuitive cognition can be guaranteed by using the arbitrary signs of language in such a way that they themselves approach the status of natural signs: 'And certainly you don't want to claim that there necessarily lies a wavering, crooked meaning beneath flowery words rich in imagery? that no one can think correctly and precisely unless he employs the most literal, common, plain expression? that to attempt to give cold, symbolic ideas something of the warmth and life of natural signs can't help but damage the truth?' (XIII, 149). Figural language, primarily metaphors and similes, is characterized here as a sort of secondary operation which converts arbitrary signs into natural signs and which thereby conveys not an unefficacious symbolic cognition but a vivid and vital intuitive apprehension of the signified ideas. The passage represents what is perhaps the central tenet of the *Laocoon* – the proposition that poetry in general is a variety of language use in which arbitrary signs acquire the status of natural signs and therefore induce in the reader an intuitive apprehension of the represented ideas. Poetry is language functioning as a natural sign. Only when it so functions does language conform to the fundamental rule of art and attain to the status of an aesthetic representation.

Oddly enough, Lessing's clearest statement of why aesthetic signification must not be arbitrary is contained in a fragment dealing with painting. While painting in general employs natural signs, there are nevertheless cases, according to Lessing, where these signs approach arbitrariness. This occurs, for instance, when the dimensions of things in reality appear in a painting as highly reduced:

> A human figure that is hand-sized or an inch in size is indeed the image of a human being; but it is still to some degree a symbolic image; I am more aware of the signs in looking at it than of the thing signified; I must first expand the reduced figure in my imagination to its true size, and this operation of my soul, however rapid and easy it might be, still prevents the intuition of the signified from occurring simultaneously with the intuition of the sign (B., 428).

When the sign is arbitrary, the resulting cognition is merely symbolic. Symbolic cognition is characterized by a foregrounding of the signifier which at the same time forces the signified to the periphery of awareness. The dissimilarity between sign and thought separates the two elements and the imagination must exert itself in order to reconstitute the signified idea. The natural sign, on the other hand, embodies qualities of the signified so that it is intuited immediately. No protracted process of decoding is required and the signified is grasped simultaneously with the signifier. The advantage of natural signs is that, for consciousness, the signifier blends into the signified and intuitive cognition is easily achieved. Arbitrary signs, however, provide primarily a symbolic cognition in which the awareness of the sign as sign prevents direct intuition of the signified. Natural signs guarantee imaginary presence-to-intuition of the represented object; arbitrary signs force themselves to the foreground of consciousness, resulting in a symbolic cognition in which the object is not only existentially, but also imaginatively absent.

Because intuitive cognition is the necessary precondition of aesthetic pleasure, both artist and poet must endeavor to keep their signs as natural as possible. The painter will therefore avoid the reduced figures that bring his work into proximity with arbitrary signs. For his part, the poet will seek to render the arbitrary signs of language, his given medium, in such a way that they approach the status of natural signs. According to Lessing, this is accomplished in two ways: the poet utilizes those aspects of language which have a natural signification and he employs whatever devices are at his disposal for transforming arbitrary signs into natural signs. ' . . . poetry not only actually possesses natural signs, but it also has means by which it can elevate its arbitrary signs to the dignity and force of natural signs' (B., 430).

I want to consider the second aspect first. The elevation of arbitrary signs to natural signs is accomplished, as the passage from the second *Anti-Goeze* already indicated, through the use of tropes:

It [poetry], however, also has a means of elevating its arbitrary signs to the status of natural signs, namely metaphor. For, since the forcefulness of natural signs consists in their similarity with things, poetry introduces – instead of this similarity, which it doesn't possess – another similarity which the signified object has with a second object, the mental representation of which can be renewed more easily and in a more lively fashion (B., 431).

This theory of metaphor is common in the eighteenth century and can be found, for instance, in the writings of Breitinger and Sulzer. The metaphorical substitution of one term for another introduces a relationship of similarity – and therefore a natural sign – where before, in the use of the proper term, there was only an arbitrary relation of enforced contiguity.

To be sure, the arbitrary relation between the metaphorical term and its signified remains, but it does not interfere with the achievement of intuitive cognition. The metaphorical term is chosen because it conveys such a mental representation or signified as can be easily and vividly recalled. From this vivid idea the imagination can then move without difficulty along the associative path of similarity to the idea actually signified by the metaphor. The natural signification occurs on the level of the signifieds, one serving as the sign of the other.

According to Lessing, the use of tropes is exclusively the prerogative of poetry and, as such, marks an advantage of poetry over the plastic arts: 'The fact that it is impossible for painting to make use of this device gives poetry a great advantage since it has a type of sign which possesses the forcefulness of natural signs except for the fact that these signs must themselves be expressed by arbitrary signs' (B., 432). Figural language combines the efficacy of natural signs with the advantages that otherwise accrue to poetry due to the arbitrariness of its linguistic signs, e.g., immateriality, discrete syntax, freedom of selection. The point is illustrated in Lessing's discussion of the "mist" which frequently envelops the characters in the *Iliad*: 'Wer sieht aber nicht, daß bey dem Dichter das Einhüllen in Nebel und Nacht weiter nichts, als eine poetische Redensart für unsichtbar machen, seyn soll.' ('But who is there who doesn't see that in the poem "being veiled with mist and night" is meant to be nothing more than a poetic figure of speech for "make invisible"' IX, 85). The idea "enveloped in mist" is a vivid, experimental idea which naturally signifies the related idea "made invisible" and therefore allows the reader to actualize the latter idea with an immediacy that its literal designation could not have provided. The reader thus attends to the event in the sensate intuition required for poetic effectiveness. As a poetic content unit, the idea "mist" remains undetermined. It is not actualized as a visual-imaginative idea and it does not impose itself on the reader, who can therefore attend directly to the idea of invisibility which it metaphorically conveys. In a painting, however, the "mist" appears as 'realisiret' ('realized'), and as such draws the viewer's attention to itself. The metaphorical meaning "invisible" is now totally absent from the content and is represented only symbolically: ' . . . denn diese Wolke ist hier eine wahre Hieroglyphe, ein blosses symbolisches Zeichen, das den befreyten Held nicht unsichtbar macht, sondern den Betrachtern zuruft: ihr müßt ihn euch als unsichtbar vorstellen.' (' . . . for this cloud is here a genuine hieroglyph, a mere symbolic sign, which does not make the liberated hero invisible but instead calls out to the viewers: you have to represent him to yourselves as invisible' IX, 86). The painting does not present the idea of invisibility, but instead points to it in a symbolic cognition in which the sign, as sign, occupies the foreground of awareness.

The poet conveys an intuitive cognition to the reader not only by transforming arbitrary signs into natural signs through the use of metaphor but also by employing those natural signs which language as such contains. In this regard Lessing mentions onomatopoetic words which he considers the earliest linguistic signs invented:

> It is certain that in the beginning the first languages arose out of onomatopoesis and that the first invented words possessed certain similarities with the things they expressed. Such words can still be found in all languages, to a greater or lesser degree, according to whether the language has distanced itself more or less from its origins. What is called musical expression in poetry stems from the clever use of these words. Various examples have often been given of this (B., 430).

Related to onomatopoetic words, and equally close to man's primal language, are the sounds used to express emotions:

> The small words with which we express our astonishment, our joy, our pain – in short, the interjections – are pretty much the same in all languages and deserve for this reason to be regarded as natural signs. A great wealth of such particles is thus a perfection in a language, to be sure... One need only look at the variety and wealth of interjections with which Sophocles' Philoctetes expresses his pain (B., 431).

In both cases the poet draws on the remains of an original mimetic language that are preserved at the present stage of linguistic development. In this way he mobilizes those resources for natural signification available to him and thereby achieves in his poem a vivid and efficacious representation.

These points, however, were commonplaces of the eighteenth century and Lessing attends to them only in passing in the published part of the *Laocoon*.[66] Far more central to his concerns is the following remark:

> In addition, poetry not only employs individual words, but rather these individual words in a certain sequence. Thus, even if the words are not natural signs, their sequence can still possess the forcefulness of a natural sign. Namely in cases when all the words follow upon one another exactly like the things they express. This is another poetic device which has yet to be adequately treated and which deserves an explication of its own through examples (B., 431).

In this passage we find the systematic justification for the famous thesis of the *Laocoon*'s sixteenth chapter: the restriction of poetry to successive contents insures the naturalness of poetic signification. While the individual signs of language may be arbitrary, the poet deploys these signs in such a way that their arrangement yields a global iconic sign – a natural sign – of the global content substance of the poem, the imitated action. Action is the proper content of poetry because action can be embodied in the succession of poetic signs. Thus, precisely at that point in the *Laocoon* (the sixteenth chapter) where Lessing seems most forcefully to separate painting and poetry, he in fact is bringing the two art forms into the closest possible proximity. The rule of *ut pictura poesis* is not abandoned but rather is relocated on a different level of generality. Poetry does not approach painting by copying particular works but by adopting the principle of signification of all successful paintings. By using the arbitrary signs of language in such a way that their arrangement yields a global iconic sign, poetry attains to the 'forcefulness of a natural sign' and thereby renders its content in the illusionary presence-to-intuition that is the idea of painting.

This interpretation can be confirmed by looking at the formulations in the sixteenth chapter:

> Ich schliesse so. Wenn es wahr ist, daß die Mahlerey zu ihren Nachahmungen ganz andere Mittel, oder Zeichen gebrauchet, als die Poesie; jene nehmlich Figuren und Farben in dem Raume, diese aber artikulirte Töne in der Zeit; wenn unstreitig die Zeichen ein bequemes Verhältniß zu dem Bezeichneten haben müssen: So können neben einander geordnete Zeichen, auch nur Gegenstände, die neben einander, oder deren Theile neben einander existiren, auf einander folgende Zeichen aber, auch nur Gegenstände ausdrücken, die auf einander, oder deren Theile auf einander folgen.

> I deduce as follows. If it is true that painting employs in its imitations entirely different means, or signs, than poetry; namely, figures and colors in space for the former, articulate tones in time for the latter; if it is indubitable that the signs must have a fitting relationship to the signified: then signs which are ordered next to one another can only express objects which exist next to one another, or the parts of which exist next to one another, and signs which follow one another in sequence can only express objects which follow upon one another, or the parts of which follow upon one another (IX, 94).

This is the first of four syllogisms developed in the chapter, The conclusion serves as the major premise of the second, the conclusion of the second as the major premise of the third, and so forth. A single deductive series allows for the derivation of the objects proper to each art, the rule of the pregnant moment and the rule of the optimally sensate quality. If we look closely at the passage, however, it proves to contain not only one syllogism but two – one each for poetry and the plastic arts. Likewise, the entire deductive argument of the chapter consists not of four syllogisms but of eight, two sets of four, one applicable to each art form. Lessing deduces the fundamental principles of the two arts in two parallel sets of four syllogisms. The quoted passage, then, can be rewritten in two columns:

| *Painting* | *Poetry* |
|---|---|
| 1. Painting employs as signs figures and colors in space. | 1. Poetry employs as signs articulate tones in time. |

| | |
|---|---|
| 2. The signs must have a fitting relationship to the signified. | 2. The signs must have a fitting relationship to the signified. |
| 3. Therefore, painting can only express objects that exist next to one another, or the parts of which exist next to one another. | 3. Therefore, poetry can only express objects that follow upon one another, or the parts of which follow upon one another. |

This representation of Lessing's argument foregrounds the relationship between identity and difference that played such a prominent role in the opening paragraph of the 'Preface.' The emotive metaphor of the amateur is here brought to its logical truth. The major premises name the difference between poetry and painting as the difference in the constitution of their signs. The minor premise, the same for both syllogisms, names the identity of the two arts. Both employ the same principles of signification; both use signs which stand in a relation of similarity to their signified contents. The amateur's metaphor located the unity of the arts in their common effect: both painting and poetry make existentially absent objects present-to-mind. The syllogisms of the sixteenth chapter, however, *trace this effect to its semiotic condition of possibility*. Because both poetry and painting are natural signs, both can accomplish the effective mimesis that summons forth the represented object in an illusionary presence.

What we see here is the core of Lessing's aesthetic theory. The aesthetic is a general form of representation, sensate intuition, which is realized in different semiotic media. Phrased in another way, the different types of sign are used aesthetically when they yield the sensate intuition or illusionary presentation that characterizes the aesthetic in general. This is the universal pragmatic criterion of aesthetic efficacy familiar to us from Enlightenment aesthetic theory. Lessing pursues the point further than this, however. He attempts to enunciate a semiotic principle which could guarantee the achievement of the specifically aesthetic form of representation, and here he arrives at conclusions which, while anticipated by both Meier and

Mendelssohn, had not before been formulated with such clarity or systematic rigor. According to Lessing, the principle common to all forms of aesthetic signification is the motivation of signs, the reduction of arbitrariness and therewith the achievement of an optimal degree of naturalness (similarity) in the relation between expression and content.[67] This naturalness in signification – whether accomplished through metaphor, onomatopoesis, the alignment of the sign sequence with the thought sequence, or through the material-visual signs of painting – guarantees an unhindered imaginative glide from perception of the sign to imaginative constitution of the aesthetic object so that 'intuition of the signified' can occur 'simultaneously with the intuition of the signifier.'[68]

The proposition that poetry attains to the status of a natural sign by imitating action, and thereby coordinating its successive signs with a content unfolding in time, lies at the theoretical center of the *Laocoon*. Poetry is shown to be not merely discourse – which, indeed, is capable of representing bodies – but discourse that functions as a natural sign. To be sure, this naturalness is not exactly the same as the naturalness of the material signs of painting. In painting, the *figurae* and sub-signs are themselves natural signs, whereas in poetry the sub-signs (individual words and phrases) stand in an arbitrary relation to their signifieds. This arbitrariness is the source of the greater imaginative freedom that distinguishes poetry from painting. It allows the poet, for instance, to combine content units which in painting would be mutually exclusive (for example, "robe" and "body"), to select only those aspects of his content material which are aesthetically propitious, to introduce invisible beings and events and therewith to afford the reader a more expansive imaginative experience. As verbal discourse, that is, as communication via arbitrary signs, poetry has eliminated the restricting effects of worldliness (e.g., dense syntax, materiality, restriction to perceptual contents, full determinateness of content units, existential presence) characteristic of the plastic arts. The notion of poetry as a natural sign which appears in the sixteenth chapter does not elide these important distinctions between the two arts. Rather, what Lessing suggests is the possibility of a *formal naturalness* in signification. Painting signifies naturally both in terms of form (spatial arrangement) and material (it employs visual material things as expression material). The naturalness of poetic signification, however, is only formal. It is the temporal arrangement of the signs which is similar to the content and therefore it is only the form of perception which the poem simulates, not the actual content of the perception. The content of a poem remains ideal – a series of linguistic meanings – and even when it is concretized as a perceptual-imaginative experience, as in the Homeric style, the resulting image is a product of the reader's imaginative activity and not of the perceptual experience of the expression substance. (This is no longer true of the 'musical painting' Lessing mentions in Chapter thirteen.) One could say that poetry stands to the plastic arts in general as drawing stands to oil painting. Poetry signifies naturally, but only in terms of formal arrangement. The poem is, to borrow a term from Peirce, a diagrammatic icon.[69]

With the proposition that poetry is a formal natural sign Lessing manages to reconcile the two basic assumptions of his aesthetic theory, that poetry must provide an intuitive cognition in order to qualify as aesthetic and that poetry employs signs that are substantially different from those of painting. As a natural sign, poetry avoids the aesthetically deleterious effects of symbolic cognition and recovers for language the intuitive immediacy that is characteristic of perception. At the same time, it avoids the restrictions which material natural signs impose upon the imagination. The most important feature of the *Laocoon*, however, is that it does not remain on this level of generality but proceeds to the discussion of particular works and genres. It is essential to see how Lessing applies the fundamental principle of his aesthetic semiotics to the actual analysis and evaluation of individual poems. As is well known, Lessing uses the insights gained in the course of his inquiry to attack the practice of descriptive poetry such as that of Albrecht von Haller (1708–77) and therewith to criticize the poetic theory of Haller's most important advocate, Johann Jacob Breitinger. The following section elucidates the issues involved in this discussion.

### Lessing and Breitinger. Description and narration

What astonishes one upon reading Breitinger's *Critische Dichtkunst* (*Critical Poetics*, 1740) is its close proximity in so many respects to Lessing's *Laocoon*. Like Lessing, Breitinger ascribes to both poet and painter the same intention: ' . . . to represent absent things to the human being as present and to offer them up, as it were, to be felt and sensed.'[70] Thus Breitinger, like Lessing, sees the unity of the arts as the 'equivalence in the effect of the two arts' (I, 29). This effect, which emerges from the presence of the aesthetic object to the imagination, is described in terms perfectly consonant with Lessing's views – 'delight of the fantasy' and 'the awakening of that pleasure which the human heart immediately senses in the movement and conflict of the affects' (II, 403). Finally, Breitinger too is attentive to the difference between the simultaneous representations of painting and the successive representations of poetry. Regarding this point, a close interpretation of the *Critical Poetics*, especially the first and fifth chapters, would be useful. Here I must restrict myself to a brief review of the essentials.

The highest perfection of painting, according to Breitinger, is its ability to present objects with the same efficacy 'as the original would have if it were present' (I, 22). The reception of a painting coincides with the perceptual apprehension of the object. But this perfection of painting is, at the same time, a severe limitation, for it entails the consequence that painting, as a mode of representation, is characterized by the same inadequacies as perception. This is one of Breitinger's central themes, the very starting point of his poetic theory: perception is a highly inadequate means of representing the world. In part, the deficiencies of perception stem from the automatization of our representations, what Breitinger terms 'habit,' which 'binds the senses, robs us of all feeling, and sinks us into an inattentive stupor' (I, 107–8). Breitinger's theory contains implicitly a notion of the deautomatization and renewal of perception. But the problematic nature of perception reaches deeper than this and is ultimately grounded in the structure of perception itself. 'Both nature and the skillfully imitating painter display their works as simultaneities, complete and fully assembled, but they must leave it to the viewer what sort of impression these works will have on his mind' (I, 27–8). The simultaneous presentation of all the features of the object, that is, the form of perceptual apprehension, requires extreme attentiveness on the part of the viewer if those features are to have their proper effect. This condition, though, is rarely met. Presented with so many aspects at once, the viewer is set into 'distraction' (I, 22). He tends 'to wander about leisurely with a superficial and uncertain mind's eye or to get confused in the mixture of the manifold parts' (I, 22–3). Due to the confusion, distraction and lack of guidance that characterizes the simultaneous presentation of perceptual objects, the viewer does not attain to an adequate and differentiated idea of what he has seen. 'Ask someone who has seen a broad vista either in nature or in the artistic representation of a painting what sort of idea the same has left behind in his mind and how superficial, obscure and uncertain will his description turn out' (I, 22).

The advantage of poetry is that it replaces the confusing, distracting and overwhelming simultaneity of features in perception with the successive unfolding of these features as represented in the successive signs of the poem. Where the painting leaves the viewer total freedom to attend to the objects as he pleases and thereby runs the risk of communicating only an obscure and undifferentiated idea of the object, poetry controls the reception of the individual features by presenting them one at a time to the reader, in the order and with the emphasis that is proper to them.

For, insofar as the artistic painter gradually achieves his painting with every word, as if with a new stroke of the brush, in the fantasy of the reader, constantly adding a new idea to the others, he allows the reader no freedom whatsoever to wander about leisurely with a superficial and uncertain mind's eye or to get confused in the mixture of the manifold parts; rather, he ties the reader's attention to the peculiar characteristics of the object, the artful organization of which he points out according to its proper order, and he occasionally adds brief, but useful lessons, through which not a little light and clarity must arise in the representation; and in this way he always remains the master who can intensify or moderate the impression which every trait in his depiction is meant to cause in accordance with his main intention (I, 22–3).

The poem elicits in the reader a protracted attitude of attentiveness in which his focus moves successively from one feature to the next, following the poet's certain guide. What results is not a vague impression, but a heightened awareness of the individual features, their peculiar characteristics, and their relative importance. The movement from painting to poetry, as described by Breitinger, corresponds to the transition from clear to distinct cognition in Wolff. For Wolff, as I argued in the first chapter, distinct cognition emerges when the individual features that are con-fused in clear cognition are unfolded in a process of successive attentiveness (reflection). In this process the object is prepared for an intellectual as opposed to perceptual comprehension. What perception knows only as a coalescence of indistinguishable features, the intellect grasps as a set of explicitly distinguished aspects. From this perspective, the central point of Breitinger's comparison of the arts becomes apparent. The successive attentiveness of the reader, which the successivity of the poem's signs ensures, leads to an awareness of each of the manifold parts of the object, a distinct awareness of the whole: 'Although the ideas which the painter, with colors and through the eye, awakens in the mind are much more sensate and more strongly felt – especially since they are more crude, and for that reason more common – the other ideas [i.e., those communicated by poetry] are much more refined, and for that reason more distinct as well, which indicates a higher degree of perfection' (I, 20–1).

Breitinger's concept of poetry as descriptive poetry, then, does not attempt to equate poem and painting. Rather, Breitinger attempts to prove the superiority of poetry over painting, a superiority he derives from the successivity of poetic representation as opposed to the simultaneity of direct perception. Poetry masters the con-fusion of things in perception by distributing the individual features across a succession of signs, each of which communicates a discrete quality of the object. Thus, poetry conveys a distinct idea of the object and presents the object to the understanding: '...it is up to the intellect and not the senses to understand, untangle, and combine with one another the ideas which words represent' (I, 20).

One final point must be touched upon. The movement from perception to linguistic representation distinguishes painting from poetry and establishes the superiority of the latter. In addition to this distinction, Breitinger also attempts to define the difference between poetry and prose, and he locates this difference in the innovativeness, force and color of poetic expression: 'This novelty of emotional colors moves the spirit much more strictly than does common language due to the fact that the poetic painter can, through figural presentation, through witty figures, splendid products of fantasy, and pleasant sounding words and periods, enlarge things as he pleases, and therefore make them much more noble, or terrible, or beautiful than they are when represented with common expressions' (II, 404–5). It is a double distinction which defines poetry: on the one hand its difference from painting that stems from its linguistic nature; on the other hand, its difference from ordinary language that stems from its forcefulness and freedom of expression. As regards the former point, Breitinger reveals himself to be a follower of Wolff insofar as he emphasizes the link between language and distinct cognition. But as regards the latter aspect, Breitinger continues to think within the confines of the performance theory-type. What distinguishes poetry is the use of the ornaments and tactics of *elocutio*, the deployment of verbal artistry in order to heighten or intensify the poetic message. The *Critical Poetics* is characterized by an overlapping of theoretical paradigms: it allows us to observe the first movements toward the establishment of representational theory. Be that as it may, having made *both* of his points regarding poetic language, Breitinger quotes those lines from Haller's 'Alpen' ('The Alps') which Lessing cites in the *Laocoon* (IX, 102–3). Thereupon follows the assertion which Lessing likewise, though distortedly, quotes: 'One need only compare this [i.e., Haller's poetic description] with the most precise historical description by a botanist or the most accurate drawing of a painter and one must concede that, in comparison to this poetic description, they are pale and dull' (II, 407). The superiority of the poetic description over a scientific description is Breitinger's central concern here and the comparison with a painting is merely mentioned as a well-established truth. It is the latter comparison, however, that Lessing seizes upon. In examining Lessing's argument, we will do well to keep in mind the basis of Breitinger's remark: for Breitinger, Haller's description is superior to a painting precisely because language is an altogether different mode of representation than perception, because language guides the attention successively from feature to feature and affords, at the end of this process, a distinct idea of the object.

Lessing's entire disagreement with Breitinger and all the force of his criticism of Haller's verse is contained in the simple question he raises after quoting the lines from the 'Alpen': 'Ich frage ihn nur, wie steht es um den Begriff des Ganzen?' ('I would merely ask him: what about the idea of the whole?' (IX, 103). In this question is buried the changing perspective on poetic language that develops across the work of Baumgarten, Meier and Mendelssohn and finds its most rigorous formulation in Lessing's *Laocoon*. What makes Lessing's question possible is the theory of aesthetic representation as a global and intuitive representation. Breitinger's theory of poetic language, at least as regards the comparison of painting and poetry, corresponds to Wolff's notion of language as the vehicle in and through which our confused perceptual representations are rendered progressively distinct. Lessing's 'what about the idea of the whole?' presupposes that the priority of distinctness has been eliminated, that the global representation of the object as an instantaneous totalization of all the features in their interconnection has replaced distinctness as an aesthetic ideal.

Lessing's argument – and the thrust of his question – can be approached most easily from the characterization of perception at the beginning of Chapter seventeen:

Wie gelangen wir zu der deutlichen Vorstellung eines Dinges im Raume? Erst betrachten wir die Theile desselben einzeln, hierauf die Verbindung dieser Theile, und endlich das Ganze. Unsere Sinne verrichten diese verschiedene Operationen mit einer so erstaunlichen Schnelligkeit, daß sie uns nur eine einzige zu seyn bedünken, und diese Schnelligkeit ist unumgänglich nothwendig, wann wir einen Begriff von dem Ganzen, welcher nichts mehr als das Resultat von den Begriffen der Theile und ihrer Verbindung ist, bekommen sollen.

How do we arrive at a distinct representation of an object in space? First we contemplate the parts individually, then the connection of the parts, and finally the whole. Our senses accomplish these different operations with such astonishing speed that they seem to us a single operation, and this speed is absolutely necessary if we are to acquire an idea of the whole, which is nothing more than the result of the ideas of the parts and their connections (IX, 101–2).

Note the distance between this account of perception – which quotes, by the way, from Mendelssohn's remarks on the first draft of the *Laocoon*[71] – and Breitinger's discussion of the same subject. Where Breitinger is concerned with the possibility of gaining an explicit awareness of the parts, Lessing's entire interest is directed at the wholeness of the representation. (One must not be misled by the term 'deutlich' in the passage.

It has nothing to do with 'distinct' in the strict philosophical sense.) In perception we move from parts to the whole, but this operation is accomplished by the senses and takes place beneath the threshhold of awareness. Consciousness seizes only the result of this rapid operation, the totalized image of the object as a unity of manifold parts. For consciousness, then, perception presents the idea of the whole in a single instant. To the one instant of perception corresponds the oneness of the object; the manifold parts coexist within that instant and, in their peculiar interconnection, constitute the object as a whole. Perception *comprehends*: in the present instance of its occurrence, it *makes present* to consciousness the whole of its object.

From this account of perception as the presence of the whole within the single present instant, Lessing's argument against descriptive poetry becomes intelligible:

...ich spreche nicht der Rede überhaupt das Vermögen ab, ein körperliches Ganze nach seinen Theilen zu schildern; sie kann es, weil ihre Zeichen, ob sie schon auf einander folgen, dennoch willkührliche Zeichen sind: sondern ich spreche es der Rede als dem Mittel der Poesie ab, weil dergleichen wörtlichen Schilderungen der Körper das Täuschende gebricht, worauf die Poesie vornehmlich gehet; und dieses Täuschende, sage ich, muss ihnen darum gebrechen, weil das Coexistirende des Körpers mit dem Consecutiven der Rede dabei in Collision kommt, und indem jenes in dieses aufgelöset wird, uns die Zergliederung des Ganzen in seine Theile zwar erleichtert, aber die endliche Wiederzusammensetzung dieser Theile in das Ganze ungemein schwer, und nicht selten unmöglich gemacht wird.

... I do not deny speech in general the capacity of depicting a corporeal whole according to its parts; speech can accomplish this because the signs, although they follow one another in sequence, are nevertheless arbitrary signs: rather, I deny this capacity to speech as the medium of poetry because such verbal depictions of bodies lack the element of illusion which is the primary aim of poetry; and this element of illusion, I claim, must be lacking in them because the coexisting nature of the body collides with the consecutive nature of speech; and, insofar as the former is dissolved into the latter, the dismemberment of the whole into its parts is indeed made easy for us but the final recombination of these parts into the whole again is made uncommonly difficult, indeed often impossible (IX, 104).

A description is an enumeration of parts. The individual features, which inhere in the object as it manifests itself to perception, are strung out along a chain of disjoint signs. This process may illuminate individual features, making us explicitly aware of them as we weren't when perceiving the object. In the movement from perception to description we have a case of the movement from the globality and simultaneity of clear cognition to the disjointness and successivity of distinct cognition. This is precisely the point that Breitinger had emphasized and from which he derived the superiority of poetry over painting. Lessing makes exactly the same observation as Breitinger, but he interprets it in an entirely different way. Through the activity of description, 'the coexisting nature' of the body given to perception is dissolved ('aufgelöst') in successivity. Coexistence, however, is the form in which the wholeness of the object shows itself: a corporeal whole is grasped as a whole only insofar as the parts or features coexist within a single moment and manifest themselves as a spatial unity of parts. The successivity of the description destroys the unity of the object.

As a result of this process, the reader never has the whole, never grasps the unity of the object, but instead he has to do only with individual parts. The presentation of each part in the successive phases of the description is accompanied by the erasure of the other parts. Each present moment of the reader's experience corresponds only to a part; the whole never emerges. Therefore, a symbolic cognition is all that is attained. The whole object is referred to, but it is not made present. At no point does the intelligibility of the object, as it is perceived, replace the intelligibility of words. At no point does the reader have the sense of directly comprehending the object in its integrity.

For Lessing, then, the notion of descriptive poetry is contradictory. The idea of description entails reference to an object. But it is the nature of description to dissolve the simultaneity and unity of the object in the successivity of its signs. The wholeness of the object no longer shows itself in the representation and the only integrating factor remaining is our linguistic understanding, our merely symbolic cognition of what is being described. To fulfill the idea of poetry, however, descriptive poetry should aim for illusion, the imaginary presence of the object to intuition. But illusion is only attained when the object's wholeness is grasped. For illusion to take place, there must be a single moment in which the unity of the object is comprehended. That is, the form of perception, the full presence of the object within the single present moment, must be simulated. As description, descriptive poetry makes impossible the very thing that, as poetry, it ought to achieve. For this reason it matters not at all to Lessing that Haller's description differs from the 'description of a botanist' by virtue of the local poetic features it contains. As description, it dissolves the unity of the object and can therefore provide no adequate answer to the question: 'what about the idea of the whole?'

It is important to emphasize this point, because much of what Lessing has to say regarding Homer follows from it. Description makes comprehension of the whole impossible. Descriptions are – from an aesthetic point of view – *meaningless*, in the sense that the successivity of the signs suspends the unity and integrity of the object and leaves us merely with parts. No instant is privileged, provides access to the whole. We would have to have the object itself – which language has made absent – in front of us, if we were to comprehend the parts in their interconnection. 'Sie [Haller's verses] mögen sich, wenn man die Blume selbst in der Hand hat, sehr schön dagegen recitiren lassen; nur vor sich allein sagen sie wenig oder nichts.' ('They [Haller's verses] might be very lovely to recite if one has the flower itself in hand; by themselves, however, they say little or nothing' IX, 104).

Lessing's analysis, which shows that description is antithetical to the nature of poetry, is balanced by his claim that narrative is a type of language use that fulfills the aesthetic function. This is how I interpret his discussion of Homer's 'Kunstgriff,' the ' . . .einzeln Gegenstand in eine Folge von Augenblicken zu setzen, in deren jedem er anders erscheinet, und in deren letztem ihn der Mahler erwarten muß, um uns entstanden zu zeigen, was wir bey dem Dichter entstehen sehn.' ('device of placing the individual object into a sequence of moments in each of which it appears different and in the last of which the painter is waiting in order to present to us as already existing what we have seen coming into existence in the poem' IX, 96). The poet does not describe an object, but narrates an action in which that object is involved. On the basis of what has been argued up to this point, we can grasp what Lessing means here and understand why he could make this claim.

Narrative alleviates the problem of dissolution that confronts us in description. To be sure, in narrative too we have a succession of signs, and, one might suppose, a succession of parts. This is true to a degree, but requires some important qualifications. The object of narrative is action, but the parts of an action are not parts in the same sense as the parts of an object are. Rather, as regards action, each part is itself a whole. The parts of an object, one could say, are like the petals that combine to form a flower. Take them apart and distribute them across a table: the flower will be destroyed. The parts of an action, though, correspond themselves to individual flowers. The action is a bouquet.

In other terms, the individual moments of the succession have a different function in narrative and in description. In description, each corresponds to a fragment, to a part that is only a part and, as such, is aesthetically (i.e., intuitively) unintelligible. In narrative, the present moments correspond to wholes which are intelligible as such and which combine additively to form a whole that is a unity of many wholes. This point can be made clear by recalling what has been said about the relation of painting and poetry. Painting presents a whole object. Poetry corresponds to single paintings only in terms of individual contents; a poem as a whole is like 'eine ganze Gallerie von Gemählden' ('a whole gallery of paintings,' IX, 89). A description, however, does not present us a series of paintings, but rather goes into and takes apart a single one.

*Narrative fulfills the aesthetic function because it maintains the structure of perception, the totalizing regard within the present instant.* It is not necessary that we actually see the object. In fact, as so many other arguments in the *Laocoon* show, it is often preferable that our 'seeing' not be actualized as a visual-imaginative experience. The 'seeing' afforded by poetry is of an ideal sort: rather than replicating visual perception in every way, it merely replicates the structure of perception – the equivalence between the one present instant and the oneness of the object. As narrative, poetry attains to the idea of painting.

To be thoroughly poetic, the text should be purely narrational. This entails the positive requirement that, as far as is possible, each new moment in the textual sequence must deliver a new contentual whole, a new phase of the action, to the reader. Negatively interpreted, the statement proscribes the accumulation of predicates, which, while presenting no new contentual unity, begin to dissolve the object they characterize into a series of mere parts. In Lessing's formulation: 'Likewise, poetry, in its successive imitations, can only make use of one property of bodies and it must therefore select that one which excites the most sensate image of the body from the perspective useful to the poem.' The specification that the selected quality (predicate) evoke the most sensate image is a rule of content selection ensuring optimal concretization. The stipulation that there only be a single predicate, however, guarantees that the instants of the textual sequence will not provide mere parts, but ever new wholes.

No poet, of course, follows this rule to the letter, not even Homer. There are places, Lessing admits, where Homer employs three, sometimes even four, epithets for a single object (IX, 109). Such an accumulation of modifying adjectives would seem to violate the rule of single predicates and therefore bring the text close to description. Lessing argues, however that, although such passages do not conform literally to the rule, they nevertheless have the same effect as the rule wa designed to guarantee: '. . .and so here too in the poem the several traits for the different parts and properties in space follow upon one another in such compressed brevity that we believe we hear them all at once' (IX, 109–10). Though the object is indeed distributed across several signs and is therefore represented sequentially, this sequence is so rapid that (like the operations of the senses in perception) it appears to conscious ness as a single moment. The symmetry between the one instant and the oneness of the object is maintained. Lessing then proceeds to show how the syntax of Homer's language specifically the ordering of nouns and modifying adjectives allows Homer to ignore the letter of the rule while stil achieving poetic effect: 'It [Homeric Greek] not only affords him optimal freedom in the accumulation and combination of adjectives, but it also has a most felicitous order for these accumulated adjectives such that the disadvantageous suspen sion of their relationship is eliminated' (IX, 110). The suspension of the relation of the parts so that only parts remain – precisely this is what occurs through description Greek word order mitigates this aesthetically deleterious effect by presenting us at once with the whole object: 'The Greek immediately combines the subject with the first predicate and then has the other predicates follow; he says: "round wheels strong and eight-spoked." Thus we know immediately what he is talking about and we first become acquainted with the thing and then with its accidental properties, according to the natural order of thought' (IX, 110). The word order / adjective, noun, adjective, adjective/ provides us with an initia and instantaneous comprehension of the whole, and thereby resists the fragmentation characteristic of description. A note omitted from the published version of the *Laocoon* approaches the same problem from a different angle: 'Indeed, when

Homer depicts a beautiful or sublime object by describing its individual, coexisting parts, he makes use of an artistic device worthy of note; that is to say, he immediately adds a simile in which we view the dismembered object reassembled again and which erases the distinct representation we have achieved and gives the object nothing more than a sensate clarity' (B., 357). Here Lessing goes further than usual in admitting descriptive passages to poetry, but he does so only under the stipulation that the distinctness (here used in its philosophical sense) of the description be ultimately eliminated and replaced by a moment in which the whole object appears. After the disintegrating work of the description is completed, the simile reintegrates the parts and presents us with a totalizing comprehension of the object.

Lessing's distinction between bodies and actions as the objects of description and narrative, respectively, and his assertion that narrative alone qualifies as poetry (that is, fulfills the aesthetic function), are not based on a facile opposition of static and dynamic representations. Rather, it is a question here of the function served in each type of discourse by the present moment of textual reception. In narrative alone does the present moment correspond to a wholeness of content. Thus, narrative attains to illusion by duplicating the structure of perception: within the individual instant of textual reception the reader attends to a comprehensible whole, just as in actual perception the whole object is viewed at once. The following moments in the textual sequence do not take that whole apart, but show it in a new phase of the action or present another object as a unity. At each point in the textual sequence the instantaneous comprehension of the object as a totality is maintained, even though the object is not necessarily concretized as something actually seen. It is not perception as such that poetry attempts to duplicate, but the structure of perception or, as I phrased it earlier, the idea of painting.

Narrative approaches the status of a natural sign. This, the central claim of the *Laocoon*, can now be fully understood.

It is not merely the similarity between textual sequence and action sequence that interests Lessing, but the structural correspondence between the sequential comprehension of contentual wholes in narrative and the sequential perception of wholes when we actually witness an action. This correspondence effects in the reader the sense that he is actually seeing the narrated action, that he is not reading signs but that he is in the actual presence of the unfolding event. The poet ' . . . will die Ideen, die er in uns erwecket, so lebhaft machen, daß wir in der Geschwindigkeit die wahren sinnlichen Eindrücke ihrer Gegenstände zu empfinden glauben, und in diesem Augenblicke der Täuschung, uns der Mittel, die er dazu anwendet, seiner Worte bewußt zu seyn aufhoren.' (' . . . wants to make the ideas he excites in us so lively that we believe, in this rapidity, that we are feeling the genuine sensate impressions of the objects of those ideas, and that we cease, in this moment of illusion, being conscious of the means he employs to this end, namely his words' IX, 101). The *Sinnlichkeit* (sensateness) or *Lebhaftigkeit* (liveliness) of the ideas is in part brought about through content selection, as exemplified by the Homeric style which stimulates a visual-imaginative concretization. This is, however, a secondary issue. The more fundamental point is that all genuine poetry, regardless of style, is sensate in the sense that the reader forgets he is attending to words and therefore feels himself in the presence of the things designated.

Is it possible to account for those features of a text which led Lessing to his distinction between description and narrative in terms of the logic of part and whole? I think that it is, but in order to do so it is necessary to change our perspective somewhat. Rather than speak of description and narrative globally, we can approach the matter by distinguishing between descriptive and narrative content units. The former belong to that class of minimal units which Roland Barthes calls 'indices.'[72] The latter are what he terms 'functions.' The essential aspect of Barthes' distinction, at least for my purposes here, is that indices and functions each appeal to a different type of comprehension.[73] Indices are integrative; that is, they are understood as referring to a meaning located at a higher level of generality and including the indices. For instance, a description is understood when the several indices that constitute it are related to a more inclusive semantic unit. Functions, however, are distributive; they refer to another unit of the same level. "Opening the door" may be completed by "closing the door," "departing" by "returning." The functions constitute the narrative syntagm and form the armature of the narrated action. If we consider reading as a process of rewriting a given text, then the basis for Lessing's distinction becomes clear. The indices will be represented as a set of single terms, mainly nouns and adjectives, subsumed beneath a super-term. Within this lexical group there will be no necessary order. The functions, however, will be rewritten as a definitely ordered sequence. Furthermore, the functions will appear in the reader's text as propositions, e.g., "x opens the door." In other words, the decoding of functions leaves us with a set of fairly comprehensible meanings embodied in whole propositions. In themselves, functions make syntactic-semantic sense. The indices, however, are single lexical units, or, at most, noun phrases that are not integrated within the higher unity of a sentence. Here, I think, we can see how Lessing arrived at his analysis. His contention that the present instant of a description offers only a part derives from the way indices are understood (by relating them to a more inclusive term) and the way they are represented in the reader's text (as noun phrases or even as single adjectives). Likewise, Lessing's claim that the individual moments of a narrative provide us with wholes stems from the fact that individual functions within a narrative sequence tend to possess the autonomy of a sentence when decoded by the reader and that the overall structure of the sequence possesses a forseeable logic.

To be sure, this analysis employs an entirely different vocabulary than Lessing's, which is infused with referential notions. Lessing speaks of parts and wholes as aspects of real or imaginary objects. According to him, when we read the lines,

> He sat upright and put on his tunic, beautiful, fresh-woven and threw the great mantle over it. Underneath his shining feet he bound the fair sandals and across his shoulders slung the sword with the nails of silver, and took up the sceptre of his fathers, immortal forever.[74]

we experience the event as if it were taking place before us. 'Wir sehen die Kleider, indem der Dichter die Handlung des Bekleidens mahlet...' ('We see the clothes while the poet paints the act of dressing...' IX, 97). For Lessing, reading is emphatically not a matter of decoding or rewriting, but of seeing. This 'seeing,' I believe, is not to be taken literally, at least not in every case. Rather, it designates the ideal vision, the correspondence between the single instant of reading and the comprehension of a contentual whole, which Lessing felt to be necessary if poetry is to bring its objects to an illusionary presentation. My discussion was designed to show how it was possible that Lessing could so evaluate these verses. In fact, Homer's text is replete with functions – "he sat upright," "he put on his tunic," "he threw over the mantle," "he bound his sandals," "he slung the sword across his shoulders," "he took up the sceptre." These functions do not occupy each individual moment of the text, but it can nevertheless be roughly said that our decoding of the text moves primarily from function to function. Furthermore, this horizontal movement is so compelling that we hardly notice the vertical movement which accompanies it, the grouping of the indices "beautiful," "great," "fair," "nails of silver," "of his fathers," "immortal forever," beneath the global signified "ancient royalty." It is this forward movement from function to function that allows the action to unfold, in Lessing's phrase, 'mit dem Flusse der Rede' ('with the flow of speech,' IX, 100), and which brings about the illusion of a successive seeing that Lessing held to be the mark of genuine poetry.

Homer's text, and the essentially syntagmatic decoding of functions which it elicits, can be fruitfully contrasted with a passage from Haller's 'Alpen' quoted by Lessing in the seventeenth chapter:

> Dort ragt das hohe Haupt vom edeln Enziane
> Weit übern niedern Chor der Pöbelkräuter hin,
> Ein ganzes Blumenvolk dient unter seiner Fahne,
> Sein blauer Bruder selbst bückt sich, und ehret ihn.
> Der Blumen helles Gold, in Strahlen umgebogen,
> Thürmt sich am Stengel auf, und krönt sein grau Gewand,
> Der Blätter glattes Weiss, mit tiefem Grün durchzogen,
> Strahlt von dem bunten Blitz von feuchtem Diamant.
> Gerechtestes Gesetz! daß Kraft sich Zier vermähle;
> In einem schönen Leib wohnt eine schönre Seele.

> There the high head of the noble gentian rises
> Far above the lowly chorus of common plants,
> A whole population of flowers serves beneath his banner,
> Even his blue brother bows down, and honors him.
> The bright gold of the flowers, refracted into rays,
> Towers up the stalk and crowns his grey mantle,
> The smooth whiteness of the leaves, streaked with a deep green,
> Glistens with the bright lightening of a moist diamond.
> Law most just! that force be married with grace;
> In a fair body there dwells a soul fairer still (IX, 102).

Here we see the classical form of a description: deictic ('There' – the following strophe begins with 'Here') plus proper name or other identifier ('gentian') plus description itself as an accumulation of predicates. Not only does the passage fail to meet the criterion of simulating a perceptual experience, but such a criterion is entirely foreign to its specific textual practice. The entire passage culminates in and serves to demonstrate the correspondence between inside and outside posited in the final line. This is accomplished by equating the terms for external features (spatial position, color, number, etc.) with terms designating spiritual-political values. The entire activity of the reader consists in collecting the indices beneath the proper connotative value, a decoding process which results in the constitution of two paradigms, a paradigm of spiritual-political 'nobility' ("one," "high," "noble," "banner," "crowns," "gold," "diamond," etc.) and a paradigm of spiritual-political "commonness" ("many," "lowly," "population," "common,") while verbs like 'bow down' and 'honor' indicate the relation between the two paradigms. The text does not describe (in the sense of relating purely empirical observations) but interprets. It translates the text of nature (outside) into another text organizing spiritual-political hierarchies (inside) and thereby asserts the identity between the two. The relationship between king and people is shown to be natural, the relations between natural things to be spiritual. The two texts are interwoven so that practically each word receives a double reading. 'Pöbelkräuter,' for instance, is read in the natural text as 'Kräuter' ('plants') in the spiritual text as 'Pöbel' ('common folk') while 'gold' designates a color in the natural text and "wealth" (and therefore "royalty") in the spiritual text. 'Banner' is a metaphor for the outside meaning "something colorful on high" and a metonym for the inside meaning "king" or "ruler."

Breitinger was entirely correct when he asserted that the sequentiality of the poetic signs allows the poet to bring 'useful lessons' into the representation of the object and to direct the reader's attention to the significance and order of the parts. For Breitinger, the text of nature is not truly understood when it is perceived, but is only brought to its truth when the reader grasps its identity with the spiritual-political text. Breitinger could assert the superiority of the poem over a painting because for him seeing was in its truth a kind of reading. The poet interprets the text of nature for the reader and thereby allows the reader to read and see the truth of that text.

For Lessing, this identity of reading and seeing has fallen apart. Nature is its appearance, not its interpretation, and therefore the only question that can be directed at a text purporting to represent flowers is the question which asks after the adequacy of the reading experience to a possible perception: 'what about the idea of the whole?' From this standpoint,

Lessing arrives at the following characterization of Haller's verses and Breitinger's praise of them:

Sie [diese poetische Schilderey] bleibet unendlich unter dem, was Linien und Farben auf der Fläche ausdrücken können, und der Kunstrichter [Breitinger], der ihr dieses übertriebene Lob ertheilet, muß sie aus einem ganz falschen Gesichtspunkte betrachtet haben; er muß mehr auf die fremden Zierrathen, die der Dichter darein verwäbet hat, auf die Erhöhung über das vegetative Leben, auf die Entwickelung der innern Vollkommenheiten, welchen die äussere Schönheit nur zur Schale dienet, als auf diese Schönheit selbst, und auf den Grad der Lebhaftigkeit und Aehnlichkeit des Bildes, welches uns der Mahler, und welches uns der Dichter davon gewähren kann, gesehen haben.

It [this poetic descriptivism] is infinitely inferior to what lines and colors on a canvas can express and the critic who accords it such exaggerated praise must have regarded it from an entirely false perspective; he must have looked more at the alien ornaments, which the poet has interwoven into his description, at the exaltation beyond the level of plant life, at the elaboration of the inner perfections for which the external beauty serves as a mere shell – he must have looked more at these features than at the beauty itself and at the degree of liveliness and likeness that poet and painter are capable of offering us in their images of that beauty (IX, 103–4).

The passage is remarkable for its descriptive accuracy as well as for the inappropriateness of the evaluative criteria it employs. Lessing correctly identifies Haller's textual practice as an 'interweaving' in which terms for 'outside' things are equated with terms for 'inside' things. He is aware that the 'inside' values are what the text primarily aims to communicate. But for Lessing, these values do not constitute the truth of the natural phenomenon, they are 'alien ornaments.' That is, they are extrinsic to the imitated object and obscure its natural value. The poet does not bring the flower, in its intrinsic beauty, to illusionary presence, but he uses the flower as a pretext for the transmission of cultural values. The 'Schönheit selbst' ('beauty itself') of the flower is the only value quality to which Lessing is willing to accord aesthetic legitimacy, and, since beauty is what appears to a global intuition, he must conclude that the flower is an object for the painter and not the poet. Nothing could make more apparent the distance between Breitinger and Lessing: whereas for Breitinger seeing is, in its truth and perfection, a kind of reading, for Lessing reading leads to an aesthetic experience when it becomes a kind of seeing.

Haller's description interferes with the intuitive apprehension of its object and brings the text itself to the foreground of attention. 'Ich höre in jedem Worte den arbeitenden Dichter, aber das Ding selbst bin ich weit entfernet zu sehen.' ('I hear with every word the laboring poet, but I am far from seeing the thing itself' IX, 104). The same experience awaits the reader of the *Aeneid* at the point where Virgil describes Aeneas' shield. Again we have a text written for the sake of the 'Zierrathen' ('ornaments,' IX, 114) that it contains. Again we have a case where the text *as performance*, and not the imaginary object itself, occupies the reader: ' . . . der witzige Hofmann leuchtet überall durch, der mit allerley schmeichelhaften Anspielungen seine Materie aufstutzet, aber nicht das grosse Genie, das sich auf die eigene innere Stärke seines Werks verläßt, und alle äussere Mittel, interessant zu werden, verachtet' (' . . . the witty courtier, who lends support to his material with all sorts of flattering allusions, shines through everywhere, but nowhere the great genius who relies on the inner strength his work itself possesses and who disclaims all extrinsic means for becoming interesting' IX, 113–14). Virgil does not furnish an intuition of the shield, but uses the description of the shield as an occasion to allude to the values and ideology of the court he serves. Finally, Ariosto too fails in his depiction of Alcina for similar reasons: 'Was nutzt alle diese Gelehrsamkeit und Einsicht uns Lesern, die wir eine schöne Frau zu sehen glauben wollen, die wir etwas von der sanften Wallung des Gebluts dabey empfinden wollen, die den wirklichen Anblick der Schönheit begleitet?' ('What use is all this learnedness and knowledge to us readers, who want to believe we are seeing a beautiful woman, who want to feel in doing so something of the gentle motion of the blood that accompanies the actual perception of beauty?' IX, 126). Ariosto's text does not present Alcina in her appearance, but weaves into her description another text, the discourse of painting theory (proportion, coloration, etc.). In each of these cases Lessing's response is identical. He recognizes that the texts do not merely describe, but he rejects their other functions as extra-aesthetic elements, as ornament, flattery, or allusion. At every point where the text refers to other texts, where the activity of decoding remains in symbolic cognition, Lessing denies the text aesthetic value. This he had to do, for he could only admit a text as poetic so long as it was more than text, so long as it brought its object to intuitive presentation. Aesthetic experience, for Lessing, is not situated within the domain of cultural texts; rather, it conveys the recipient beyond the cultural sphere and recovers, in doing so, the immediacy, richness, and presence of nature.

Lessing's preference for Homer's narrative art over the textual practice of Haller, Ariosto and Virgil is related to the equivalence between narrative and natural signs that is the central proposition of the Homer chapters. In narrative the sign sequence stands in a relation of similarity to the action sequence and the individual moments of textual reception deliver contentual wholes. In both of these respects narrative simulates the structure of perception and thereby approaches the status of a formally natural sign. The reader loses the explicit awareness of the signs as signs and believes himself in the presence of the unfolding event. The text acquires optimal transparency and a genuinely intuitive aesthetic cognition is achieved. Clearly, though, Lessing, with his remarkable critical 'acumen,' could not be satisfied with a theory which amalgamates all forms of poetry beneath the concept narrative. In addition to sequence, narrative is characterized by the difference between the enunciation of the message and the actors and events referred to. Plato, therefore, called narrative 'diegesis' and defined it as the reporting of actions in which the poet speaks in his own person.[75] This he distinguished from 'mimesis,' in which the characters speak for themselves.

Narrative presupposes a discrepancy between discourse and action which is not present in all forms of poetry. It is important to ask whether Lessing's theory is able to accommodate this distinction between narrative and mimesis.

With Homer as his primary example, Lessing develops his theory of poetry as a natural sign in terms of the distinction between narrative and description. There are, however, passages in the *Laocoön* where he attends to other genres and evaluates them positively. One of these responds to a criticism of the first *Laocoon* sketch which Mendelssohn had raised. To Lessing's assertion that corporeal beauty is the object of painting alone, Mendelssohn objected: 'If we banish painting from poetry altogether, then we condemn some beautiful passages in the ancient poets. Anacreon's ode to his painter is a picturesque description of beauty.'[76] In the twentieth chapter of the *Laocoon* Lessing takes up Mendelssohn's example:

> I must not forget here the two odes of Anacreon in which he analyzes the beauty of his maiden and of his Bathyllus. The twist he gives to the matter redeems everything. He believes he has a painter in front of him and he orders him to work right before his eyes. Make me the hair this way, he says, and the brow that way, and the eyes like this, the mouth so, so the throat and breasts, so the hips and hands! That which the painter could only assemble part by part could only be prescribed for him part by part in the poet's words. His intention is not that we should know and feel in these oral instructions to the painter the entire beauty of the beloved objects; he himself senses the inadequacy of verbal expression and it is precisely for this reason that he calls on the aid of the other art form, the illusionary quality of which he exalts to such an extent that the entire ode seems to be in praise of art rather than of his maiden (IX, 127–8).

The passage begins by admitting that the girl's beauty is the object of the poem and that the poem analyzes her beautiful appearance by successively mentioning her individual features. It would seem, then, that Lessing is compelled either to admit Mendelssohn's criticism or to declare the poem unsuccessful. The remainder of the analysis, however, goes on to show that it is not a simultaneous arrangement of features which the poem relates but the successive phases of an action. The poet imagines he is addressing a painter and the successive statements he makes thereby correspond to the painter's execution of the painting in successive phases. In other words, the poem is not an imitation of the girl's *Gestalt* – which it could not satisfactorily render present – but of the painter's action. The technique appears to be identical to Homer's device of transforming descriptions into narrations. But Lessing's final statement opens up the possibility of distinguishing between the Homeric and the Anacreontic poems. The latter, Lessing suggests, is a 'Lobgedicht auf die Kunst,' a poem of praise which, as such, is decisively different than a narrative. Anacreon's poem does not imitate something from which it, as discourse, is distinguished. It is a performative speech act which accomplishes an action through its own enunciation. It does not designate a reality but creates that reality in the very act of speech. Lessing does not see this distinction between performance or mimesis (the poet's speech is like the speech of characters in a drama) and narrative. The action which Anacreon imitates is not – as would be the case with Homer – distinct from the enunciation itself, but is the series of commands, exclamations, and praises constituted in the language of the poem. Lessing can accept Anacreon's 'description' precisely because it is not a description, but the mimesis of a speech act.

We are compelled to make Lessing's position in the *Laocoon* more precise than he himself did. The fundamental semiotic principle of Lessing's theory is that poetry functions as a natural sign. Naturalness in signification can be accomplished in two types of speech: where the speech is distinct from the actions or objects referred to, as in both description and narrative, then narrative alone qualifies as a natural sign; where the speech itself is the action, as in performative speech acts, then sign and object are not only similar, but coincide. A poem such as Anacreon's is a natural sign of other linguistic signs. Its mimesis is total.

As I mentioned, Lessing did not arrive at this distinction between mimetic speech and narrative speech in the *Laocoon* itself although his discussion of Anacreon's poems – as well as his praise of Ovid in Chapter twenty-one – presupposes it. In a letter to Friedrich Nicolai from 1769, however, Lessing re-evaluates his earlier position. The decisive passage begins:

Nun noch ein Wort von der Poesie, damit Sie nicht missverstehen, was ich eben gesagt habe. Die Poesie muß schlechterdings ihre willkührlichen Zeichen zu natürlichen zu erheben suchen; und nur dadurch unterscheidet sie sich von der Prosa, und wird Poesie. Die Mittel, wodurch sie dieses tut, sind der Ton, die Worte, die Stellung der Worte, das Silbenmass, Figuren und Tropen, Gleichnisse u.s.w. Alle diese Dinge bringen die willkührlichen Zeichen den natürlichen näher;

One more word about poetry so that you don't misunderstand what I have just said. Poetry simply must attempt to elevate its arbitrary signs to the status of natural signs; only in this way does it differentiate itself from prose and become poetry. The means through which it does this are tone, words, the position of the words, the meter, figures and tropes, similes, etc. All these things allow arbitrary signs to approach natural signs (XVII, 291).

Up to this point the letter merely resumes the theory elaborated in the *Laocoon*. Then, in a manner typical of his relentless pursuit of a principle, Lessing offers the following consideration:

aber sie [the 'Dinge' of the previous clause] machen sie nicht zu natürlichen Zeichen: folglich sind alle Gattungen, die sich nur dieser Mittel bedienen, als die niedern Gattungen der Poesie zu betrachten; und die höchste Gattung der Poesie ist die, welche die willkührlichen Zeichen gänzlich zu natürlichen Zeichen macht. Das ist aber die dramatische; denn in dieser hören die Worte auf willkührliche Zeichen zu seyn, und werden *natürliche* Zeichen willkührlicher Dinge.

but these things do not make them into natural signs: as a result, all the genres that make use of these means are to be considered the lower genres of poetry; and the highest genre of poetry is the one which makes arbitrary signs completely into natural signs. That, however, is dramatic poetry; for in dramatic poetry words cease being arbitrary signs and become *natural* signs of arbitrary things (XVII, 291).

Only in dramatic poetry does the poet's language function as a natural sign and therefore only in the drama does poetry achieve its ideal. As performative speech (Lessing still fails to accord certain lyric forms the status of performative or mimetic speech), the poem is the very reality it designates, for this reality itself is the activity of speaking. The poem no longer tries to embody a reality from which it is separate, as in narrative. Perfected mimesis is not the imitation of an object or action, it is the action itself.

With this assertion Lessing not only relativizes the theses of the *Laocoon*, he completely abandons the model of aesthetic signification he had developed there. For in that model the reality of discourse was never given serious attention. The task of the poet was considered to be the rendering present of an object or action existing independently (even if only imaginatively) of the discourse itself. If we call this object or action the referent, then we can say that the poet embodies the referent in his discourse and thereby stimulates an intuitive apprehension of the referent on the part of the reader. In painting this embodiment is formal and material, while in poetry it is only formal. Despite this difference – as well as all the others elucidated in the course of Lessing's argument – the fundamental identity of the two arts remains. *In the Laocoon poetry is still viewed in terms of the paradigm of painting*. As narrative, it provides a sort of moving, ideal painting, the illusion of a developing action. In the letter to Nicolai, Lessing forces his insistence on the naturalness of signification, on the embodiment of the referent, to the point where it loses all meaning. The only referent which discourse can perfectly imitate turns out to be not a real or imaginary object or action, but discourse itself. At that point where the difference between sign and referent is overcome, the referent disappears, and the poet is left the task of dramatizing language itself, of setting it into action.

# CONCLUDING REMARKS: ENLIGHTENMENT AESTHETICS FROM THE STANDPOINT OF TODAY

The decisive factor in evaluating the achievements of eighteenth-century aesthetics, it seems to me, is to understand them as part of a larger cultural matrix. As I have argued here, this matrix can be accounted for as a particular 'metasemiotic,' a structured set of attitudes toward language and signs. The most important features of this metasemiotic can be summarized as follows:

(1) *The primacy of the sphere of mental representations.* In the Enlightenment language is viewed as a set of arbitrary signs. The being of language is entirely functional so that talk of signs is always talk of means or media. As sounds or written characters employed for the purpose of marking and communicating positive ideas, signs yield all dignity and importance to the ideas or meanings they serve to convey. It is our ideas which represent the world, which evince evidence, which are true or false. The paradigm of cognition, the only self-sufficient form of cognition, is intuition. Compared to intuitive cognition, figural (Wolff) or symbolic cognition (Baumgarten, Meier, Mendelssohn, Lessing) is secondary and derivative. Symbolic cognition is legitimate only in view of the intuitive cognition it was derived from and into which, ultimately, it should be converted. The entire philosophy of the sign – and 'Classical thought,' according to Foucault, 'was through and through a philosophy of the sign'[1] – rests on the primacy of intuition, the direct apprehension of our mental representations.

(2) *The arbitrary nature of the sign.* Wolff's doctrine of the arbitrary sign celebrates the inaugural moment of intuition in which meanings are directly seized. He grounds discourse in an 'arché beyond discourse' (Wilfrid Sellars), a moment in

which the world manifests itself to the reflective soul as a series of 'enunciables.' Intuition grasps those meanings or ideas which are later marked by signs of man's free choice. In this way, knowledge is based on a type of cognition that exists outside of language, in the direct encounter with things. At its origin, the sign is an arbitrarily selected name for an immediately apprehended mental representation. It is this act of naming, the institution of freely chosen signs, which is at the very root of culture.

(3) *The critical impulse of the theory of signs.* The functional definition of the sign is experienced as a liberation from the disputes and misunderstandings of the past. Once it is realized that language is only signs, then the business of finding truth can be pursued expeditiously. The confusions of the past are viewed as the products of a simple, but far-reaching error – the confusion of signs with the ideas they designate or the things they refer to, the adherence to the merely functional surface of discourse as if it were thought itself. To be sure, the possibility of this error is given in the nature of signs themselves. Related to their signifieds only by virtue of an arbitrary connection, they reveal nothing of the thoughts they designate. The basic texts of Enlightenment semiotics inevitably touch on this problem, Wolff, for instance, in his remarks on 'empty tones' or John Locke in the chapters of his *Essay Concerning Human Understanding* entitled 'Of the Imperfection of Words' and 'Of the Abuse of Words.'[2] But the difficulties and confusions arising from the arbitrariness and opacity of signs are looked upon as eminently curable. Optimism *vis-à-vis* language prevails, so that Locke adds to the above mentioned chapters a third, 'Of the Remedies of the Foregoing Imperfection and Abuses,' and Antoine Arnauld and Pierre Nicole, in their fundamental *Logic or the Art of Thinking* (1664), insert a chapter entitled: 'Of the Remedy for the Confusion which is born in our thoughts and discourses from the confusion of words; . . .'[3]

(4) *Signs and the economy of thought.* The signs which

man employs are themselves discrete sense ideas of articulate sounds or written characters and, as such, they can be recalled and manipulated with greater facility than the ideas they designate. The ease and economy of thought are made possible by sign use. By substituting signs for his actual ideas of things, man expands the scope of his representations. Reasoning, the unfolding and logical linking of representations, is carried out in language alone. We acquiesce on the level of sign comprehension, of symbolic cognition, in order to give our thought speed and efficiency. Language acquires an additional value because it represents things more distinctly than perception. The qualities of objects are distributed along an articulate chain, allowing us to distinguish the various features the object contains as we couldn't when perceiving them in their con-fusion. For this reason, language is the vehicle for distinct thought, that which makes the use of the intellect possible. As our reasoning and analysis progress, sign use gains in importance. Signs allow us to recall abstract ideas which otherwise would be lost for us, to form judgements and to reason syllogistically. Thus, man's mastery and comprehension of his experience are inextricably linked to the sign. Sign-use allows man to elevate himself beyond immediate sense experience and to grasp the world intellectually; it is the vehicle of cultural progress.

(5) *Progressive semiosis*. Language defines the field of human knowledge that reaches from man's pre-semiotic knowledge in intuition to his post-semiotic experience of the world as a logical structure. This latter type of knowing exists only as an ideal, the *ars characteristica combinatoria* or perfect philosophical language in which the logical nature of things is displayed. Here our 'cognitio symbolica' is converted 'quasi in intuitivam' and the concepts of things are exhibited as if before our eyes. Unrealized as yet for man, this perfectly distinct and yet intuitive form of knowing coincides with divine cognition. God is the locus where the semiotic mediations of our reasoning are reconverted into the direct apprehension of things.

Sign-use is situated, then, between two types of intuition, the sensate intuition of our perceptual experience and the intellectual intuition of divine knowledge. The sign demonstrates man's intellectual superiority – indeed is the very possibility of this superiority – over the mute creatures, and, at the same time, points out his inadequacy, his essential finiteness. The sign is the moment of externality that necessarily remains in man's knowing and his dependence on it signals his limitation. Mendelssohn expresses the matter most clearly: 'But precisely this necessity of abstraction and signification (that is, of symbolic cognition) proves that we are dust.'[4] The Enlightenment myth of the sign localizes sign use between two experiences of plenitude and presence – an original perceptual experience in which the world reveals itself directly, the *arché* which grounds man's subsequent symbolic representations, and the *telos* of divine cognition in which the world is again experienced intuitively, but with total distinctness. The movement from one pole to the other, the advancement of culture itself, is a process of progressive semiosis.

This metasemiotic, as I believe the preceding chapters have demonstrated, thoroughly informs Enlightenment aesthetics. Of course, this is no accident. Aesthetic theory participates in those major historical-cultural displacements which eighteenth-century sign theory itself both reflects and helps bring about: the critical dismantling of traditional, hierarchical symbolism and the establishment of uniform, methodical procedures of inquiry for all domains of knowledge. If Enlightenment semiotics provides a theoretical codification of language as a secularized, indeed neutral medium of intellectual debate and exchange (the vital element in which the emerging bourgeois public sphere can flourish[5]), then aesthetic theory can be said to accomplish an analogous operation in terms of a local area of cultural activity. The aestheticians construe art as a special form of representation and thereby draw it into the mental immanence of the ideational realm. It therefore becomes

231

possible to offer a theoretical account of aesthetic value based no longer on particular, class-specific factors, but rather on universal features of representational activity. Since the organ of aesthetic experience is an analogue of reason (Baumgarten), then the laws governing such experience are as universal as those of logic. *In one and the same movement, art becomes the subject matter of theory and aesthetic experience is transformed into something that takes place between subjects and their representations, without the mediation of inherited bodies of erudition and independently of a locally defined cultural site.* The development of the sub-discipline of aesthetic semiotics is entirely consistent with this cultural trend. To conceive as signs the material vehicles that convey aesthetic representations is to submit them to the constraints of a sort of grammar, a set of rules governing various aspects of aesthetic sign use.

But, in addition to this general process of rationalization, aesthetic theory, with its semiotic sub-discipline, expresses another essential aspect of Enlightenment culture. What the foregoing analysis of Baumgarten, Meier, Mendelssohn and Lessing has repeatedly pointed up is that, in the Enlightenment, culture itself becomes a problem the culture has to deal with. The widespread discussion of signs and sign-related issues – especially as it enters into the discussion of art – shows the culture in the process of diagnosing itself. Mendelssohn's work is a case in point. We have seen that he associates sign-use with the finitude of human reason and that he speculates on the primitive forms of signification that first made language possible. It could also be shown that his prize-winning *Treatise on Evidence* (1763) traces the lack of evidence – and hence the errors, false starts, and cumbersomeness – of philosophical discourse to its reliance on arbitrary signs.[6] In a similar fashion, his *Jerusalem, or On Religious Power and Judaism* (1783) locates the source of religious idolatry in the problematic nature of semiotic instruments.[7] But the sign not only troubles philosophy and religion, it is also the aggravating factor in much of our contemporary cultural malaise. The literary and philosophical scene of 1762 appears to Mendelssohn as 'words without spirit, method without inner illumination, figures of speech without feeling...'[8] And some twenty years later he finds that our alphabetical culture 'displays the symbolic cognition of things too openly on the surface, relieves us of the effort of penetration and study, and creates between doctrine and life a breach that is far too wide.'[9] As these statements make clear, the Enlightenment possessed a problematic awareness of culture, a suspicion of its stultifying, deadening, burdensome qualities; and at the origin of these negative factors was the sign, the very thing which made cultural development – 'the progress and improvement of concepts, opinions and knowledge'[10] – possible.

It is in this context that the idealization of poetry and of aesthetic representation generally, which the preceding chapters have documented, must be interpreted. Enlightenment culture begins to make the aesthetic domain into *a compensatory field of activity*, an area in which the problems of culture are alleviated momentarily and in which the present state of cultural malaise is eliminated. For this reason, poetry receives the twofold significance – at once archaic and anticipatory or utopian – that I have often referred to. It is poetry which renews culture by regaining contact with its natural origins; and it is poetry which anticipates the full recovery of nature that awaits the culture at the end of its progressive development. This idealization occurs in two ways. First of all, in the theory of the wholeness of the human being: in aesthetic experience, man recovers that harmonious interaction of the faculties, that rich and energetic representational-conative activity that characterizes him in terms of his natural human potential. And secondly, in the theory of transparent discourse: in poetry, language regains the vividness and transparency that characterized its first beginnings and – this aspect especially emerges in Lessing – that constitutes the aim of cultural progress. The arbitrary signs of human institution, with all their attendant problems, are transformed into natural signs and symbolic cognition is rendered intuitive.

The rationalization and idealization of the aesthetic – the two cultural trends which I hold to be central to the development of aesthetic theory in the Enlightenment – receive in Lessing's *Laocoon* their most systematic elaboration. Of course, Lessing is dealing with a particular thematic problem, the relationship between poetry and the plastic arts. To solve this problem he makes use of a twofold strategy. On the one hand, he examines the differences between the arts that derive from the different types of sign they employ; on the other, he demonstrates the underlying unity of the arts. In the pursuit of this double task, however, he charts the constellation of values characterizing the Enlightenment metasemiotic and defines the position of art within the culture at large. Lessing's *Laocoon* – this is the thesis I have argued – is the Enlightenment's most complete statement on the semiotics of poetry and art.

To accomplish the first of his tasks, Lessing attends with unprecedented scrupulousness to the components of each of the arts and develops a global model of aesthetic signification in which the differences between the arts at each level of the aesthetic sign are clearly set forth. Among the factors which Lessing considers are the material constitution and syntax of the aesthetic signs, the spheres of content available to each sign type, the different modes of selection and arrangement of contents, the different status of the individual content units, and the various types and causes of possible concretizations. The comparative classification of the arts in terms of these differences then becomes the basis for an evaluation of the arts as regards the freedom of imagination each affords. Poetry is shown to be superior to painting because of the 'Geistigkeit' (spirituality) of its contents, their purely imaginary nature, while painting and sculpture, as material arts, do not allow for the same purely imaginative experience. The central thrust of Lessing's aesthetics moves toward the elimination of the material element, the moment of sensuous, existential presence, within the arts; the purest form of the aesthetic is localized entirely within the sphere of ideal contents. Lessing's comparison of the different types of aesthetic sign shows how the refined form of semiosis characterizing poetry (e.g., discrete expression-tokens, relative immateriality of the expression-plane, arbitrariness of the individual signs, pre-segmentation of the content material allowing for greater freedom of selection and purity of meaning, etc.) enables poetry to provide an imaginative experience that is independent of the limitations of worldliness characterizing the plastic arts. In this aspect of his aesthetic theory, Lessing actualizes key tenets of Enlightenment semiotics: the notion of language as the vehicle through which mastery over sense experience is attained and through which man progressively moves toward an approximation of divine cognition reappears in Lessing's supposition of a progress in the arts through various stages of semiosis. Indeed, Lessing's suspicion of painting – because of its materiality and sensuous presence painting compels the viewer to remain on the level of sensation – has its parallel in the fundamental text of Enlightenment semiotics, the above mentioned *Logique* of Arnauld and Nicole.[11] It is not sensuous presence which Lessing demands of art, but the intuitive presence of an ideal content, a spiritual or mental product.

Lessing's insistence on the basic unity of the arts derives from the notions of intuition and natural sign employed in the aesthetics of Baumgarten, Meier, and Mendelssohn. The intuitive presence of an existentially absent object and the aesthetic pleasure which emerges from the intuition of the object's value qualities are taken to be the definitive features of aesthetic experience. This experience is most apparent in painting, where the object is given as it would appear to direct perception. It is important to emphasize, however, that it is not painting as such which serves as an aesthetic norm for Lessing, but the *enargia* ('picture power' – Geoffrey Hartman[12]) of painting. That is to say, Lessing does not use painting in all its aspects to derive his central criterion for poetry, but only the ability of painting to present objects to intuition. From painting in its full specificity Lessing abstracts the form or idea – intuitive presence – which he then adapts as his central aesthetic principle. Only when we grasp this aspect of Lessing's method can we understand how he could simultaneously assert the inferiority of painting *and* the unity of the arts. It is not painting *per se* which poetry ought to approximate according to Lessing, but the idea of painting, the form of intuitive presence.

This attention to principle, to the form as opposed to its particular instantiation, is especially characteristic of Lessing's work. In the sixteenth chapter of the *Laocoon*, Lessing attempts to identify the common principle of signification which makes possible the attainment of intuitive presence in all the arts. This principle is sign motivation or, in Lessing's terms, the use of natural signs. In natural signification, the referent, which is to be brought to an intuitive representation, is embodied in the sign vehicle. As a result, the perception of the sign easily moves toward an intuitive apprehension of the referent: the 'Intuition des Bezeichneten' (intuition of the signified) occurs simultaneously with the 'Intuition des Zeichens' (intuition of the sign). Poetry and painting share in this structure of signification and therefore both accomplish the effective mimesis which defines the aesthetic in general. The signs of painting are motivated both materially and formally. Their spatial structure corresponds to the spatial structure of the corporeal object represented and the individual signs duplicate the material nature of that object insofar as they are solid, colored and fully determined as material things. The motivation of poetic signs, however, is only formal. The sign vehicles bear no similarity to the action-referent except as regards their successivity. The poem replicates only the form of perception, not its content. Poetry is a natural sign only because its signs present themselves to the reader in the same successive form as would the action itself. Poetry, therefore, maintains the advantages provided by its more advanced stage of semiosis; its individual signs remain arbitrary. The distinguishing feature of poetry is that it recovers for language the form of intuitive presence because the poem as a whole attains to the status of a natural sign. The lack of material motivation is not at all problematic since it is not the material specification of painting which poetry aims to simulate, but only the idea of painting, the form of presentation abstracted from painting as such.

The same method of seeking a formal or structural equivalence between poetry and painting can be seen in Lessing's distinction between narrative and description in terms of the logic of part and whole. Narrative presents a series of comprehensible wholes and thereby corresponds to a perceptual experience in terms of structure alone. As in perception, a contentual whole is given to comprehension within a single moment. Lessing does not insist on the concretization of narrative content units so as to yield a perceptual-imaginative experience, although his preference for the Homeric style shows that he attributed high aesthetic value to a text which stimulates such a quasi-perceptual actualization. He merely insists that the present moment of textual reception (and perhaps this 'present moment,' given the findings of contemporary psycholinguistic research, could be expanded to include the reception of about seven words)[13] function so as to yield a contentual whole and thereby to approximate the structure of perception. Poetry accomplishes ideally – in terms of structure – what painting does materially.

In this way, poetry sheds its semiotic character – the symbolic cognition ordinarily provided by the arbitrary signs of language – and regains the experience of presence, the transparency to intuition, which language left behind. As a diagrammatic icon or formally natural sign, poetry proves to be an ideal language, at once free of the disadvantages of worldliness and yet maintaining the immediacy – the intuitive nature – of perceptual experience. Here Lessing departs from Baumgarten and Meier. Whereas they tend to view poetry as moving back toward man's pre-semiotic experience, Lessing sees poetry as post-semiotic. The advancements and advantages of semiosis are preserved; the representation remains ideal. But, in contrast to ordinary language, the perfected language of poetry recovers the experience of presence and communicates its contents immediately to intuition. In poetry, as in the *ars characteristica combinatoria* which was the semiotic dream of the century, 'cognitio symbolica convertitur quasi in intuitivam.' Baumgarten locates poetry at the origin of our linguistic experience, Lessing, boldly, at its end.

With Lessing's *Laocoon*, the semiotically based aesthetics of the Enlightenment, ideally at least, comes to an end. Herder, in his 'On Studiousness in Several Learned Languages' of 1764, already begins to elaborate the hermeneutic-philological paradigm for the study of cultural artifacts that it was his great intellectual achievement to inaugurate.[14] For Herder, inquiry focuses on the individual uniqueness of languages and texts as it emerges from and reflects the historical specificity of a people's, or genial individual's, spirit (*Geist*), not on the adequacy of a language or text to an ideal form of representation. The very being of language and art begins to shift: no longer means for conveying mental representations, they become expressions of an antecedent subjectivity. We can take Herder's work to mark the commencement of a transformation in the way language and other cultural objects are experienced and conceptualized, a profound revolution in the way culture thinks of itself. This new way of thinking is related to the development of historicism generally and in aesthetics to the articulation of what I called in the introduction to Chapter 2 the expressive theory-type. In the more than two hundred years since Herder's first publications, our cultural consciousness has become so thoroughly historicized that a direct appropriation of Lessing's *Laocoon* is no longer possible: Lessing and his contemporaries were quite simply speaking a different language – that is, a different theoretical language – about art, language, and signs from that which we speak. Furthermore, this problem of historical distance is aggravated by the fact that the twentieth century has witnessed (and continues to do so) a second paradigm shift in the study of language and culture. Since the Saussurean revolution in linguistics '...a process restructuring the historical sciences of spirit [*historische Geisteswissenschaften*] as systematic sciences of culture has begun and to some extent been completed. The transformation of the historical study of language into structural linguistics and recently the at least partial transformation of literary history into a structural science of literature [*strukturale Literaturwissenschaft*] should be seen in this connection.'[15] Thus, two massive reorganizations of thought – the historicist revolution and the structuralist revolution – separate us from representational aesthetics and the eighteenth-century theory of the sign. For this reason, the appraisal of Enlightenment aesthetics from the standpoint of today is a very complex matter.

Of course, this talk of intellectual revolutions gives only a schematic account of what is in fact a dense and multi-faceted situation. The contemporary theoretical scene contains several competing traditions and discourses each of which has different genealogical affiliations. Thus, while it is certainly true that Enlightenment aesthetics speaks a language that is different – and is addressed to different problems – from that of most schools of aesthetic thought today, it is likewise the case that certain directions of contemporary theory have constituted themselves by reactivating particular dimensions of the eighteenth-century discourse on language and art. Just as there is no way of eliminating the historical and theoretical distance that separates us from Lessing, there is likewise no simple answer to the question: what is the relevance of Lessing's work today? To evaluate Enlightenment aesthetics from a contemporary standpoint is not to look for those still valid truths the aestheticians discovered, but rather to determine those areas of contemporary thought that continue to operate with eighteenth-century instruments.

One such area, I believe, is phenomenology. Like eighteenth-century philosophy generally, phenomenology stakes out as its particular domain of inquiry the sphere of mental representations. (*Cogitationes* is the Latin term Husserl sometimes uses to denote these ideational units.)[16] There are two ways in which these representations can be subjectively attended to, through the mediation of signs or in direct intuition. Husserl calls these modes of intentionality 'signitive and intuitive intentions,'[17] an opposition which parallels that between symbolic and intuitive cognition. As in the eighteenth-century texts we have examined, in phenomenology as well the positive valorization falls entirely on the side of the intuitions. Using terminology that rings very familiar, Husserl explicates the difference as follows: 'The content [*Gehalt*] is in each case different; in the one case I see [*schaue*], and in this seeing the state of affairs is itself given; in the other case I have a symbolic opinion [*symbolische Meinung*]. In the one case I have an intuition, in the other an empty intention [*Leerintention*].'[18] Only in the direct, intuitive 'seeing' of the object of consciousness is the intentional act fulfilled. Here too we find that the paradigm of mental activity is essentially specular.

The point I wish to make here is that there runs through phenomenological discourse a conceptual strand deriving from eighteenth-century patterns of thought: the positing of an immanent representational domain, the use of visual models to characterize intellectual operations, the opposition symbolic/intuitive with positive valorization of the second element in the pair. I do not mean to equate or identify phenomenological research with eighteenth-century thought (which would be absurd), but merely to trace the genealogy of some of the conceptual instruments used in that research. (Of course, this hypothesis implicitly calls into question the 'evidence' of phenomenological insight: the language, which according to phenomenologists neutrally describes states of affairs that immediately present themselves to reflective phenomenological 'seeing' [*Schauen*], proves to be a redaction of Enlightenment

philosophical discourse.) The interesting aspect of this link between the semantic systems of phenomenology and eighteenth-
century thought is that it carries over to the field of aesthetics.
The complex model of the literary work which Roman
Ingarden develops in his two major studies in aesthetic theory
exhibits remarkable similarities with Lessing's global model of
signification in poetry.[19] In both cases we find a layered
structure consisting of an abstract linguistic stratum and a
stratum of concrete objects making up the fictional world.
In both cases we find a conception of reading as a passage from
the intellectual comprehension of the linguistic level to the
quasi-perceptual experience of the designated world of objects.
Like Lessing, Ingarden juxtaposes the intellectual-linguistic
comprehension of theoretical discourse with the intuitive
actualization of artistic texts.[20] Indeed, Ingarden even identifies as a special structural feature of the work certain 'schematized views,' which, when imaginatively ramified by the reader,
transform the 'signitive' apprehension of the fictional world
into an experience of that world as intuitively given.[21] In terms
of their theoretical function, these triggers setting off the
process of intuitive actualization correspond almost exactly to
the 'optimally sensate qualities' described by Lessing. Thus,
phenomenological aesthetics proves to be a contemporary area
of inquiry that resonates with eighteenth-century terms.

One theme from Enlightenment aesthetics which phenomenology does *not* pick up is the historical-philosophical
(*geschichtsphilosophisch*) one of progressive semiosis. That is
to say: the operative concepts which phenomenology borrows
from the eighteenth century are employed for the technical
analysis of representational processes and not for the solution
of long-range, orientational questions such as: what is the aim
of cultural development? I have argued in this study that one
of the functions aesthetic theory attributes to poetry involves
precisely this question. Poetry, as transparent discourse, anticipates the transparency of the philosophical language which is
the goal of progressive inquiry. This particular intertwining of

semiotic-linguistic theory and the philosophical interpretation of history does not, however, lack contemporary relevance. On the contrary, the notions of an 'ideal speech situation' or an 'ideal communication community,' which have in recent years emerged with such forcefulness in the work of Jürgen Habermas and Karl-Otto Apel, seem to me to continue this line of Enlightenment thought.[22] The ideal of transparency, which in the Enlightenment was conceived in semantic terms, reappears in the work of Habermas and Apel as a pragmatic ideal: a communicational interchange in which 'subjects are transparent to themselves and others as regards what they are actually doing and saying...'[23] This ideal speech situation is presupposed (counter-factually) by every effort at rational argument. It is thus both present (as an effective norm) and anticipated (as an ideal that is not yet realized) – which is to say that its status resembles that of poetry in Enlightenment theory. The philosophical interpretation of history relies on an aesthetic ideal, or the equivalent of such an ideal, in order to define and make present its regulative idea of transparent communication free of compulsion. 'The anticipation of the ideal speech situation has, for every possible communication, the significance of a constitutive semblance [*Schein*], which is simultaneously the pre-semblance [*Vorschein*] of a form of life.'[24] The terms with which Habermas accounts for the status of his regulative principle are borrowed from the philosophy of art, in particular from Ernst Bloch's 'aesthetics of pre-semblance.'[25] As was the case in Enlightenment theory, aesthetic representations point forward to a state of freedom in which the compulsions and opacities of speech are finally overcome.

Phenomenology and universal pragmatics, then, each echo a different dimension of the Enlightenment discourse on signs and art. And yet beneath this difference there is a fundamental sameness: both contemporary movements are characterized by the same polarized relationship between philosophical theory and art that comes into being with the emergence of the discipline of aesthetics in the eighteenth century. This event does not simply mean that art becomes the subject matter of philosophical analysis. Rather, as I think the previous chapters have shown, philosophical discourse creates 'art' (the aesthetic) as its 'other,' as something radically different from and yet profoundly related to philosophical discourse itself. There are two functions which this 'other' can fulfill for philosophy, both of which are present together in eighteenth-century thought but which appear separate in phenomenology on the one hand and universal pragmatics on the other. This separation, however, ought not obscure the fact that in both cases art functions for philosophy as a guarantee of ultimate values. For phenomenology, art serves to exemplify that contact with the origins of experience upon which the phenomenological method itself rests. Hence the insistence on intuition, on fulfilled acts of representation, on what Ingarden calls 'bringing-to-appearance.'[26] For universal pragmatics, it is not access to the primordial richness of experience that art provides, but rather an anticipatory glimpse – a pre-semblance – of an ideal future situation which, in turn, can serve as an orientation for the present. In both cases, the aesthetic is characterized by its compensatory function; it makes attainable that which the culture of reason either no longer possesses or cannot yet reach. This is the structural position within the culture at large which was first ascribed to art by eighteenth-century aesthetic theory. From the Enlightenment to the present, then, the same pattern or strategy has been maintained: philosophy, representing the rational essence of the culture, projects an image of art as its other, as that which is excluded from the space of rational discourse but which at the same time guarantees the truth of that discourse and serves as its reference point and orientation.

The final area of thought and research I want to consider here is contemporary semiotics, which entertains an extremely complex relationship to the Enlightenment discipline of the same name. As I have already noted in the first chapter, the premises of sign theory today are fundamentally different from those of the eighteenth century. The point that I want to emphasize here is that contemporary semiotics also breaks with the pattern which the foregoing paragraphs have described: it no longer distinguishes between art and philosophy as between two *essences*, playing one off against the other in a discursive game of mirrors. Rather, it sees in each an historically variable, institutionalized bundle of signifying practices. From the standpoint of contemporary semiotics, philosophy and art no longer occupy the representative and authoritative positions within the culture as a whole that have been attributed to them since the eighteenth century. The reasons for this change in perspective most likely have their source in modifications that are taking place in the very structure of our cultural life and that are extremely difficult to grasp.[27] Be that as it may, the theoretical reason for the shift in viewpoint is clear: since the beginning of contemporary semiotic research in the work of Peirce, the teleological framing of sign-use between originary intuition and final, fully adequate translation has been abandoned. In a theoretical context defined by the notion of unlimited semiosis, aesthetic signification loses its privileged position and becomes instead one among several interrelated mechanisms of signification through which the culture maintains and transforms itself. Thus, from the standpoint of today, the Enlightenment definition of the aesthetic appears as a mythological figure of thought, a device with which the culture attempts to make sense of itself. In the preceding three chapters I have tried to describe how this device worked, that is, how the Enlightenment theoreticians located the aesthetic within an array of values having to do with language and signs.

However, even though semiotic theory today can no longer follow Enlightenment semiotics in its thematic treatment of aesthetic questions, it nevertheless faces related theoretical tasks. The problem is to restate these tasks so that they can be productively pursued within the current theoretical framework. In this way, contemporary theory, in the act of grasping the limitations of another system of thought, enters into a new relationship with itself. I want to conclude by briefly sketching how this process of theoretical innovation might work in terms of the Enlightenment material I have analyzed in the foregoing pages. Lessing's work, it seems to me, suggests three potential areas of research:

1. *The comparative analysis of the arts in terms of a typology of modes of sign production.* Thanks to pioneering work by Nelson Goodman and Umberto Eco, the greater 'freedom' which Lessing attributed to poetry as compared to the plastic arts can now be seen to result from a variety of factors: the means by which the sign tokens are physically produced, the articulation of the expression plane, the types of coding employed.[28] What remains to be done in this area – and here Lessing can serve as an example – is to describe how these modes of sign production are deployed for aesthetic use. This is a project which would have to be carried out historically rather than in the normative, classificational manner of the Enlightenment. The result would be something like an evolutionary semiotic of the arts: an account of changes in the mode of sign production within individual arts (for example, the introduction of montage in film which involves a rearticulation of the expression plane) as well as in the distribution of semiotic labor among the arts.

2. *The general theory of narrativity.* The analysis of narrative has perhaps been the most successful area of recent semiotic research. The basic trend of this work can be fairly characterized, I think, as the replacement of a mimetic view of narrative with a logical view. Narrative processes are no longer conceived as imitations of real-world or imaginary actions, but as transformations operating between logically opposed terms. In this sense, what seemed to be a sheerly temporal process to Lessing, now can be understood as resting on a simultaneous logical order or grid. And yet, Lessing's simplistic, cinematic view of narrative time does provoke reflection on how to conceptualize the role of time in narrative. Even if the narrative operates with a simultaneous order of logical terms, it never-

theless does require that these terms be instantiated in a processual form. At present, we know very little about what is specific to this level of temporal instantiation. Indeed, one could even say that the notation systems for the mapping of narrative processes which are presently in use tacitly presuppose the linear conception of time that Lessing himself relied on. What is needed is a model of narrative time that goes beyond Lessing and that allows us to capture the forms of temporal discontinuity that are an irreducible component of story-telling: innovation and repetition. Such a model would enable us to grasp narrative time not merely as the linear axis onto which a set of logically related terms are projected, but as a dimension of semiosis endowed with its own possibilities of efficacy and productivity.[29]

3. *The semiotic definition of the negative.* Lessing makes three related points in his comparison of poetry and the plastic arts: that poetry can represent negative states of affairs, that poetry can represent metaphorical states of affairs, and that poetry can represent past states of affairs; painting, by contrast, is limited to the positive, the literal, and the present. There can be no question but that Lessing is wrong here. We know today that painting can employ metaphorical processes and that it can be used narratively (that is, representing transitions from one temporal point to another so that the painting includes both past and future: cf., for example, Correggio's 'Leda with the Swan') to a far greater degree than Lessing thought possible. But this does not mean that Lessing's view is entirely unfounded; it merely needs to be rethought in a less absolutist and abrupt manner. I would suggest the following reformulation of the problem: the three capacities Lessing attributes to poetry can all be said to operate with some form of negation. This is obvious in the case of linguistic negation. In addition, metaphor can be said to negate or neutralize certain aspects of the metaphorically employed term and the past tense can be considered as involving some form of negative marker. The problem that Lessing's theory raises is: what are

the different types and degrees of negation and to what extent can they be realized in different semiotic systems? Not accidentally, this problem is related to the first area of research I listed insofar as it correlates the extent and diversity of semiotic negation with the mode of sign production characteristic of a particular semiotic system such as representational painting.

These open research questions provide, I think, an appropriate conclusion to a study of the *Laocoon* and its cultural and intellectual background. Lessing himself viewed publication as a stage in an ongoing, communal process of inquiry (XVI, 293); in order to be adequate to his intentions, then, it is necessary to go beyond his findings. Lessing's work remains current only to the degree that it challenges contemporary thought to reflect on its own limitations. To perceive this challenge, however, presupposes understanding that work as embedded in a specific cultural framework that is different from our own. What I have tried to do in this study is to outline such an understanding.

# NOTES

In the notes, I have employed the following abbreviations:

Christian Wolff, *Gesammelte Werke*, ed. J. École, J. E. Hoffman, M. Thomann, H. W. Arndt, 3 divisions, 57 vols. (Hildesheim/New York: Georg Olms, 1962– ):

Division I, Vol. I, *Vernünftige Gedanken von den Kräften des Menschlichen Verstandes und ihrem richtigen Gebrauche in Erkenntnis der Wahrheit* (1713), ed. Hans Werner Arndt = *German Logic* (references are to chapter and paragraph).

Division II, Vol. III, *Philosophia Prima sive Ontologia* (1729), ed. J. École = *Ontologia*.

Division II, Vol. V, *Psychologia Empirica* (1732), ed. J. École = *Psy. Rat.*

Division II, Vol. VI, *Psychologia Rationalis* (1734), ed. J. École = *Psy. Rat.*

*Vernünftige Gedancken von GOTT, der Welt und der Seele des Menschen, auch allen Dingen überhaupt* (Halle: Rengerische Buchhandlung, 1720) = *German Metaphysics*.

Alexander Gottlieb Baumgarten, *Reflections on Poetry*, trans. Karl Aschenbrenner and William B. Holther (Berkeley: University of California Press, 1954) = *Reflections on Poetry*.

*Aesthetica* (Hildesheim: Georg Olms, 1961) (Unaltered, photomechanical reproduction of the original edition in two volumes, Frankfurt, 1750–8) = *Aesthetica*.

*Metaphysica* (Hildesheim: Georg Olms, 1963) (Unaltered, photomechanical reproduction of the seventh edition, Halle, 1779) = *Metaphysica*.

*Ethica Philosophica* (Halle: Carl Hermann Hemmerde, 1763³) = *Ethica*.

Georg Friedrich Meier, *Theoretische Lehre von den Gemüts-*

*bewegungen überhaupt* (Frankfurt a.M: Athenäum, 1971), (unaltered, photomechanical reproduction of the first edition, Halle, 1744) = *Theoretische Lehre*.

*Anfangsgründe aller schönen Künste und Wissenschaften*, 3 vols. (Halle: Carl Hermann Hemmerde, 1748–1750) = *Anfgr*.

*Auszug aus der Vernunftlehre* (Halle: bei Johann Justinius Gebauer, 1752), (reproduced in: Immanuel Kant, *Gesammelte Schriften*, ed. Koniglich Preussischen Akadamie der Wissenschaften, vol. XVI [Berlin: Druck und Verlag von Georg Reimer, 1914]) = *Vernunftlehre*.

*Betrachtungen über den ersten Grundsatz der schönen Künste und Wissenschaften* (Halle: Carl Hermann Hemmerde, 1758) = *Grundsatz*.

*Versuch einer allgemeinen Auslegungskunst* (Dusseldorf: Stern Verlag, 1965), (unaltered, photomechanical reproduction of the original edition, Halle, 1757' = *Auslegungskunst*.

Moses Mendelssohn, *Gesammelte Schriften*, Jubiläumsausgabe, ed. F. Bamberger, H. Bordianski, S. Rawidowicz, B. Strauß, L. Strauß, I. Elbogen, J. Guttmann, E. Mittwoch and continued by Alexander Altmann, 17 vols. (Stuttgart-Bad Constatt: Friedrich Fromann Verlag, 1971 – ) = *J.A.*

*Gesammelte Schriften*, ed. G. B. Mendelssohn, 7 vols. (Leipzig: F. A. Brockhaus, 1843–5) = *Schriften*.

## INTRODUCTION

1 Arthur C. Danto, *The Transfiguration of the Commonplace. A Philosophy of Art* (Cambridge, Mass.: Harvard University Press, 1981), p. 135.

2 Algirdas Julien Greimas and Joseph Courtés, *Sémiotique. Dictionnaire raisonné de la théorie du langage* (Paris: Hachette, 1979), p. 129. The works by Foucault and Lotman which most clearly rest on the two hypotheses mentioned and to which my own work is most indebted are: Michel Foucault, *The Order of Things. An Archaeology of the Human Sciences* (New York: Vintage Books, 1973); Jurij M. Lotman, 'Das Problem des Zeichens und des Zeichensystems und die Typologie

der russischen Kultur des 11.–19. Jahrhunderts,' in J.M.L., *Aufsätze zur Theorie und Methodologie der Literatur und Kultur*, ed. Karl Eimermacher (Kronberg Ts.: Scriptor Verlag, 1974), pp. 378–411.

3 Cf. Juri M. Lotman, 'Problèmes de la typologie des cultures,' in *Essays in Semiotics/Essais de sémiotique*, ed. Julia Kristeva, Josette Rey-Debove, Donna Jean Umiker (The Hague: Mouton, 1971), p. 50: 'Culture is superimposed upon natural language and its relation to this language is one of its essential parameters. The articulation of cultures in view of the type of relations they entertain with the sign will permit an eventual classification of cultures.'

4 The original printing of Baumgarten's *Meditationes philosophicae de nonnullis ad poema pertinentibus* is reproduced in: Alexander Gottlieb Baumgarten, *Reflections on Poetry*, translated, with the original text, an introduction and notes by Karl Aschenbrenner and William B. Holter (Berkeley and Los Angeles: University of California Press, 1954). The term 'aesthetica' occurs at par. 66. The quotation is from: Jean Paul, *Vorschule zur Ästhetik*, ed. Norbert Miller (München: Hanser, 1963), p. 22.

5 For the development of aesthetics in England and France the reader is referred to the following works: Ernst Cassirer, *Die Philosophie der Aufklärung* (Tübingen: J. C. B. Mohr (Paul Siebeck), 1932); Jacques Chouillet, *L'Esthétique des lumières* (Paris: Presses Universitaires de France, 1974); Monroe C. Beardsley, *Aesthetics from Classical Greece to the Present: A Short History* (New York: Macmillan, 1966); Harold Osborne, *Aesthetics and Art Theory. An Historical Introduction* (New York: E. P. Dutton, 1970); and René Wellek, *A History of Modern Criticism*, vol. 1, *The Later 18th Century* (New Haven, Conn.: Yale University Press, 1955).

6 *The Transfiguration of the Commonplace*. pp. 149–60.

7 As 'creative interpretive responses' I would especially call attention to: Wilfried Barner, Gunter Grimm, Helmut Kiesel, Martin Kramer, *Lessing. Epoche – Werk – Wirkung* (München: C. H. Beck, 1975), which contains the best summary of the *Laocoon* available; and Friedrich A. Kittler, 'Erziehung ist Offenbarung'. Zur Struktur der Familie in Lessings Dramen,' in *Jahrbuch der deutschen Schillergesellschaft* XXI (1977), pp. 111–37.

8 *Grosses vollständiges Universal-Lexikon aller Wissenschaften und Künste*, vol. 61 (Leipzig und Halle: Verlegts Johann Heinrich Zedler, 1749), article 'Zeichen,' pp. 545–75.

9 Johann Heinrich Lambert, *Philosophische Schriften* I–II, *Neues Organon* (Hildesheim: Georg Olms, 1965) (Reprint of the original edition, Leipzig, 1764).

10 Indeed, the genesis of the *Critique of Judgement* can be observed in Kant's marginal notes, made for the purpose of teaching, to Georg Friedrich Meier's *Auszug aus der Vernunftlehre* (Halle: bei Johann Justinus Gebauer, 1752). Both Meier's handbook and Kant's notes are reprinted in: Immanuel Kant, *Gesammelte Schriften*, ed. Königlich

Preussischen Akadamie der Wissenschaften, vol. XVI (Berlin: Druck und Verlag von Georg Reimer, 1914).

11 Johann Christoph Gottsched, *Versuch einer Critischen Dichtkunst* (Darmstadt: Wissenschaftliche Buchgesellschaft, 1962) (Reprint of the Fourth edition, Leipzig, 1751); Johann Jacob Breitinger, *Critische Dichtkunst*, 2 vols. (Stuttgart: J. B. Metzlersche Verlagsbuchhandlung, 1966) (Reprint of the original edition, Zurich, 1740).

12 For a recent statement of this view see Rolf Grimminger, 'Die Utopie der vernünftigen Lust. Sozialphilosophische Skizze zur Ästhetik des 18. Jahrhunderts bis zu Kant,' in: *Aufklärung und literarische Offentlichkeit*, ed. Christa Bürger, Peter Bürger and Jochen Schulte-Sasse (Frankfurt a.M.: Suhrkamp, 1980), pp. 116–32.


CHAPTER 1

1 See Martin Heidegger, 'Die Zeit des Weltbildes,' in *Holzwege* (Frankfurt a.M.: Vittorio Klostermann, 1952), pp. 69–104; Michel Foucault, *The Order of Things*, pp. 46–214; Ian Hacking, *Why Does Language Matter to Philosophy?* (Cambridge, London, New York, Melbourne: Cambridge University Press, 1975), pp. 15–53, 163–70.

2 *German Metaphysics*, par. 751.

3 *Psy. Emp.* pars. 35 and 268. See also *German Metaphysics*, par. 273.

4 *Vernunftlehre*, par. 10.

5 See Michel Foucault, *The Birth of the Clinic* (London: Tavistock, 1973), p. xiii; Ian Hacking, *Why Does Language Matter to Philosophy?* pp. 32–3.

6 See Nelson Goodman, *Languages of Art* (Indianapolis/New York: Bobbs-Merrill, 1968).

7 This is Ian Hacking's term for the age of the representational paradigm. See *Why Does Language Matter to Philosophy?* pp. 15–53, 163–70.

8 The diagram summarizes distinctions drawn in *German Logic*, I, pars. 9–17.

9 *German Logic*, I, par. 9.

10 *Ibid.*, I, par. 13.

11 Johann Heinrich Lambert, *Neues Organon*, 'Dianologie,' par. 9.

12 See *Psy. Emp.*, par. 37.

13 *German Logic*, I, par. 16.

14 *German Metaphysics*, par. 277.

15 *Ibid.*, pars. 282–5.

16 Ferdinand de Saussure, *Course in General Linguistics*, trans. Wade Baskin (New York, London, Toronto: McGraw-Hill, 1966), pp. 68–9.

17 See Jonathan Culler, *Ferdinand de Saussure*, Fontana Modern Masters (London: Fontana Books, 1976), pp. 12–22.

18 Umberto Eco, *A Theory of Semiotics*, Advances in Semiotics (Bloomington, London: Indiana University Press, 1976), p. 49. See Jurij M. Lotman, *Die Struktur literarischer Texte*, trans. Rolf-Dietrich Keil

(München: Wilhelm Fink Verlag, 1972), pp. 59–60, where the systematic character of the sign is also emphasized.

19  *German Metaphysics*, par. 294.

20  *Ontologia*, par. 958.

21  *Course in General Linguistics*, pp. 71–2.

22  *Psy. Emp.*, par. 266.

23  *Psy. Emp.*, pars. 280–1.

24  *Psy. Emp.*, pars. 234 and 281.

25  Wolff is one of those philosophers who, in Wilfrid Sellars' phrase, endeavor 'to break out of discourse to an *arché* beyond discourse.' 'Empiricism and the Philosophy of Mind,' in W.S., *Science, Perception and Reality* (New York: The Humanities Press, 1963), p. 196. Jacques Derrida analyzes this derivation of the sign as a classical philosophical strategy. See J. D., *La Voix et le phénomène* (Paris: Presses Universitaires de France, 1967), p. 57.

26  See Étienne Bonnot de Condillac, *Essai sur l'origine des connaissances humaines*, texte établi et annoté par Charles Porset, précédé de 'L'archéologie du frivole,' par Jacques Derrida (Paris: Galilée, 1973), pp. 128–33.

27  See Johann Gottfried Herder, *Sprachphilosophische Schriften*, ed. Erich Heintel (Hamburg: Felix Meiner, 1960), pp. 19–30.

28  *Essai sur l'origine des connaissances humaines*, p. 133.

29  *Ibid.*, pp. 194–9.

30  'Sendschreiben an den Herrn Magister Lessing in Leipzig,' *J.A.*, II, pp. 83–109. The passage on the origin of language is on pages 102–9.

31  Mendelssohn touches on this point himself: 'One finds in all languages the clearest indications that they once consisted entirely of imitative tones [*nachahmenden Tönen*]. The emphatic words which the poets know how to use with such effect are all characterized by a certain imitative sound by virtue of which they designate objects in a most sensate manner.' *Ibid.*, p. 109.

32  *German Metaphysics*, par. 316. See also *Psy. Emp.*, pars. 286 and 288.

33  *Ontologia*, par. 959.

34  *German Metaphysics*, par. 323.

35  *German Logic*, I, par. 4.

36  *German Logic*, II, par. 15.

37  I borrow the phrase from J. N. Findlay. See Gilbert Ryle and J. N. Findlay, 'Use, Usage and Meaning,' in *Readings in Semantics*, ed. Farhang Zabeeh, E. D. Klemke and Arthur Jacobson (Urbana: University of Illinois Press, 1974), pp. 479–97, here p. 488.

38  See *German Logic*, II. par. 5.

39  Berkeley makes this very clear in *Principles of Human Knowledge* (1710): 'It were, therefore, to be wished that every one would use his utmost endeavors to obtain a clear view of the ideas he would consider, separating from them all that dress and incumbrance of words which so much contribute to blind the judgement and divide the attention. In vain do we extend our view into the heavens and pry into the

entrails of the earth, in vain do we consult the writings of learned men and trace the dark footsteps of antiquity – we need only draw the curtain of words, to behold the fairest of knowledge, whose fruit is excellent and within reach of our hand.' *Selections from Berkeley*, ed. Alexander Campbell Fraser (Oxford: Clarendon Press, 1891), p. 35.

40 See Michel Foucault, *The Order of Things*, p. 56: 'Language has withdrawn from the midst of beings themselves and has entered a period of transparency and neutrality.' The same point is made at p. 79: 'From an extreme point of view, one might say that language in the Classical era does not exist. But that it functions: its whole existence is located in its representative role, is limited precisely to that role and finally exhausts it.'

41 *Ontologia*, par. 952.

42 See Wilhelm von Humboldt, *Gesammelte Schriften*, ed. Königlich Preussischen Akademie der Wissenschaften, 17 vols. (Berlin: B. Behr's Verlag, 1903–36), III, p. 331; VI, p. 119.

43 *Ontologia*, par. 956.

44 *Ibid*.

45 Meier, *Anfgr.*, par. 163.

46 John Locke, *An Essay Concerning Human Understanding*, collated and annotated by Alexander Campbell Fraser, 2 vols. (New York: Dover, 1959), I, Book II, Ch. 8.

47 *Selections from Berkeley*, pp. 71–2.

48 See Foucault, *The Order of Things*, p. 59: 'From now on, however, it is within knowledge itself that the sign is to perform its signifying function; it is from knowledge that it will borrow its certainty or its probability.'

49 John Freccero summarizes Augustine's view as follows: 'All of creation is a discourse leading to Love, just as all desire is ultimately a desire for the Word. The theology of the Word binds together language and desire by ordering both to God, in whom they are grounded.' 'The Fig Tree and the Laurel: Petrarch's Poetics,' *Diacritics* 5 (1975), p. 35.

50 *Metaphysica*, par. 358. See also Meier, *Auslegungskunst*, par. 35.

51 *Auslegungskunst*, par. 38.

52 *Auslegungskunst*, par. 54. See also Baumgarten, *Metaphysica*, par. 349.

53 *Auslegungskunst*, par. 54.

54 *Ontologia*, par. 967.

55 Meier, *Anfgr.*, par. 519.

56 Meier, *Theoretische Lehre*, par. 220.

57 *German Metaphysics*, par. 318.

58 *German Logic*, I, par. 13.

59 *Ibid*.

60 *Psy. Emp.*, par. 329.

61 *German Metaphysics*, par. 319.

62 Johann Christoph Schwab, *Von den dunkeln Vorstellungen, ein*

*Beytrag zu der Lehre von dem Ursprunge der menschlichen Erkennt-niss, nebst einem Anhang über die Frage: in wie fern die Klugheit eine Tugend sey?* (Stuttgart: bey J. F. Steinkopf, 1813), pp. 34-5.

63  *Psy. Emp.*, par. 351. See also *German Metaphysics*, par. 321.

64  *Psy. Rat.*, par. 461.

65  Jean-Jacques Rousseau, *Essai sur l'origine des langues* (Paris: Biblio-thèque du Graphe, 1970), esp. chapters 4 and 5. The progressive-regressive movement of this myth has been analyzed by Jacques Derrida, *Of Grammatology*, trans. Gayatri C. Spivak (Baltimore, Md.: Johns Hopkins University Press, 1976).

66  On this point see Hans Werner Arndt, 'Die Semiotik Christian Wolffs als Propädeutik der ars characteristica combinatoria und der ars inveniendi,' *Zeitschrift für Semiotik* 1 (1979), pp. 325-31, esp. pp. 328-9.

67  Johann Gottfried Herder, *Sämtliche Werke*, I, pp. 361-414.

68  *Psy. Emp.*, par. 312. See the article by Hans Werner Arndt cited above (note 66) for further details on the *ars characteristica combinatoria*.

69  *The Order of Things*, p. 66.

70  'Das Problem des Zeichens und des Zeichensystems und die Typologie der russischen Kulture des 11.-19. Jahrhunderts,' p. 401.

71  The notion of aura I have in mind here is derived from Walter Benjamin. According to Benjamin, aura, or a sense of the un-approachability of objects, is what is lost when those objects become mechanically reproducible. For Enlightenment culture, language is a set of reproducible tokens (of a conventionally established type) which in themselves are of no significance. See Walter Benjamin, *Das Kunstwerk im Zeitalter seiner technischen Reproduzierbarkeit* (Frankfurt a.M.: Suhrkamp, 1963), pp. 13-19.

72  René Descartes, *Discours de la méthode*, avec introduction et notes par Étienne Gilson (Paris: Librairie Philosophique J. Vrin, 1970), pp. 70-1.

73  Wolff, *Philosophia rationalis sive Logica*, par. 139, quoted after Hans Werner Arndt, 'Die Semiotik Christian Wolffs,' p. 327.

74  Baumgarten, *Metaphysica*, par. 347. Meier, *Auslegungskunst*, par. 7.

75  *German Logic*, II, par. 1.

76  *Anfgr.*, par. 711.

77  John Locke, *An Essay Concerning Human Understanding*, II, p. 12.

78  *Psy. Rat.*, par. 342.

79  This is the opening sentence of Rousseau's *Essai sur l'origine des langues*.

80  Condillac, *Essai sur l'origine des connaissances humaines*, p. 128.

81  Wolff, *Psy. Rat.*, par. 461.

82  *German Metaphysics*, par. 323.

83  *German Metaphysics*, par. 956-63.

84  *Sämtliche Werke*, XXXII, p. 180: 'A completely philosophical language would have to be the language of the gods who looked on as the things of the world were formed, who saw beings in their state of

becoming and origination and therefore created every name for an object genetically and materially.'

85  *Psy. Emp.*, par. 312 (my emphasis).
86  Moses Mendelssohn, *Schriften*, IV/2, p. 346.
87  Wolff, *Psy. Emp.*, par. 312.

## CHAPTER 2

1  This is a fair appraisal, I think, of the following works: Armand Nivelle, *Kunst- und Dichtungstheorien zwischen Aufklärung und Klassik*, revised German edition (Berlin: de Gruyter, 1960); Fritz Bamberger's introduction to Mendelssohn, *J.A.*, I, pp. lx–lxvii; Lieselotte Richter, *Philosophie der Dichtkunst. Moses Mendelssohns Ästhetik zwischen Aufklärung und Sturm und Drang* (Berlin: Chronos Verlag, 1948). It is true, with modifications, of: Alfred Baeumler, *Kants Kritik der Urteilskraft. Ihre Geschichte und Systematik*. Vol. I. *Das Irrationalitätsproblem in der Aesthetik und Logik des 18. Jahrhunderts bis zur Kritik der Urteilskraft* (Halle: Max Niemeyer Verlag, 1932). Bäumler is followed by Hans Böhm, 'Das Schönheitsproblem bei G. F. Meier,' *Archiv für die gesamte Psychologie* LVI (1926), 177–252. An important exception is the exquisite study by Alexander Altmann, *Moses Mendelssohns Frühschriften zur Metaphysik* (Tübingen: J. C. B. Mohr [Paul Siebeck], 1969).

2  The notion of theory-type is adapted from Michel Foucault's notion of 'discursive formation,' which I have modified to suit the study of theories of art. See M.F., *The Archaeology of Knowledge*, trans. A. M. Sheridan Smith (New York: Harper & Row, 1976), pp. 21–76.

3  See Christa Bürger, *Der Ursprung der bürgerlichen Institution Kunst. Literatursoziologische Untersuchungen zum klassischen Goethe* (Frankfurt a.M.: Suhrkamp, 1977). Christa Bürger sees *divertissement* and 'Repräsentation' as the primary functions of the courtly-aristocratic institution of art (passim). This concept of representation has to do with the exhibition of hierarchical social values, not with representation in the sense I employ it.

4  *Herders Sämtliche Werke*, ed. Bernhard Suphan, 33 vols. (Berlin: Weidmannsche Buchhandlung, 1877–1913), VIII, p. 208. The German term Herder employs here is *Divination*.

5  See Erich Auerbach, ' "La Cour et la Ville," ' in E. A., *Scenes from the Drama of European Literature* (New York: Meridan Books, 1959), pp. 131–79, esp. p. 159: 'The notion of *bienséance* comprises a mixture of ethical and aesthetic considerations, cemented by a subtly developed sense of tact. In it morality, rules of social conduct, and aesthetic measure are scarcely distinguishable. Practical morality, the morality that deals in ethical and inethical behavior, is in any case the weakest element in *bienséance*, while the strongest is a purely social prudery, largely in regard to vocabulary.'

6  The term hermeneutics (*hermeneutica, Auslegungskunst*) was, of course,

current in representational theory, as Meier's *Versuch einer allgemeinen Auslegungskunst* illustrates. But hermeneutics is here a subdivision of semiotics or characteristic. It is the codification of the 'rules whose observation allows meanings to be cognized from signs.' (*Auslegungskunst*, par. 1.) The meanings in question are 'connected representations' (par. 103); they have nothing to do with the hidden essence of an author's individuality.

7   *Aesthetica*, par. 14.

8   *Ibid.* Similar definitions are given by Meier (*Anfgr.*, par. 23) and Mendelssohn (*J.A.*, I, p. 170, 431).

9   Max Dessoir, *Aesthetics and Theory of Art*, trans. S. A. Emery (Detroit: Wayne State University Press, 1970), p. 35. The original German edition is from 1906.

10  *Schriften*, IV/1, p. 314.

11  *J.A.*, I, p. 431. Since it is a question of a definition here, it is perhaps advisable to provide the original German formulation: 'Das Wesen der schönen Künste und Wissenschaften besteht in einer *künstlichen sinnlich-vollkommenen* Vorstellung, oder in einer *durch die Kunst vorgestellten sinnlichen Vollkommenheit.*'

12  *Grundsatz*, par. 20.

13  Wolff, *Psy. Emp.*, par. 580.

14  *Aesthetica*, par. 1.

15  *Metaphysica*, par. 521. See also *Aesthetica*, par. 17.

16  See *Aesthetica*, pars. 557, 560; *Anfgr.* par. 312.

17  See *Metaphysica*, par. 517.

18  *Theoretische Lehre*, par. 194 (my emphasis).

19  Bernhard Poppe, *Alexander Gottlieb Baumgarten. Seine Bedeutung und Stellung in der Leibniz-Wolffischen Philosophie, nebst Veröffentlichung einer bisher unbekannten Handschrift der Ästhetik Baumgartens* (Borna-Leipzig: Buchdruckerei Robert Noske, 1907), p. 167.

20  Meier claims that the arts 'enliven the whole human being' (*Anfgr.*, par. 15) and that they enable us to 'disseminate truth as human beings among human beings.' (*Anfgr.*, par. 14.) We have here the origins of the aesthetic humanism that culminates in the work of Kant and Schiller. Exactly how aesthetic representation engages the whole person will become clear in my discussion of Mendelssohn's theory.

21  *Aesthetica*, par. 37.

22  The centrality of the category of cognitive life or vitality in Baumgarten's aesthetics has been overlooked in the past. Nivelle, who wants to make Baumgarten all too Kantian, insists that Baumgarten conceives of the aesthetic 'without any relationship to the will,' (*Kunst- und Dichtungstheorien*, p. 12), that is, without any affective dimension. Böhm recognizes the centrality of the category in Meier's work, but assumes it would have played little role in Baumgarten's thinking even if the fragmentary *Aesthetica* had been completed. ('Das Schönheitsproblem bei G. F. Meier,' pp. 200–3, pp. 211–22.) A look at *Ethica*, par. 66, demonstrates that Baumgarten thought

cognitive life to be of extreme importance. Likewise, the manuscript reprinted by Poppe (*Alexander Gottlieb Baumgarten*, p. 210) indicates unequivocally (as does *Aesthetica*, par. 22) that the aesthetic is characterized by an affective-conative dimension.

23 *Metaphysica*, par. 652. See also *Ethica*, par. 669; Meier, *Theoretische Lehre*, par. 57.

24 The fact that these perfections apply to all types of thought, not just aesthetic representations, is seldom noticed. Meier's logic (*Vernunftlehre*) insists on them no less strongly than his aesthetics (*Angfr.*). The six perfections accrue, of course, to God in the highest degree (*Metaphysica*, par. 873). What Aron Gurwitsch writes of Leibniz is equally true of Baumgarten: 'Whereas Arnauld wants to regard human knowing purely in and of itself, Leibniz relates it to the infinitely perfect and complete knowing of God, which provides the measure and norm for human knowing.' (Leibniz, *Philosophie des Panlogismus* [Berlin/New York: Walter de Gruyter, 1974], p. 24.) Thus, it is an ethical obligation to maximize in oneself the six cognitive perfections, that is, to illustrate in oneself the 'glory of god.' (*Ethica*, par. 11.) This is a point of some importance: *the aesthetic is first conceptualized in terms of ethical-theological values*.

25 *J.A.*, I, p. 384.

26 *J.A.*, I, p. 169. Meier holds the same position: 'The drive springs of the soul, therefore, are appeal (*Gefallen*) and repulsion (*Mißfallen*), pleasure and displeasure.' *Theoretische Lehre*, par. 56. As Meier's account shows, all the affects, emotions and passions – all the forms of affective-conative activity the soul exhibits – have their source in these basic appraisive responses to the value qualities (perfections and imperfections) of the represented object.

27 The text of the treatise is available in *J.A.*, II, pp. 149–55. The complete correspondence is reproduced in *Lessing, Mendelssohn, Nicolai. Briefwechsel über das Trauerspiel*, ed. Jochen Schulte-Sasse (München: Winkler, 1972). A recent account of the debate which summarizes the earlier literature is: Arnold Heidsieck, 'Der Disput zwischen Lessing und Mendelssohn über das Trauerspiel,' *Lessing Yearbook* XI (1979), pp. 7–34.

28 'Rhapsodie, oder Zusätze zu den Briefen über die Empfindungen,' *J.A.*, I, pp. 383–424.

29 There is a line of theoretical development involved in Mendelssohn's distinction between desire and feeling which ought to be briefly mentioned here. These two dimensions of affectivity were not distinguished in the traditional monist account of the soul that runs from Leibniz across Wolff and Baumgarten to Meier. Mendelssohn's work through the years exhibits an increasingly severe elaboration of the distinction. The 'Reflections on the Sources and Combinations of the Fine Arts and Letters' ('Betrachtungen über die Quellen und Verbindungen der schönen Künste und Wissenschaften,' 1757) repeats the position of 'On Mastery over our Inclinations.' (Cf. *J.A.*, I, p. 170.)

But four years later, in his 'Remarks on the Philosophical Writings' ('Bemerkungen zu den Philosophischen Schriften, 1761'), Mendelssohn redefines the two spheres: 'Pleasant feeling is, as it were, a positive judgement of the soul as regards its actual condition; willing, however, is the effort of the soul to make this condition real.' (*J.A.*, I. p. 225). Finally, the well-known essay 'On the Capacities of Cognition, Feeling, and Desire' ('Über das Erkenntniss-, Empfindungs-, und Begehrungs-vermögen, 1776, *J.A.*, III/1, pp. 276–9,) sees in wanting and feeling two fundamentally different activities of the soul. In my view, this line of theoretical development has been overemphasized in the literature, primarily because it seems to approach the Kantian system. As I shall show, Mendelssohn's most fully elaborated accounts of aesthetic experience refer to the soul's total – representational and conative – activity.

30  *J.A.*, II, p. 149.

31  *Reflections on Poetry*, pars. 16–17.

32  The 'Letters on the Feelings' ('Briefe über die Empfindungen,' 1755) describes this extensive clarity in the following words: 'All representations of beauty must be enclosed within the borders of clarity. Indeed, one can go even further. The clearer the representation of the beautiful object is, the more lively will be the feeling, the more fiery the pleasure that arises from it. A clearer representation allows us to perceive a greater manifold and more internal relationships within the manifold.' *J.A.*, I, p. 50.

33  *J.A.*, III/1, p. 273.

34  *J.A.*, II, p. 150.

35  'Betrachtungen über die Quellen und die Verbindungen der schönen Künste und Wissenschaften,' *J.A.*, I, pp. 165–90.

36  *J.A.*, I, p. 168.

37  *J.A.*, I, p. 168.

38  The argument against Charles Batteux' *Les Beaux-Arts réduits à un même principe* (1746) is presented at *J.A.*, I, p. 169.

39  *J.A.*, I, pp. 169–70.

40  Meier, *Theoretische Lehre*, par. 57. See also Baumgarten, *Metaphysica*, par. 652; *Ethica*, par. 669. Mendelssohn held the same position: 'But I am speaking here about a perception and cognition of the *object*, or about an *intuitive cognition*, not about a mere consciousness of signs and words by which the properties of the object are indicated: for the latter leaves the soul in an indifferent state and excites neither pleasure nor displeasure.' *J.A.*, I, p. 385.

41  *J.A.*, I, p. 170.

42  *J.A.*, I, p. 170.

43  *Theoretische Lehre*, par. 97.

44  'Über die Hauptgrundsätze der schönen Künste und Wissenschaften,' *J.A.*, I, pp. 426–52.

45  *J.A.*, I, p. 170.

46  *J.A.*, I, p. 431.

47  *J.A.*, I, p. 431.

48 Similar shifts in the location of the perfection – from the object to the representation – can be found elsewhere in Mendelssohn's writings. See *Schriften*, IV/1, p. 577 (a review of Johann Georg Sulzer's *Hand Lexicon, or Brief Dictionary of the Fine Arts and Letters*, 1759) and IV/2, p. 29 (a review of Johann Adolf Schlegel's translation with commentary of Batteux' *The Fine Arts Reduced to a Single Principle*, 1759). As the latter example shows, Mendelssohn realized that his revised concept (sensately perfect representation) was in accord with Baumgarten's view.

49 *J.A.*, I, p. 386.

50 *J.A.*, I, p. 389.

51 *J.A.*, I, p. 389.

52 I use the term 'transcendental' in the Kantian sense, which, though foreign to Mendelssohn, seems to me applicable here.

53 The remarks contained in this and the following paragraph involve a highly condensed interpretation of the following texts: 'On Mastery over the Inclinations,' especially the section on 'illusion,' *J.A.*, II, pp. 154–5; parts of the 'Rhapsody,' *J.A.*, I, pp. 386–92; 'Answers to Some Questions regarding the Art of Acting' ('Beantwortung einiger Fragen in der Schauspielkunst,' 1770), *Schriften*, IV/1, pp. 26–8; the review of J. A. Schlegel's Batteux commentary, *Schriften*, IV/2, pp. 9–27.

54 Mendelssohn discusses the classical, Aristotelian example of the snake at *J.A.*, II, pp. 154–5.

55 On Baumgarten's classification of the philosophical disciplines in general and of the subdivisions of aesthetics in particular, see Ursula Franke, 'Die Semiotik als Abschluß der Asthetik. A. G. Baumgartens Bestimmung der Semiotik als ästhetische Propädeutik,' *Zeitschrift für Semiotik* 1 (1979), pp. 345–60.

56 This is the evaluation of Tzvetan Todorov, 'Esthétique et sémiotique au XVIIIᵉ siècle,' *Critique* XXIX (1973), pp. 29–39. Baumgarten's fragmentary *Aesthetica*, of course, does not include a section on semiotics. Meier's *Anfgr.* does, but it is restricted mainly to a discussion of the stylistic virtues. In his review of an excerpt from Meier's *Anfgr.*, Mendelssohn criticizes the fact that the semiotics of aesthetic signification is given such short shrift. See Mendelssohn, *Schriften*, IV/1, pp. 313–18.

57 Marie-Luise Linn, 'A. G. Baumgartens "Aesthetica" und die antike Rhetorik,' *Deutsche Vierteljahrsschrift für Literaturwissenschaft und Geistesgeschichte* XLI (1967), pp. 424–43. Reprinted in: *Rhetorik. Beiträge zu ihrer Geschichte in Deutschland vom 16.–20. Jahrhundert*, ed. Helmut Schanze (Frankfurt a.M.: Fischer-Athenäum, 1974), pp. 105–25.

58 For an interpretation of rhetorical doctrine that emphasizes this communicational aspect, see Dieter Breuer, *Einführung in die pragmatische Texttheorie* (München: Wilhelm Fink, 1974), pp. 142–220.

59 Recall Lotman's characterization of Enlightenment culture as a 'battle

against the sign.' (See above, Chapter 1, 'The Position of the Sign in Enlightenment Culture.')

60 *Anfgr.*, par. 525.

61 Hans Peter Hermann analyzes the earliest phases of this transformation as they appear in the works of Gottsched and Breitinger in his book: *Naturnachahmung und Einbildungskraft* (Bad Homburg/Berlin/Zürich: Gehlen Verlag, 1970). Michael Fried offers a brilliant discussion of the same transformation as it occurs in painting theory in: *Absorption and Theatricality* (Baltimore, Md. and London: The Johns Hopkins University Press, 1981).

62 On this recoding of the place of poetry within the culture at large, see the article by Jörg Zimmermann: 'Ästhetische Erfahrung und die "Sprache der Natur,"' in *Sprache und Welterfahrung*, ed. Jörg Zimmermann (München: Fink, 1978), pp. 234–56.

63 *Anfgr.*, par. 711. The statement is printed with special emphasis in Meier's text.

64 This and the quotation immediately preceding it are from *Schriften*, IV/1, pp. 348–9.

65 *Anfgr.*, par. 781.

66 'Vom Werthe der Reime,' foreword to Samuel Gotthold Lange, *Horazische Oden* (Halle: Carl Hermann Hemmerde, 1747).

67 'Vom Werthe der Reime,' p. 7.

68 *Ibid.*

69 *Ibid.*, pp. 7–8.

70 *Ibid.*, p. 7.

71 *Reflections on Poetry*, par. 89.

72 See Baumgarten, *Metaphysica*, par. 517, for the basic definitions. Emphatic terms are said to convey pregnant representations (*perceptiones praegnantes*), that is, representations that are replete with features. See also Meier, *Anfgr.*, par. 126.

73 See the quotation from *J.A.*, II, p. 109 at footnote 31 of Chapter 1.

74 *Schriften*, IV/1, p. 259.

75 Of course, Aristotle accords a good deal of importance to metaphor as well. Jacques Derrida has pointed up the systematic relationship between the Aristotelian concepts of metaphor and mimesis in his 'The White Mythology: Metaphor in the Text of Philosophy,' *New Literary History* 6 (1974), pp. 5–74, esp. pp. 30–46. Perhaps we have here a clue to the internal, systematic basis for the Aristotle reception of the Enlightenment: the Aristotelian model of mimesis could be easily integrated within the representational paradigm that characterizes eighteenth-century aesthetics and poetics.

76 See Johann Christoph Gottsched, *Versuch einer Critischen Dichtkunst*, pp. 257–268.

77 Johann Georg Sulzer, 'Anmerkungen über den gegenseitigen Einfluß der Vernunft in die Sprache, und der Sprache in die Vernunft,' in *J.G.S.*, *Vermischte Philosophische Schriften* (Leipzig: bey Weidmanns Erben und Reich, 1773), pp. 166–98. I use Sulzer's essay here because

it exemplifies better than any single text by Baumgarten, Meier, or Mendelssohn the systematic position of the concept of metaphor in Enlightenment thinking. The essay first appeared in French in the yearbook of the Berlin Academy in 1767. Like all of Sulzer's work, it is a compendium of views articulated by both French and German writers.

78 *Ibid.*, p. 190.
79 *Ibid.*, p. 189.
80 *Ibid.*, p. 191.
81 Mendelssohn, *Schriften*, IV/1, p. 349.
82 *J.A.*, I, pp. 437–8.
83 Cf. Jürgen Schröder, *Gotthold Ephraim Lessing. Sprache und Drama* (München: Wilhelm Fink, 1972), pp. 326–32; Tzvetan Todorov, 'Esthétique et sémiotique au XVIIIᵉ siècle,' pp. 34–5. Both view Lessing's notion of poetry as a natural sign as a singular accomplishment: Schröder sees Lessing as anticipating a new way of viewing language and Todorov sees him as achieving a unique degree of systematization.
84 Sulzer, 'On the Reciprocal Influence of Reason on Language, and of Language on Reason,' p. 188.
85 *Anfgr.*, par. 521.
86 At *Anfgr.*, par. 519, Meier argues that the use of essential signs, that is, signs which are similar to their signified objects, enhances the perfection of the poem. It is also interesting to note that Baumgarten (*Ethica*, par. 143) urges the use of essential signs in religious ceremonies. I will discuss Mendelssohn's use of the notion of natural sign in the analysis and description of poetry at the end of this chapter.
87 *Anfgr.*, par. 521. The definition repeats verbatim Baumgarten's use of the terms at *Ethica*, par. 366.
88 *Anfgr.*, par. 678. See also Baumgarten, *Aesthetica*, pars. 622–4.
89 *J.A.*, I, p. 491. This and the following remarks are taken from Mendelssohn's essay 'On the Sublime and the Naive in the Belles Lettres' ('Über das Erhabene und Naive in den schönen Wissenschaften') of 1758. I quote from the slightly revised 1771 edition of the essay (*J.A.*, I, pp. 453–94).
90 *J.A.*, I, p. 488.
91 *J.A.*, I, p. 491.
92 *Psy. Emp.*, par. 312.
93 The most important text in which Mendelssohn attempts to classify the arts is his 'Reflections on the Sources and Combinations of the Fine Arts and Letters' of 1757 (*J.A.*, I, pp. 165–90). Here I follow the revised version of the essay, 'On the Chief Principles of the Fine Arts and Letters,' from 1771 (*J.A.*, I, pp. 426–52).
94 *J.A.*, I, p. 437.
95 *J.A.*, I, p. 439.
96 Recall Mendelssohn's formulation defining the aesthetic in general: 'And, since the purpose of the fine arts is to please [*gefallen*], we can

assume the following principle as indubitable: the essence of the fine arts and letters consists in an *artistically produced sensate-perfect representation*, . . .' *J.A.*, I, p. 431.

97   Mendelssohn himself concedes as much regarding architecture. See *J.A.*, I, p. 450.

98   *J.A.*, I, p. 438.

99   *J.A.*, I, p. 438.

100  For an interesting modern interpretation of this rule, see Roland Barthes, 'Diderot, Brecht, Eisenstein,' in R.B., *Image – Music – Text*, ed. Stephen Heath (New York: Hill and Wang, 1977), pp. 69–78.

101  For Mendelssohn's formulation, see *J.A.*, I, pp. 440–1.

102  *J.A.*, III/1, p. 274.

103  *J.A.*, I, pp. 444–5.

104  *J.A.*, I, p. 448.

105  *J.A.*, I, p. 443.

106  *J.A.*, III/1, p. 242. Mendelssohn's notes on Burke were written shortly after the publication of Burke's *Inquiry* and were then sent to Lessing. For the biographical details, see the introduction to *J.A.*, III/1, pp. xli–xlv. In 1758, Mendelssohn published a review of Burke's *Inquiry* which is available in *Schriften*, IV/1, pp. 331–50.

107  Mendelssohn reiterates this point in his comments on Lessing's first *Laocoon*-plan (see especially *J.A.*, II, pp. 235, 241). Shortly after reading Burke, Mendelssohn applied his ideas regarding time and space in poetry to the discussion of descriptive poetry. The occasion was a review of Joseph Warton's *Essay on the Writing and Genius of Pope* (1756) See *Schriften*, IV/1, p. 396.

108  *J.A.*, III/1, p. 241.

109  Compare *J.A.*, III/1, p. 244: 'The sudden, the unexpected, is only a beauty in those arts which have their existence as a temporal sequence. In architecture or painting they are ugly.'

## CHAPTER 3

1  The review appeared in the ninth volume of the *Allgemeine Deutsche Bibliothek* (1769). It is reprinted as an appendix to Hugo Blümner's edition: *Lessings Laokoon*, herausgegeben und erläutert von Hugo Blümner, zweite verbesserte und vermehrte Auflage (Berlin: Weidmannsche Buchhandlung, 1880), pp. 683–703. The quotation is from this edition, pp. 686–7. Blümner's edition remains the most complete edition of the *Laocoon* and is especially valuable for its inclusion of the many fragments from Lessing's work on the problem of poetry and the plastic arts. Whenever I quote from these fragments in this chapter, I am citing from Blümner's edition. The citations will be identified parenthetically within the text with the initial B. and the page number (e.g., B., 686–7). All other quotations from Lessing's writings, including the published version of the *Laocoon*, are from the standard edition: Gotthold Ephraim Lessing, *Sämtliche Schriften*, herausgegeben von

Karl Lachmann, dritte, aufs neue durchgesehene und vermehrte Auflage besorgt durch Franz Muncker, 23 vols. (Stuttgart, Berlin, Leipzig: Göschen, später de Gruyter, 1886–1924). Quotations from this edition will be identified parenthetically within the text by volume number and page (e.g., IX, 14).

2 Jürgen Schröder – *Gotthold Ephraim Lessing. Sprache und Drama* – has provided a convincing interpretation of Lessing's work that centers on the critique of inherited terminology as the recurrent mode of operation in all of Lessing's writing.

3 On the importance of moderation to Lessing's critical procedure, see Ingrid Strohschneider-Kohrs, *Vom Prinzip des Maßes in Lessings Kritik*, Dichtung und Erkenntnis, No. 7 (Stuttgart: J. B. Metzlersche Verlagsbuchhandlung, 1969).

4 Cf. IX, 7.

5 See above, Chapter II, section 3.2.

6 This is Mendelssohn's term. See above, Chapter II, section 2.2.

7 See above, Chapter II, section 2.2.

8 The discussion of Sophocles' *Philoctetes* is strongly influenced by Mendelssohn's review of Johann Adolf Schlegel's Batteux translation and commentary. The review, quoted by Lessing elsewhere in the *Laocoon* (IX, 143 and 146–7), develops a theory of 'Ekel' (disgust or revulsion) and contains several interesting remarks on the function of the actor's movements, gestures and expressive sounds within the total dramatic construct. The following passage (*Schriften*, IV/2, pp. 15–17) is especially pertinent to my theme: 'The external action on the stage is meant to lend a helping hand to the poetic illusion and to give the poet's intention an extra degree of reality. However, as soon as it draws the spectator's attention away from the poetry and takes command for its own sake, it is used contrary to its function and disturbs the pleasant deception more than it supports it... For such external actions as are capable of attracting the spectator's attention away from the poetic illusion by virtue of the terrifying, miraculous, monstrous or base qualities that accrue to them not as signs of thoughts, but as mere pantomime – such actions must be... banished from the stage... The greater the force with which the poet affects our imagination, the more external action he can allow himself without doing damage to the poetry....' Mendelssohn's point is that those elements which are sensuously present on the stage must not assert themselves in their sensuous presence. Rather, they must function as *signs*, which point to the imaginary world of the drama. In drama, the poetic illusion – the imaginary presence of an absence – takes precedence over the sensuously present elements.

9 Here (IX, 143) Lessing is quoting Mendelssohn's remark on 'Ekel' in the above cited review (note 8). Lessing expands the application of Mendelssohn's statement to include the ugly as well as the repulsive, when it is represented in the visual arts. To say that something is always nature, never imitation, is to say that it always affects us as a

sensuous presence, never as the ideal presence of an existentially absent object.

10 Both of these examples are drawn from cultural contexts in which a *performance* model defines the situation of aesthetic reception. The doctrine of the autonomy of the aesthetic object emerges within representational theory for which art takes place not within a public context but within the mental immanence of an idealized subject. As it were, in representational theory the aesthetic object *forgets* the audience. See also Lessing's remarks on the 'witty courtier' Virgil and his strategy of flattery (IX, 113).

11 Cf. Lessing's remarks on the 'Weisheit' (wisdom) of the Laocoon artists at IX, 44.

12 On truth-to-life and expressiveness, cf. IX, 19; on communicative ends, cf. the remarks on the communication of religious doctrine at IX, 65; on the transmission of knowledge, cf. the disagreement with Ludovico Dolce at IX, 125; on appeal to the audience, cf. the discussion of the 'witty courtier' Virgil at IX, 113.

13 Cf. Fred O. Nolte, *Lessing's "Laokoon"* (Lancaster: Lancaster Press, 1940).

14 Louis Hjelmslev, *Prolegomena to a Theory of Language*, tr. by Francis J. Whitfield (Bloomington: Indiana University Publications in Anthropology and Linguistics, 1953), pp. 35–6.

15 Rather, I follow a certain interpretation of Hjelmslev as represented by Umberto Eco – *A Theory of Semiotics* (Bloomington: University of Indiana Press, 1976), pp. 50–4 – and Christian Metz – *Language and Cinema*, pp. 208–12.

16 The term 'dialectical' is common in Lessing criticism. Cf. Michael J. Böhler, *Soziale Rolle und Ästhetische Vermittlung* (Bern und Frankfurt a.M.: Verlag Herbert Lang, 1975), pp. 160–74; Wolfgang Ritzel, *Gotthold Ephraim Lessing* (Stuttgart: Kohlhammer, 1966), pp. 140–56; Peter Heller *Dialectics and Nihilism. Essays on Lessing, Nietzsche, Mann and Kafka* (Amhearst: University of Massachusetts Press, 1966), pp. 1–68. Jürgen Schröder (*Gotthold Ephraim Lessing*, passim) touches on a similar idea in his emphasis on the dialogical nature of Lessing's writing.

17 See Herder, *Sämmtliche Werke*, IV, pp. 62–9.

18 This gives me an opportunity to mark my divergence from the [most] recent book-length study of Lessing's *Laocoon*, Elida Maria Szarota *Lessings "Laokoon": Eine Kampfschrift für eine realistische Kunst und Poesie* (Weimar: Arion Verlag, 1959). Szarota asserts that Lessing was a 'Materialist' (p. 17, for instance) in his methodology, a contention I can no more agree with than her major thesis according to which the *Laocoon* contains the program of a realist aesthetics (socialist realism). On the other hand, Szarota's book has been extremely helpful to me in seeing Lessing in relation to his contemporaries and successors, especially Winckelmann.

19  Cf. Gottfried Wilhelm Leibniz, *Monadologie*, trans. Hermann Glockner (Stuttgart: Reclam, 1957), par. 49.

20  Cf. Immanuel Kant, *Kritik der Urteilskraft* (Frankfurt: Suhrkamp, 1974), par. 14.

21  Cf. B., 469: 'Indeed, I would like to ask whether it wouldn't have been preferable if the art of painting with oils had never been invented.'

22  Ritzel (*Gotthold Ephraim Lessing*, p. 111) speaks of Lessing's 'subjective bias' regarding this point. Lessing's personal taste is, however, impersonal and systematic on two accounts: first, it coincides with the classicist preference for form and outline over color; second, it coincides with the systematic preference for the intelligible over the sensual that runs through all of Lessing's aesthetic thought.

23  Cf. B., 446: 'As a consequence of the confines of the plastic arts, all their figures are immobile. The life of movement which they seem to have is the addition of our imagination; art does nothing except set our imagination in motion.'

24  Cf. Lessing's analysis of the funereal nature of Egyptian art, the stationary figures of which were suggestive of death. Daedalus created genuine art by calling these figures to life (B., 452–3). Beauty in the arts is for Lessing the appearance of life. Quietude is the form that this appearance must take so that there will be no conflict between the immobility of the figure and vitality. The effort to capture movement, however, necessarily deadens it by materializing it. If poetry is a 'higher' form of art than the plastic arts, then this is in part because poetry can present movement without these deadening results.

25  At times the opposition material/immaterial appears on the surface or lexical level of Lessing's texts as the opposition material/poetic. Cf. IX, 89; IX, 92.

26  In describing the transition from 'Einbildungskraft' (imagination) and 'Anschauung' (perception) to memory via the sign, Hegel underlines this aspect of verbal language. Cf. Georg Wilhelm Friedrich Hegel, *Enzyklopädie der philosophischen Wissenschaften im Grundrisse* (1830), hrsg. von Friedhelm Nicolin und Otto Pöggeler (Hamburg: Felix Meiner, 1969), par. 459: 'The mediation of representations through *the less sensate element of tones* [*das Unsinnliche der Töne*] will reveal itself in the following transition from representation to thought – memory – in its own full importance' (My emphasis).

27  For the term 'figurae,' see Hjelmslev, *Prolegomena*, p. 29.

28  See Charles F. Morris, *Foundations of a Theory of Signs*, Encyclopedia of Unified Science, Vol. I (Chicago: University of Chicago Press, 1938), pp. 13–20.

29  Morris (*Foundations*, p. 8) speaks of 'semiotical terms.'

30  At this point it is helpful to introduce the following typographical convention: oblique lines surrounding a term, e.g., /cloak/, indicate that the expression token is being referred to. Double quotation marks, e.g., "cloak", indicate that the content unit is being referred to. Normal quotation marks enclose the words or statements of others.

31 Jonathan Swift, *Gulliver's Travels and Other Writings*, ed. by Louis A. Landa (Boston, Mass.: Houghton Mifflin, 1960), pp. 150–1 (Riverside edition *Gulliver's Travels*, Part II, Chapter V).

32 See Baumgarten, *Reflections on Poetry*, par. 41.

33 I am representing Lessing's point of view here. One could conceivably argue that the sculpted robe suggests the contortions of the body and thereby acquires a kind of transparence.

34 This explains why the primary activity of poet and painter is localized differently for each. The poet can attend to imaginative invention (the level of content) while the painter must concentrate on material execution (the level of expression): 'With the artist, execution seems more difficult to us than invention; with the poet, however, it's the reverse and execution seems to us, in comparison to invention, the easier of the two.' (IX, 77) It is a question here of the labor involved in sign production. The easily replicable tokens of language place so little claim on the poet that his energies are freed for imaginative invention.

35 *Psy. Rat.*, par. 342.

36 The term 'dissolve' is a translation of Lessing's verb 'auflösen.' Cf. IX, 104, where it is said that 'das Coexistirende des Körpers' (the coexisting nature of bodies) is dissolved into 'das Consecutive der Rede' (the consecutive nature of speech).

37 Rather than go back to Wolff for this figure of thought, one could go forward, to Hegel: 'Perception, immediately and initially something given and spatial, acquires, insofar as it is used as a sign, the essential determination that its being is that of sublated perception. The intelligence is its negativity; thus, the truer form of perception, which a sign is, is an existence in *time* – a disappearance of existence in its very existence, and, according to its further external, psychic determination, it is a *posited being* of the intelligence which emerges out of its own (anthropological) naturalness – the *tone*, the fulfilled expression of the internality which announces itself.' (Hegel, *Enzyklopädie*, p. 459). Translated into Hegelian terms, the central point of Lessing's distinction between poetry and the plastic arts is that poetry, by virtue of the type of sign it employs, is the negation and preservation on a higher level (*Aufhebung*, sublation) of the plastic arts.

38 Cf., for instance, the following example: 'The misfortune of Laocoon and the destruction of the city are not two paintings next to one another in the poem; they do not together constitute a whole which our eye could, or should, survey at once; and only in such a case would one have to worry that our regard might now fall more on Laocoon, now more on the burning city. The descriptions of each follow upon one another and I fail to see what disadvantage the second one would suffer no matter how much the first might have affected us' (IX, 48). Within the single space of a painting heterogeneous elements can simultaneously make claims on the beholder. This leads to distraction and disruption of the imaginative focus. The sensuous presence characteristic of the plastic arts, therefore, not only is not equivalent

to imaginative presence-to-mind, but it also prevents its achievement. Simultaneity of sensuous presentation can lead to a non-simultaneity of imaginative comprehension. Cf. also Lessing's critique of Michael-angelo's *Last Judgement* at B., 446.

39 Cf. E. H. Gombrich, 'Lessing,' *Proceedings of the British Academy*, XLII (1957), pp. 133–56, esp. p. 140 on the *Laocoon*: 'It has often been said that Lessing did not know very much about art. I am afraid the truth may be even more embarrassing to an historian of art who has been charged with the task of celebrating Lessing: he had not much use for art.'

40 Jürgen Schröder, *Gotthold Ephraim Lessing*, p. 90.

41 Cf. Wilhelm Dilthey, *Das Erlebnis und die Dichtung* (Leipzig: Druck und Verlag von B. G. Teubner, 1906), pp. 34–5, on the combination of induction and deduction in the *Laocoon*.

42 The greater range of poetry, attributable to the arbitrariness of its signs, was pointed out, for instance, by Baumgarten (*Reflections on Poetry*, par. 40) and Mendelssohn (*J.A.*, I, p. 438).

43 'Corporeal beauty has its origin in the harmonious effect of manifold parts which can be surveyed at once. It requires, therefore, that these parts be positioned next to one another; and, since things, the parts of which are positioned next to one another, are the proper object of painting, then painting, and only painting, is capable of imitating corporeal beauty' (IX, 120).

44 Cf. IX, 121.

45 The relevant remarks of Mendelssohn's are as follows: '...but the poet is all the more perfect, the more determinate his images are and the easier it is for the imagination to fill in the omitted traits and to form for itself clean and extensive ideas of the fictional entities. Homer and Virgil allowed themselves only a few such images as cannot be thoroughly represented by the imagination. But all the fictional entities of Milton are of this sort. The force we exert in representing them in their completeness seems to exhaust our imagination. The first en-counter with them astonishes us unusually and arouses a sort of wonderment peculiar to the sublime. But their effect is not so lasting; for as soon as we recover ourselves and begin to activate our imagina-tion, we sense all too clearly our inability to form them fully and they begin to become unpleasant. Milton will astonish us more the first time, but Homer will be read all the more often' (*J.A.*, II, p. 245).

46 Cf. the quotation above, note 45.

47 Lessing's assumption is, of course, that painting necessarily has a definite subject matter.

48 'Although the poet likewise makes us think of a goddess as a human figure, he has nevertheless removed all ideas of course and heavy matter and he has enlivened her body with a force which exempts it from the laws of human locomotion. But how could painting distinguish the corporeal figure of a goddess from the corporeal figure of a human being in such an excellent way that our eye would not be offended

when it found entirely different rules of locomotion, gravity and equilibrium observed in the one case as compared with the other?' (IX, 55).

49 For the most important result of these commutational experiments, see IX, 82: 'The worst thing in such a change is just this: that, due to the painterly elimination of the distinction between visible and invisible beings, all those characteristic traits by virtue of which the latter transcend the former are lost as well.'

50 Cf. IX, 91: 'To be sure, Milton can't fill any galleries. But, if, so long as I had my bodily eye, its sphere had to be the sphere of my inner eye as well, then I would, in order to become free of this limitation, place a great deal of value on the loss of the former.'

51 Gombrich, 'Lessing,' p. 140.

52 For an example of Lessing's formulation of this distinction, cf. IX, 143: 'Die Mahlerey, als nachahmende Fertigkeit kann die Häßlichkeit ausdrücken: die Mahlerey, als schöne Kunst, will sie nicht ausdrücken.' ('Painting, as an imitative skill, can express ugliness; painting, as a fine art, doesn't want to express it.') The distinction parallels – and is an outgrowth of – Mendelssohn's distinction between the essence of an art and the special rules of efficacy that obtain for each art.

53 Cf. IX, 43.

54 '...this much, then, is beyond question: that, since the whole immeasurable realm of perfection is available for his [the poet's] imitation, this visible shell, beneath which perfection becomes beauty, can only be one of the most unimportant means through which he knows how to interest us for his characters' (IX, 22).

55 This discussion of Lessing's concept of 'Mitleid' is based on his famous letter to Mendelssohn from February 2, 1757. See Lessing, Mendelssohn, Nicolai. Briefwechsel über das Trauerspiel, hrsg. Jochen Schulte-Sasse (München: Winkler Verlag, 1972), pp. 102–3.

56 An event acted out on the stage has greater existential presence, but Lessing's analysis of Philoctetes shows that he considered it possible to maintain the imaginary status of the action despite the sensuous presence of the hero's cries and gestures. Cf. above, n. 8.

57 Cf., for example, Blümner's commentary (B., 512–20).

58 Baumgarten, Aesthetica, pars. 115–28.

59 Cf. above, Chapter 2, pp. 75–7.

60 Here again a consequence of the identification of the two arts is perceptible, but here it seems sculpture provides the paradigm which is transposed to painting. Garve touches on this in his critique of the Laocoon, pointing out that paintings can depict scenes and circumstances as well as bodies (B., 700). Translated into my terms, Garve's argument is that the global content substance of a painting is not necessarily a body with its visible qualities but a scene or situation. This places painting between sculpture and poetry. What this distinction illustrates is that selection and arrangement are indeed separate opera-

tions in painting, contrary to Lessing's view. In other words, a painting is more like a text than Lessing would allow.

61  On the poetics of verisimilitude – what Lessing terms 'Wahrscheinlich-keit' – viewed in terms of the question of motivation, see Gérard Genette, 'Vraisemblance et motivation,' *Communications*, XI (1968), pp. 5–21.

62  Mendelssohn, *J.A.*, II, p. 245 (my emphasis).

63  Cf. above, section 2.3.2, as well as the long fragment on Milton's blindness (B., 442–4).

64  The failure to distinguish between content material and content substance has led to misrepresentations of Lessing's position on this point. For instance, Szarota (*Lessings Laokoon*, pp. 218–19) argues that poetry can represent ugliness because it is an aspect of life. But the role of ugliness has nothing to do with the intrinsic realism of poetry, but rather is a function of the type of sign poetry employs.

65  The issue is discussed in Victor Anthony Rudowski, 'Action as the Essence of Poetry: A Reevaluation of Lessing's Argument,' *PMLA*, LXXXII (1967), pp. 333–41.

66  Cf. the discussion of interjections in *Philoctetes* (IX, 7–8) and the mention of Homer's 'musikalischer Mahlerey' ('musical painting,' IX, 89).

67  This point has been made by Tzvetan Todorov ('Esthétique et sémiotique au XVIII^e siècle,') pp. 34–5.

68  Charles Morris' definition of art from the point of view of his behaviorist semiotics exhibits obvious similarities to Lessing's view. According to Morris, in the interpretation of aesthetic signs '...there is the direct apprehension of value properties through the very presence of that which has the value it designates.' 'Esthetics and the Theory of Signs,' *The Journal of Unified Science* (*Erkenntnis*), VII (1939/40), p. 136.

69  See *Philosophical Writings of Peirce*, ed. Justus Buchler (New York: Dover Publications, 1955), p. 105, 116.

70  *Critische Dichtkunst*, I, pp. 14–15. References hereafter in parentheses.

71  Cf. *J.A.*, II, p. 235.

72  For what follows see Roland Barthes, 'Introduction à l'analyse structurale des récits,' *Communications*, VIII (1966), pp. 1–27. Cf. also Gerard Genette, 'Frontières du récit,' *Communications*, VII (1966), pp. 152–63, and Philippe Hamon, 'Qu'est-ce qu'une description?' *Poétique*, III (1972), pp. 464–485. Hamon makes passing reference to Lessing's *Laocoon* (p. 471).

73  Cf. Hamon, 'Qu'est-ce qu'une description?' p. 474: 'As regards its interior functioning, description certainly does not appeal to the same "linguistic consciousness" (of the author or of the reader) as does narration.'

74  *The Iliad of Homer*, translated and with an introduction by Richmond Lattimore (Chicago and London: The University of Chicago Press, 1951), Bk. III, ll. 42–6.

75 *Republic*, Bk. III, 393a. On the notion of diegesis, see Genette, 'Frontières du récit,' p. 153.

76 *J.A.*, II, 237.


CONCLUSION

1 Michel Foucault, *The Order of Things*, p. 66.

2 John Locke, *An Essay Concerning Human Understanding*, ed. Alexander Campbell Fraser, 2 vols. (New York: Dover, 1959).

3 Antoine Arnauld and Pierre Nicole, *La Logique ou L'Art de penser*, ed. Pierre Clair and François Girbal (Paris: Presses Universitaires de France, 1965).

4 *Schriften*, IV/2, p. 346.

5 On the bourgeois public sphere (*bürgerliche Öffentlichkeit*), see Jürgen Habermas, *Strukturwandel der Öffentlichkeit* (Neuwied and Berlin: Luchterhand, 1962).

6 See especially *J.A.*, II, pp. 290–1.

7 See Moses Mendelssohn, *Schriften zur Philosophie, Aesthetik und Apologetik*, ed. Moritz Brasch, 2 vols. (Hildesheim: Georg Olms, 1968) (reprint of the edition Leipzig, 1880), II, pp. 434–54, where Mendelssohn gives a detailed analysis of the problem.

8 *Schriften*, IV/2, p. 342.

9 *Schriften zur Philosophie, Aesthetik und Apologetik*, II, p. 451.

10 *Ibid.*, p. 442.

11 See the remarks of Louis Marin on the distinction between arbitrary linguistic signs and material natural signs in the *Logique* in his *Étude sémiologiques* (Paris: Klincksieck, 1971), pp. 127–8.

12 Geoffrey Hartman, *Beyond Formalism* (New Haven and London: Yale University Press, 1970), p. 342.

13 See George A. Miller, 'The Magical Number Seven, Plus or Minus Two: Some Limits on our Capacity for Processing Information,' in G.A.M., *The Psychology of Communication* (Baltimore, Md.: Penguin Books, 1967), pp. 14–44.

14 Herder, *Sämtliche Werke*, I, pp. 1–7.

15 Karlheinz Stierle, *Text als Handlung. Perspektiven einer systematischen Literaturwissenschaft* (München: Wilhelm Fink, 1975), p. 189.

16 See Edmund Husserl, *Cartesianische Meditationen und Pariser Vorträge*, ed. S. Strasser (The Hague: Martinus Nijhoff, 1963), p. 8.

17 The distinction is elaborated in Edmund Husserl, *Logische Untersuchungen*, 2 vols. (Tübingen: Max Niemeyer Verlag, 1968), II, pp. 53–9, 90–4.

18 Edmund Husserl, *Die Idee der Phänomenologie*, ed. Walter Biemel (The Hague: Martinus Nijhoff, 1964), pp. 59–60.

19 See Roman Ingarden, *Das literarische Kunstwerk* (Tübingen: Max Niemeyer Verlag, 1960²); *Vom Erkennen des literarischen Kunstwerks* (Tübingen: Max Niemeyer Verlag, 1968). Ingarden himself has written an essay on Lessing, which is unfortunately only available in Polish.

20  See *Vom Erkennen des literarischen Kunstwerks*, pp. 158–73.
21  *Ibid.*, pp. 56–8.
22  See Jürgen Habermas, 'Vorbereitende Bemerkungen zu einer Theorie der kommunikativen Kompetenz,' in J. H. and Niklas Luhmann, *Theorie der Gesellschaft oder Sozialtechnologie* (Frankfurt a.M.: Suhrkamp, 1971), pp. 101–41; Karl-Otto Apel, 'Das Apriori der Kommunikationsgemeinschaft und die Grundlagen der Ethik,' in K.-O. A., *Transformation der Philosophie*, vol. II, *Das Apriori der Kommunikationsgemeinschaft* (Frankfurt a.M.: Suhrkamp, 1973), pp. 358–435.
23  Habermas, 'Vorbereitende Bemerkungen,' p. 138.
24  *Ibid.*, p. 141.
25  See Ernst Bloch, *Ästhetik des Vor-Scheins*, ed. Gerd Ueding (Frankfurt a.M.: Suhrkamp, 1974).
26  Ingarden, *Vom Erkennen des literarischen Kunstwerks*, p. 56.
27  Friedrich A. Kittler's essay 'Nietzsche' (in *Klassiker der Literaturtheorie*, ed. Horst Turk [München: C. H. Beck, 1979], pp. 191–205) discusses Nietzsche's work in aesthetics and literary theory in terms of such deep-structural transformations in the culture.
28  See Nelson Goodman, *Languages of Art*; Umberto Eco, *A Theory of Semiotics*. The idea of a typology of modes of sign production is Eco's.
29  For an interesting attempt to analyze the role of temporal discontinuity in narrative, see Michel de Certeau, 'On the Oppositional Practices of Everyday Life,' *Social Text* 1/3 (1980), pp. 3–43, esp. pp. 33–43. A typology of institutionalized temporal forms in the novel is developed in M. M. Bakhtin's essay, 'Forms of Time and of the Chronotope in the Novel,' in *The Dialogic Imagination. Four Essays by M. M. Bakhtin*, ed. Michael Holquist, trans. Caryl Emerson and Michael Holquist, (Austin, Texas and London: University of Texas Press, 1981), pp. 84–258.

# INDEX